A Research Reader in
Universal Design for Learning

# A Research Reader in Universal Design for Learning

*Edited by*

GABRIELLE RAPPOLT-SCHLICHTMANN
SAMANTHA G. DALEY
L. TODD ROSE

HARVARD EDUCATION PRESS
Cambridge, Massachusetts

Library of Congress Control Number 2012943108

Paperback ISBN 978-1-61250-501-5
Library Edition ISBN 978-1-61250-502-2


Published by Harvard Education Press,
an imprint of the Harvard Education Publishing Group

Harvard Education Press
8 Story Street
Cambridge, MA 02138

Cover Design: Perry Lubin

The typefaces used in this book are Sabon for text and Myriad Pro for display.

# Contents

# Foreword

Historically, many studies of learning and teaching have suffered from erroneous assumptions so deeply rooted in our culture that scholars were not even aware that they were basing their work on these false beliefs:

- Most learners are "okay," but some learners are "broken" (disabled).
- The inability to learn a skill (e.g., reading) is centered in the learner (e.g., dyslexic) rather than in the methods and media of instruction (e.g., print is a disabling medium for some people).

Research in Universal Design for Learning (UDL) has shown that these dichotomies are inaccurate and lead to suboptimal educational interventions for both "disabled" and "okay" students.

Research for learning and teaching is increasingly moving to different assumptions championed by UDL:

- Depending on the skill to be learned, every person can appear "okay" or "broken" (Howard Gardner's framework for multiple intelligences implies that a person may have "disabilities" in the intelligences not manifested).
- Depending on the methods and media of instruction, every person can appear "okay" or "broken" (e.g., people labeled as dyslexic can often read with little difficulty when provided electronic supports that are not possible on the printed page).

In other words, learning is best characterized by continua, not dichotomies: all of us are a mixture of "okay" and "broken," depending on our individual strengths and weaknesses, and all of us can benefit from appropriate methods and media. UDL research centers on understanding these two precepts.

The statements above are not meant to imply that every person faces equal challenges in learning. We know that some learners face profound difficulties that may be physical, cognitive, emotional, social and that they need special supports beyond the norm. But these people are not different in kind but, rather, in degree; labeling them as distinct and assuming that what benefits them cannot be of use to every learner undercuts the value of what UDL research provides. It is important to remember in this regard that Maria Montessori developed her educational methods for children seen as disabled by their contemporaries; yet now we understand the tremendous value of those methods for all learners.

As this book demonstrates, UDL is valuable both as a scholarly method and as a set of findings to inform learning in general for all people. For the first time in history, we have neuroscience that allows us to better understand the ways our individual minds shape how we learn and digital technologies that can help us compensate for ways in which our particular minds may struggle.

We stand at the beginning of an exciting era in research in which UDL can benefit us all—and can help us all to see every learner, no matter how many challenges that person may face, as like us. This valuable and wide-ranging book indicates the wide terrain of current UDL-related research and points us to fruitful paths for the crucially important research yet to come.

*Chris Dede*
*Timothy E. Wirth Professor in Learning Technologies*
*Harvard Graduate School of Education*

# INTRODUCTION

GABRIELLE RAPPOLT-SCHLICHTMANN,
SAMANTHA G. DALEY, AND L. TODD ROSE

Over the last five years, we have seen exponential growth in interest surrounding the Universal Design for Learning (UDL) framework, primarily within education policy and practice. Notably, the Higher Education Opportunity Act of 2008 established the statutory definition of UDL while emphasizing that preservice teacher training incorporate instruction on strategies consistent with UDL. And the U.S. Department of Education's (2010) National Technology Education Plan, which is meant to guide the use of technologies in transforming education, refers to UDL ubiquitously as a framework that reduces barriers and maximizes learning opportunities for all students.

The interest around UDL is understandable because the framework provides a strong answer to the growing call for more "personalized" curricular materials that can accommodate the full diversity of learners and teachers within the education system. In short, UDL is gaining traction because it offers a means to provide opportunities for deep learning through the design of highly flexible methods, materials, and assessments (Rose & Meyer, 2002; Rose, Meyer, & Hitchcock, 2005). Interest notwithstanding, we believe that educational scholars are rightly skeptical about reform initiatives. Is UDL just one more fad in a long line of educational fads that will come and go without any lasting impact? And, if not, how will UDL be different than all the reform ideas that came before?

As research scientists, it is our position that the long-term potential of UDL to transform education—and what differentiates it from previous and current reform efforts—lies less in the practical content of the current UDL guidelines (CAST, 2011) and more in the unique opportunity that the framework affords for effectively facilitating the connection between research and practice in education.

With that in mind, this book is meant to articulate some of the core concepts and assumptions of the UDL framework from the learning sciences that are not articulated explicitly in the guidelines. Our aim is to highlight ways in which UDL is uniquely situated to act as a continuously improving bridge between research and practice and thus catalyze the next generation of research within the learning sciences, as well as the next generation of best and evidence-based practices within education. Finally, our hope is that readers will gain a richer understanding of the UDL framework, including its capacity to change and develop as our knowledge of learning and teaching improves.

## FRAMING UDL FROM A RESEARCH PERSPECTIVE

Given the scope and magnitude of the challenges facing contemporary education, it is not surprising that policy makers and practitioners are increasingly looking to research from the learning sciences as a means of improving education (National Research Council, 2002). However, this is an ambitious proposition, given both the complexity of the educational challenges and the fact that most learning science research to date has been divorced from the educational context. As such, we believe that success will depend in large part on building genuinely reciprocal value-add relationships between education and research in the fields of learning and development. Key to this effort is the development of an explicit conversation among researchers, practitioners, and policy makers, where the generation of research deals directly with the problems of practice and operates in direct collaboration with practitioners.

UDL is uniquely positioned to serve this catalytic role, facilitating deeper connections between research and practice in education because its core principles are in essence a synthesis of transdisciplinary insights drawn from across the learning sciences (Rose & Gravel, in press). Although the emphasis has been on practice, we contend that within the UDL framework important opportunities exist to explore, examine, and inform theory and research concerning the nature of learning and development. However, to realize this potential, it will be important to appreciate both the challenges inherent in working in transdisciplinary and translational science and the unique opportunities that the UDL framework affords for stimulating interconnected, mutually beneficial, forward-moving collaborative work.

Historically, transdisciplinary work meant to bridge learning science and education has been hampered by serious philosophical, methodological, and epistemological differences between the research science and education fields (Overton, 2003; Rappolt-Schlichtmann, Ayoub, & Gravel, 2009; Samuels, 2009). There are no easy solutions to resolving disciplinary differences; however, such a resolution may not be necessary for productive interchange to occur and for the generation of usable knowledge. Indeed, the UDL framework has been effective primarily because it offers a fertile space where researchers and educators can productively interact, not through a common theoretical perspective or methodology but, rather, "a common issue to which all apply their own particular expertise with the goal of reaching a more holistic understanding of the issue" (Samuels, 2009, p. 49).

## UDL AS PROBLEM-CENTERED THINKING

With the advent of the Internet, disciplinary boundaries have loosened, and as a result scientists have become increasingly interested in and accepting of interdisciplinary perspectives. These conditions provide for a unique opportunity to build a genuinely bidirectional and iteratively improving translational framework in education. But to be successful, this work should be organized around meaningful problems, not disciplinary assumptions or methods. When this kind of productive cross-collaboration works best, a self-improving cycle can be established whereby theory and research from the learning sciences informs the practice of education and, importantly, information from educational practice feeds back to inform and influence research and theory about the nature of learning. The history of the development of the UDL framework offers a nice example of the value of being problem centered, particularly in terms of how the UDL framework itself has been able to inform education while at the same time adapt in response to new insights from research and practice.

## PAST IS PROLOGUE

In the mid 1980s, David Rose and Anne Meyer, co-founders of CAST, worked directly with students with disabilities. They became frustrated doing neuropsychological evaluations and writing support plans for students that seemed to have little impact. They were focused on the problem of students with disabilities experiencing recurrent failure in educational environments that were one-size-fits-all—schools designed to meet the needs of the "average" student and not adaptable to support all students in our education system. Focused on this "problem," Rose and Meyer, along with their colleagues at CAST, collaborated with many scientists and practitioners. They were resourceful in their use of the research literature, looking across many disciplines to inform their thinking, including, and most centrally: developmental psychology, neuroscience, clinical neuropsychology, computer science, and even architecture. In each instance they were able to gain a new and varied perspective on the problem of students with disabilities in schools.

Eventually, a critical insight led to the emergence of the UDL framework: students weren't really the problem at all; rather, the education system (goals, methods, materials, and assessments) was too narrowly conceived, defined, and constructed to accommodate the diversity of learners in the school system (Meyer & Rose, 2000; Rose & Gravel, 2010; Rose & Meyer, 2002; Rose, Meyer, & Hitchcock, 2005). Rose and Meyer, along with their colleagues at CAST, began to describe the curriculum as "disabled." For instance, students with dyslexia were only disabled when they had to learn and perform in print-oriented contexts. They could certainly learn and excel but would run into trouble if the only way to gain access to learning was through print-based materials. Thus, print-based materials are disabled; they don't work for everyone. This idea had a lot of traction with advocates and practitioners, taking the burden from individual children and placing the onus on curriculum and the education system writ large.

UDL then became an actionable construct. The UDL principles and guidelines (CAST, 2008, 2011; Rose & Gravel, in press) were created so that instructional designers and teachers could systematically anticipate and reduce or eliminate barriers to learning by making curricula and assessments flexible. Three principles underlie the framework of UDL: (1) multiple means of representation, (2) multiple means of expression and action, and (3) multiple means of engagement (Rose & Meyer, 2002).[1]

The generation of the UDL principles and guidelines was the direct result of a careful synthesis of relevant research from across the learning sciences—in essence, a concrete representation of our best and current understanding of the variables most salient in the process of learning. For example, the principles stem from the realization that three broad divisions are often made in the research literature when learning is described. Lev Vygotsky (1978) and Benjamin Bloom (1984) both adopted a similar three-part framework when writing about the process of learning, and within cognitive neuroscience we often find reference to three networks broadly representing: (1) pattern recognition processes in the posterior regions of the cortex, (2) motor and executive capabilities in the frontal regions of the cortex, and (3) affective capabilities in the medial regions of the nervous system (Luria, 1973).

The three-principle framework may seem in some ways like a gross over-simplification. But, like most phenomena in science, learning, and especially as it is represented with the brain sciences, is far too complex to study productively in its full form. We rely on models to simplify complexity, highlighting what we think is most relevant. In developing a good model, we have to find a balance between two extremes—too complex or too simplistic. Because UDL means to be a framework whereby research is successfully translated to practice, and vice versa, it was important to adopt the simplest model possible that still managed to expose in common language our most fundamental and current understanding of learning. By 2008, and with the creation of the guidelines, UDL was a research-based framework to support productive cross-talk between research and practice.

## AN EVOLVING FRAMEWORK

Of course, UDL has necessarily continued to change over time as the research literature evolved and as new tools and strategies were developed, put into practice, and researched. There have been many such changes that have shaped and refined the UDL framework today. One such influence has come from the dramatic shift that has taken place within the fields of modern learning and developmental science. At the heart of this shift is dynamic systems theory, a flexible meta-theoretical framework for analyzing how many factors act together in natural systems in disciplines as diverse as physics, biology, and education.

A complete treatment of dynamic systems is beyond the scope of this book; here it is sufficient to point out that, in contrast to classic, static models that have dominated work in learning for decades, the dynamic systems approach assumes that learning is variable and context dependent (e.g., Fischer & Bidell, 2006; Thelen & Smith, 1994; van Geert, 1998). This approach has reoriented theory and research in many fields relevant to education—including learning science and developmental psychology—and fueled discoveries that have overturned longstanding beliefs about the nature of behavior and learning. We believe that the dynamic systems approach offers tremendous potential for guiding new lines of research and practice around the UDL framework. Indeed, in part in response to knowledge and ideas from research and substantive collaborations with practitioners to inform the framework, in recent years the UDL framework has adapted to represent a more dynamic perspective, putting interaction at the center of the paradigm.

Specifically, in assuming that the child and curriculum are a dynamic system, the UDL framework now holds that neither the child nor the curriculum is disabled. Instead, they are two limits on the same system, where learning occurs in the interaction between the child and the context (Meyer, Rose, & Gordon, in press; Rose & Gravel, in press). Most of education practice and curriculum design still implicitly assumes a top-down, child-as-container approach, where educators impart knowledge and students are meant to absorb or acquire but not necessarily learn it. Taking the idea further, we argue that learners and the curriculum will mutually influence each other, forming a social and educational system that has characteristics that are both stable and changing at any given point in time (Fischer & Lerner, 1994; Wertlieb, 2003; Lerner et al., 2003; Fischer & Bidell, 1998; Thelen & Smith, 1998). Interestingly, Dewey made this point in 1902 in his article "The Child and The Curriculum" (reprinted in this volume), but nearly a century of theory, research, and mathematics were required to develop the concept of dynamic systems to where it was finally tractable as an accepted and accessible lens on development and learning within developmental psychology. Still a nascent idea, UDL as a transdisciplinary and continuously improving framework could effectively provide the infrastructure needed to bring the dynamic systems point of view to the center of education research, practice, and policy.

## RESEARCH IN UDL

What should research within the context of UDL look like? In 2011 CAST adopted a more explicit structure to our research and development efforts following a model adopted by the National Science Foundation, among others (American Statistical Association, 2007; National Science Foundation, 2005; RAND, 2003). Our goal was to better define the process of transdisciplinary, or problem-centered, research so as to be more systematic in our work. We now define our research activities within five categories:

**FIGURE I.1    CAST's Cycle of Innovation and Development Through Research**

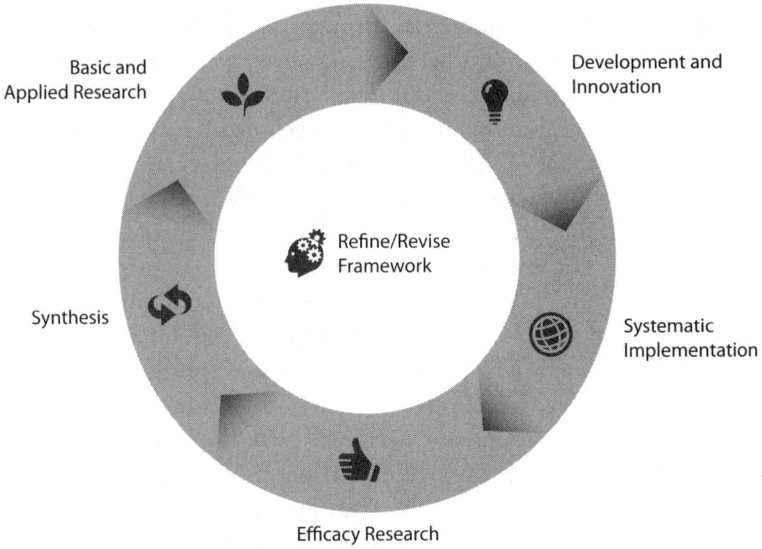

*Source:* Adapted from the National Science Foundation via RAND (2003), American Statistical Association (2007), and National Science Foundation (2005).

- *Basic research.* Contributing to the knowledge base within the learning sciences
- *Research syntheses.* Providing coherent, cross-disciplinary views of the science of learning and teaching
- *Development/Innovation.* Generating UDL tools, materials, methods and assessments
- *Implementation.* Exploring best-practices in the implementation of UDL
- *Efficacy research.* Exploring and defining the relative impact of UDL tools, materials, methods, assessments, and approaches to implementation

Together these five categories provide the basis for an innovative model of development, creating the structure for UDL-centered work. Figure I.1 illustrates this process, whereby each category of the cycle enables transition to and directly informs the adjacent category.

## THE STATE OF THE FIELD

Over the last two decades, work within UDL has focused on the development of the principles and guidelines through the synthesis of the research literature described above. But there has also been a substantial amount of work in the area of development and innovation. Many UDL digital tools, books, and even a few curricula have been developed for use in classrooms, including Science Writer, SNUDLE (Science Notebooks, Universal Design for Learning edition), and ICON (Improving Comprehension Online). There are even online authoring tools that let everyone from curriculum developers to teachers and students create UDL materials.[2] Design-based research should play (and often has played) a large role in this work, allowing for the creation of knowledge and the generation of new research questions.

Design-based research is a formative evaluation approach to intervention development where the goal is to refine both existing theory from the research literature and to generate "usable knowledge" to improve educational practice (Flagg, 1990; Reeves & Hedberg, 2003; Lagemann, 2002; Collins, Joseph, & Bielaczyc, 2004). Practitioners and developer-researchers work together to create meaningful change in contexts of practice through the development of interventions that speak directly to the problems of practice (National Research Council, 2002). Within this framework, development and research take place through continuous cycles of design, implementation, analysis, and redesign (Cobb, 2001; Collins 1992). The focus is on linking process to outcomes in authentic contexts, thereby offering fertile ground for the hypotheses of potential causal accounts/mechanisms of learning and teaching.

A few studies have been done that explore the efficacy of UDL applications in applied educational settings, most often as a part of federally funded development efforts. For example, the efficacy of UDL-supported reading environments in improving the literacy outcomes of students who struggle with reading has been reported in several studies across diverse populations (Coyne, Pisha, Dalton, Zeph, & Smith, 2012; Dalton et al., 2002; Proctor, Dalton, & Grisham, 2007; Proctor et al., 2009; Rose & Dalton, 2002; Strangman & Dalton, 2005). In a quasi-experimental study of 204 students, students using the online learning tool *Strategic Reader* as a part of their reading instruction over twelve weeks gained approximately 0.53 grade equivalents versus 0.2 grade equivalents for students in the traditional instruction group.

The effect size of 0.29, equating to approximately half a grade level of reading achievement gain, was meaningful for struggling readers, including students with learning disabilities, who read at or below the twenty-fifth percentile prior to the intervention. In addition, students reading the digital novels spent significantly more time on task and had significantly more opportunities to respond to strategies than did their peers using traditional strategy instruction (Dalton et al., 2002). Because UDL is still a relatively new framework it should come as no surprise that efficacy and experimental studies are lacking. But efficacy trials and experimental research should be an important component of any program of development and innovation. More of this kind of work needs to be done on the products that are the outcomes of UDL development efforts as the framework matures.

## A CALL TO ACTION

In contrast to the work described above, very little basic and applied research has been done within or inspired by the UDL framework. This kind of work—research that is explicitly informed by the problems of education practice—is very much needed. By way of example, we take up the concept of scaffolding. Under UDL, engagement is achieved through the application of an appropriate challenge that is precisely calibrated to individual learners' specific strengths and weaknesses. Thus, scaffolding is an essential and central concept to UDL, with the engagement guidelines offering direction on how the environment can be made flexible and then manipulated by teachers to support optimal cognitive and emotional functioning within learning.

Certainly, there is a strong theoretical basis for the concept of support and scaffolding in instructional design, but the empirical basis that should support the explicit design and implementation of such environments is severely lacking (Palincsar, 1998; Puntambeker & Hübscher, 2005; Rappolt-Schlichtmann et al., 2007). Specifically, while UDL concretely identifies contextual supports within the guidelines that can be used in the context of scaffolding, there is very little knowledge (Quintana et al., 2004) as to the specific effect of those contextual supports on children's performance (Are all scaffolds created equal?) and about when such tools should be applied (Is the effect the same regardless of age or context?) and for whom (Is the effect the same for all learners, irrespective of individual differences?). It is clear that our capacity to take full advantage of UDL will rest on our ability to fill these empirical gaps. This is just one example of many areas of study that could be initiated from questions garnered within the UDL framework.

Finally, we need to innovate in the area of data analysis and research methodology so as to emphasize the centrality of variation and context in human development and learning. Historically, concepts of learning have favored simple linear progressions that tend to oversimplify and homogenize (e.g., Piaget, 1983; Freud, 1965; Kohlberg, 1969). Contemporary theories of human development and learning offer a more complex heterogeneous view (e.g., Case & Okamoto, 1996; Cicchetti & Lynch, 1993; Fischer & Bidell, 1998; Fischer et al., 1997), but approaches to research in the learning and developmental sciences have, on the whole, not followed suit; most still fail to address dynamic processes empirically. Without research methods and analysis tools that more accurately reflect education in real life, we have been unable to make any significant progress in understanding what happens when UDL is successfully implemented and when it is not. Under UDL, variability and multiple paths to success are the rule and not the exception.

## HOW THIS BOOK IS ORGANIZED

In this book, we've reached out to leading researchers in the learning sciences to help us understand the developing field of UDL and how it informs—and is informed by—new insights from research. In chapter 1 we enter into conversation with Jeremy Roschelle, director of the Center for Technology and Learning at SRI International, about the social nature of learning and its implications for UDL research, using Dewey's classic article "The Child and the Curriculum" as a springboard for the conversation. Roschelle's work has focused especially on leveraging social collaboration in learning to support the development of conceptually difficult ideas, often through advanced or emerging technologies. Early in his career, he says, the Dewey piece significantly broadened his understanding of the social nature of learning.

In chapter 2, renowned psychologist Howard Gardner discusses "constructivism, with constraints" in an introduction to his article "The Unschooled Mind: Why Even the Best Students in the Best Schools May Not Understand." Given that Gardner has spent decades developing a rich set of ideas on how learning is best fostered, we sought Gardner's insight into the balance between learners actively and somewhat freely developing their own understandings versus educators purposefully guiding or limiting the bounds of this exploration.

Affective neuroscientist Mary Helen Immordino-Yang helps us explore in chapter 3 the relationship between cognition and emotion in light of UDL. She reminds us that "thinking is at once emotional and cognitive," and the two are "co-regulated and interdependent." She also notes that emotions change with broad variability both within and among learners—a fact with significant implications for education. Our discussion leads into Justin Storbeck and Gerald Clore's "On the Interdependence of Cognition and Emotion," which systematically explores the relationship between emotion and cognition in thinking and learning.

In chapter 4 we address the dynamics of scaffolding in conversation with Kurt Fischer, cofounder of Harvard's Mind, Brain, and Education Institute. A central tenet of UDL is that learning occurs in the transaction between the person and the environment, which means many factors influence the process and outcome of learning. Contextual support and scaffolding are key components. The work of Fischer, a developmental theorist whose micro-developmental studies have captured the effects of such supports, goes beyond the original conception of scaffolding, arriving at a point of great interest for UDL: how novice learners can become expert learners when they become aware of and assume responsibility for their own learning. His work places a premium on the *dynamic* nature of learning and change. He assumes that people do not have a specific level of knowledge that is fixed; instead, knowledge and performance vary between two stable states—optimal and functional levels. Fischer and colleagues' influential piece "The Dynamics of Competence: How Context Contributes Directly to Skill" completes the discussion.

"Learning from Outliers" is the topic of chapter 5. Mike Russell, a leading researcher on assessment and computer-based testing, talked with us about learners who are "outliers"—that is, those outside the band of average learning performance that classical models of education tend to focus on. Outliers, Russell reminds us, provide meaningful insights about the nature of learning that are applicable and valuable for all learners. Well-designed assessments can help us better understand how all individuals learn, including those outside the big part of the bell curve; it can also inform instruction so we improve teaching and learning for all. The article "On the Roles of External Knowledge Representations in Assessment Design," by renowned assessment expert Robert Mislevy and colleagues, is included here.

Finally, in chapter 6 we talked with Paul van Geert of the University of Groningen in the Netherlands about the concept of variability, leading into his article "Focus on Variability: New Tools to Study Intra-Individual Variability in Developmental Data." Variability and its importance is anchored in dynamic systems theory, which has generated new insights into the many pathways of human development from infancy forward that depend on varied and interacting, individual and environmental factors. Van Geert has done pioneering work in building dynamic systems models and theories in the field of language and cognitive development, education, and social development. In this chapter, van Geert reminds us, among other things, of the need for researchers to focus not only on variability that exists among individuals (*inter*-individual variability) but also variability within the same individual that manifests over time and across different contexts (*intra*-individual variability).

## CONCLUSION

Problem-centered thinking that is resourceful and dogged with disciplinary knowledge and built through cross-collaboration can lead to novel solutions. In synthesizing the research literature to derive the first instantiation of the UDL guidelines, researchers saw the "problem" of variability as a strength and the child and curriculum as a dynamic system (CAST, 2011). We expect the UDL framework and guidelines to change on a regular basis as researchers and practitioners interact to work on problems within education: UDL is meant to be a dynamic framework, one that learns from new insights in research and practice. For the UDL guidelines to evolve productively, researchers will need to be nimble and creative, working at the level of the core concepts and evidence-based assumptions that define and support the UDL framework and not the guidelines themselves. This is because the guidelines are a concrete consequence of the transdisciplinary cross-communication between researchers and practitioners. Were researchers (and even practitioners) to allow their work to be solely bound by the guidelines, then the UDL framework would become stagnant and self-important rather than speaking to and from the most timely innovations within the learning sciences and education practice.

So what are the core concepts and evidence-based assumptions that define the UDL framework? From a UDL perspective, learning is contextual, social, emotional, dynamic, and variable. In the pages that follow we take each of these core concepts or assumptions about the nature of learning and explore their relation to the UDL framework in the context of conversations with luminaries in each domain. The scientists were selected as much for their areas of expertise as their willingness to and facility with operating at the boundaries between disciplines—people who drive their work forward with problem-centered thinking. Most have knowledge of the UDL framework, but for some the concept was new, their work having contributed to the framework in a more passive way.

## NOTES

1. Nine guidelines more specifically articulate these principles to actively support design and implementation. For a full articulation, see www.udlcenter.org/aboutudl/udlguidelines.
2. For example, see UDL Studio (http://udlstudio.cast.org), UDL Curriculum Toolkits (http://udl-toolkit.cast.org), and UDL Book Builder (http://bookbuilder.cast.org), which has more than fifty thousand users and more than one thousand publicly shared digital books authored and shared by educators, students, and parents.

## REFERENCES

American Statistical Association. (2007). Using statistics effectively in mathematics education research. Retrieved from http://www.amstat.org/education/pdfs/UsingStatisticsEffectivelyInMathEdResearch.pdf

Bloom, B. S. (1984). *Taxonomy of educational objectives*. Boston, MA: Allyn & Bacon.

Case, R., & Okamoto, Y. (1996). The role of central conceptual structures in the development of children's thought. *Monographs of the Society for Research in Child Development,6*(Serial No. 246), 1–26.

CAST. (2008). *Universal Design for Learning guidelines version 1.0.* Wakefield, MA: Author.

CAST. (2011). *Universal Design for Learning guidelines version 2.0.* Wakefield, MA: Author. Retrieved from http://www.udlcenter.org/aboutudl/udlguidelines

Cicchetti, D., & Lynch, M. (1993).Toward an ecological/transactional model of community violence and child maltreatment: Consequences for children's development. *Psychiatry, 53*(1), 96–118.

Cobb, P. (2001). Supporting the improvement of learning and teaching in social and institutional context. In S. Carver & D. Klahr (Eds.), *Cognition and instruction: Twenty-five years of progress* (pp. 455–478). Mahwah, NJ: Erlbaum.

Collins, A. (1992). Toward a design science of education. In E. Scanlon & T. O'Shea (Eds.), *New directions in educational technology* (pp. 15–22). New York: Springer-Verlag.

Collins, A., Joseph, D., & Bielaczyc, K. (2004). Design research: Theoretical and methodological issues. *Journal of the Learning Sciences, 13*(1), 15–42.

Coyne, P., Pisha, B., Dalton, B., Zeph L. A., & Smith, N. C. (2012). Literacy by design: A Universal Design for Learning approach for students with significant intellectual disabilities. *Remedial and Special Education, 33*(3), 162–172.

Dalton, B., Pisha, B., Eagleton, M., Coyne, P., & Deysher, S. (2002). Engaging the text: Reciprocal teaching and questioning strategies in a scaffolded learning environment. Final Report to the U.S. Department of Education. Wakefield, MA: CAST.

Dalton, B., & Proctor, C. P. (2008). The changing landscape of text and comprehension in the age of new literacies. In J. Coiro, M. Knobel, C. Lankshear, & D. Leu (Eds.), *Handbook of research on new literacies* (pp 297–324). Mahweh, NJ: Erlbaum.

Dalton, B., & Rose, D. (2008). Scaffolding digital reading comprehension. In C. C. Block & S. R. Parris (Eds.), *Comprehension instruction: Research-based best practices* (2nd ed., pp. 347–361). New York: Guilford Press.

Dalton, B., & Strangman, N. (2007). Using technology to support struggling readers' comprehension: A review of the research. In D. Reinking, M. C. McKenna, L. D. Labbo, & R. D. Keiffer (Eds.), *Handbook of literacy and technology* (2nd ed., pp. 75–92). Mahwah, NJ: Erlbaum.

Fisher, C. B., & Lerner, R. M. (1994). Foundations of applied developmental psychology. In C. B. Fisher & R. M. Lerner (Eds.), *Applied developmental psychology* (pp. 3–20). New York: McGraw-Hill.

Fischer, K., Ayoub, C., Singh, I., Noam, G., Maraganore, A., & Raya, P. (1997). Psychopathology as adaptive development along distinctive pathways. *Development and Psychopathology, 9*(4), 749–779.

Fischer, K. W., & Bidell, T. R. (1998). Dynamic development of psychological structures in action and thought. In R. M. Lerner (Ed.) &W. Damon (Series Ed.), *Handbook of child psychology* (5th ed., pp. 467–561). New York: Wiley.

Fischer, K. W., & Bidell, T. R. (2006). Dynamic development of action and thought. In W. Damon & R. M. Lerner (Eds.), *Handbook of child psychology: Theoretical models of human development* (Vol. 1, 6th ed., pp. 313–399). New York: Wiley.

Flagg, B. N. (1990). *Formative evaluation for educational technologies.* Hillsdale, NJ: Erlbaum.

Freud, S. (1965). *New introductory lectures on psychoanalysis* (J. Strachey, Trans.). New York: Norton.

Higher Education Opportunity Act, PL 110-315 (2008).

Kohlberg, L. (1969). Stage and sequence: The cognitive-developmental approach to socialization. In D. Goslin (Ed.), *Handbook of socialization theory and research* (pp. 347–480). Chicago: Rand McNally.

Lagemann, E. C. (2002). *Usable knowledge in education.* Chicago: Spencer Foundation. Retrieved from http://www.spencer.org/publications/index.htm.

Lerner, R., Anderson, P., Balsano, A., Dowling, E., & Bobek, D. (2003). Applied developmental science of positive human development. In I. Weiner (Series Ed.), R. Lerner, M. Easterbrooks, & J. Mistry (Vol. Eds.), *Handbook of psychology: Developmental psychology* (Vol. 6, pp. 535–558). Hoboken, NJ: Wiley.

Luria, A. R. (1973). *The working brain.* New York: Basic Books.

Meyer, A., & Rose, D. (2000). Universal design for individual differences. *Educational Leadership, 58*(3), 39–43.

Meyer, A., Rose, D. H., & Gordon, D. (in press). *Universal Design for Learning: Theory and practice.* Wakefield, MA: National Center on Universal Design for Learning.

National Research Council. (2002). *Scientific research in education.* Washington, DC: National Academies Press.

National Science Foundation. (2005). The mathematics education portfolio brief (NSF 05-03). Retrieved from http://www.nsf.gov/publications/pub_summ.jsp?ods_key =nsf0503.

Overton, W. (2003). Development across the lifespan. In I. Weiner (Series Ed.) & R. Lerner, M. Easterbrooks, & J. Mistry (Vol. Eds.), *Handbook of psychology: Developmental psychology* (Vol. 6, pp. 13–42). Hoboken, NJ: Wiley.

Palincsar, A. S. (1998). Keeping the metaphor of scaffolding fresh: A response to C. Addison Stone's "The metaphor of scaffolding: Its utility for the field of learning disabilities." *Journal of Learning Disabilities, 31*(4), 370–373.

Palincsar, A. S., & Brown, A. L. (1984). Reciprocal teaching of comprehension-fostering and comprehension-monitoring activities. *Cognition and Instruction 1*(1), 117–175.

Piaget, J. (1983). Piaget's theory. In P. Mussen (Ed.), *Handbook of child psychology* (Vol. 1, pp. 703–732). New York: Wiley.

Proctor, C. P., Dalton, B., & Grisham, D. L. (2007). Scaffolding English language learners and struggling readers in a universal literacy environment with embedded strategy instruction and vocabulary support. *Journal of Literacy Research, 39*(1), 71–93.

Proctor, C. P., Uccelli, P., Dalton, B., & Snow, C. E. (2009). Understanding depth of vocabulary and improving comprehension online with bilingual and monolingual children. *Reading and Writing Quarterly, 25*(4), 311–333.

Puntambekar, S., & Hübscher, R. (2005). Tools for scaffolding students in a complex environment: What have we gained and what have we missed? *Educational Psychologist 40*(1), 1–12.

Quintana, C., Reiser, B. J., Davis, E. A., Krajcik, J., Fretz, E., Duncan, R. G., et al. (2004). A scaffolding design framework for software to support science inquiry. *Journal of the Learning Sciences, 13*(3), 337–386.

RAND, Mathematics Study Panel. (2003). Mathematical proficiency for all students: Toward a strategic research and development program in mathematics education. Santa Monica, CA: RAND.

Rappolt-Schlichtmann, G., Ayoub, C., & Gravel, J. (2009). Examining the "whole child" to generate usable knowledge. *Mind, Brain and Education, 3*(4), 209–217.

Rappolt-Schlichtmann, G., Tenenbaum, H., Keopke, M., & Fischer, K. (2007). Transient and robust knowledge: Contextual support and the dynamics of children's reasoning about density. *Mind, Brain, and Education, 1*(2), 98–108.

Reeves, T. C., & Hedberg, J. G. (2003). *Interactive learning systems evaluation.* Englewood Cliffs, NJ: Educational Technology Publications.

Rose, D., & Dalton, B. (2002). Using technology to individualize reading instruction. In (Eds.) C. C. Block, L. B. Gambrell, & M. Pressley (Eds.), *Improving comprehension instruction: Rethinking research, theory, and classroom practice* (pp. 257–274). San Francisco: Jossey-Bass.

Rose, D. H., & Gravel, J. W. (2010). Universal Design for Learning. In P. Peterson, E. Baker, & B. McGraw (Eds.), *International encyclopedia of education* (pp. 119–124). Oxford: Elsevier.

Rose, D. H., & Gravel, J. W. (in press). Universal Design for Learning. In L. Florian (Ed.), *Sage handbook on special education* (2nd ed.). New York: Sage.

Rose, D. H., & Meyer, A. (2002). *Teaching every student in the digital age: Universal Design for Learning.* Alexandria, VA: Association for Supervision and Curriculum Development.

Rose, D., Meyer, A., & Hitchcock, C. (2005). *The universally designed classroom: Accessible curriculum and digital technologies.* Cambridge, MA: Harvard Education Press.

Samuels, B. M. (2009). Can differences between education and neuroscience be overcome by Mind, Brain, and Education? *Mind, Brain, and Education, 3*(1), 45–53.

Strangman, N., & Dalton, B. (2005). Using technology to support struggling readers: A review of the research. In D. Edyburn, K. Higgins, & R. Boone (Eds.), *Handbook of special education technology research and practice* (pp. 545–569). Whitefish Bay, WI: Knowledge by Design.

Thelen, E., & Smith, L. B. (1994). *A dynamic systems approach to the development of cognition and action*. Cambridge, MA: MIT Press.

Thelen, E., & Smith, L. B. (1998). Dynamic systems theories. In W. Damon (Series Ed.) & R. M. Lerner (Vol. Ed.), *Handbook of child psychology: Theoretical models of human development* (Vol. 1, 5th ed., pp. 563–633). New York: Wiley.

U.S. Department of Education, Office of Educational Technology. (2010). *Transforming American education: Learning powered by technology* (National Technology Education Plan 2010). Retrieved from http://www.ed.gov/sites/default/files/netp2010.pdf.

van Geert, P. (1998). We almost had a great future behind us: The contribution of nonlinear dynamics to developmental science in the making. *Developmental Science, 1*(1), 143–159.

Vygotsky, L. (1978). Mind in society: The development of higher psychological processes. Cambridge, MA: Harvard University Press.

Wertlieb, D. (2003). Applied developmental science. In I. Weiner (Series Ed.) & R. Lerner, M. Easterbrooks, & J. Mistry (Vol. Eds.), *Handbook of psychology: Developmental psychology* (Vol. 6, pp. 43–64). Hoboken, NJ: Wiley.

# CHAPTER ONE

# LEARNING IS SOCIAL AND CONTEXTUAL

The Universal Design for Learning framework rests on the assumption that learning is not possible without attention to the specific environment and task through which it is pursued. Human learning is not machine learning; children are not storage containers that can be programmed to rationally manipulate and process data. Instead, learning thrives (or fails to thrive) within deep and meaningful interactions—interactions between people and their environment. The so-called "problems" encountered by learners are not, therefore, inherent to the individual child but often created by the form the content takes and other contextual factors. From a UDL perspective, all learning situations are most effectively thought of as dynamic ecologies that capture transactions among learners, teachers, and the designed curriculum. To enhance, promote, or support learning, the entirety of this system needs to be taken into account. Even when learning individually and from a static source (such as printed text), the interaction of the learner with the material is itself social and contextual.

John Dewey, in his classic piece "The Child and the Curriculum," anticipates many of these modern-day ideas about the interactive nature of learning, the importance of the child-teacher relationship, and the ongoing challenge for educators (including researchers, curriculum designers, and teachers) to avoid the oft-repeated error of reducing pedagogy to either focusing on the individual child or the content itself rather than their complex interactions. Rather, Dewey suggested in 1902 that we marry these two goals by supporting a child's motivation and engagement within the learning environment in a scientifically rigorous way. Building on his background as a high school teacher, a philosopher, and ultimately the creator of the first Lab School, Dewey speaks as philosopher and psychologist, as idealist and pragmatist, and as progressive educator.

To explore these ideas, we reached out to a leader in mathematics and science education, Jeremy Roschelle, whose work has focused on leveraging social collaboration in learning to support the development of conceptually difficult ideas, often through advanced or emerging technologies. Roschelle, the director of the Center for Technology in Learning at SRI International, researches the design and classroom use of innovations that enhance learning of complex and conceptually difficult ideas in mathematics and science. More recently, he has been addressing large-scale use of innovative technologies in education.

CAST has worked with Roschelle on a joint project funded by the National Science Foundation to transform preservice mathematics textbooks into interactive opportunities for students to co-create learning options and "social artifacts" that can be communicated with teachers and other learners. Our conversation with Roschelle was far reaching; we learned that his interest and expertise in the social and contextual nature of learning has evolved and broadened considerably since he trained as a cognitive scientist in graduate school. He agreed with our selection of Dewey's "The Child and Curriculum"—an essay he first read while auditing a course in the philosophy of education and that he says significantly broadened his thinking about the social nature of learning. His own work has been deeply collaborative, connecting across many fields and disciplines—so much so that, through this collaborative work, he no longer thinks of himself as representing a certain academic or theoretical discipline but as working to solve educationally relevant problems.

In the conversation, Dewey's ideas struck us as both timely and timeless. Roschelle reminded us that Dewey did not have access to cognitive psychology, a field not yet developed at the time, nor did he have the modern instructional tools of the twenty-first century. And yet his ideas about the nature of learning and education remain poignant and valid, and they inform Roschelle's and our work today. Five key ideas emerged in our conversation.

### Learning as Transaction

The transaction between the person and their environment is the critical element in learning. Roschelle points out that "learning occurs in interactions between people and situations, so that's where you get the cultural, social, and contextual depth out of Dewey." He emphasizes that when thinking about educational experiences, "don't just think about the kids," but consider how the tools and design of the learning experience fosters interactions and transactions between learners and adults.

### Importance of Design

In this transactional view of learning, adults play the key role of designing the curriculum to enable the most effective learning situations. "When we design," Roschelle says, "we're not just designing the teacher-student interaction, but we're designing a set of interactions—teachers with students, students with each other in small groups, students with resources, and teachers with resources. And so, we have a lot of places to design. I think of that as a system and what we're designing is a curricular activity system that is going to optimize these kinds of transactions or interactions." Drawing on the "instructional triangle" (Cohen & Ball, 1999), Roschelle strives in his work to design for teacher, student, and resource, where the resource could be a technological resource, the space in the room, or any other instructional tool, which can all be flexibly used and reconfigured.

### Neither Child-Centered nor Content-Centered Curriculum

Roschelle raises a key tension in instructional design between a flexible, child-centered curriculum, where a child could enter the curriculum at any point and through a variety of approaches, versus a more prescribed, sequential curriculum focused on a specific learning progression. He uses Dewey to suggest that this dichotomy is a false one; learning need not be either completely child centered or completely dominated by a set curricular structure. Instead, he suggests that an ideally designed curriculum should have a well-reasoned learning progression, taking advantage of knowledge of the nature and structure of the topic being taught, but also allow for multiple situations and opportunities for learners to engage with and work to understand the material. This perspective requires a complex or dynamic systems lens on design and research in service of such design.

### Teacher as Guide

Adults both design this balanced curriculum and guide learners through it. The goal of education in Dewey's work, says Roschelle, is to promote the development of children "who are inquirers and can look at problematic situations in life. They work with tools and work with others to take on really hard, ambiguous, frustrating, difficult, long-term problems and solve them. That's the population Dewey wants to build," and adults are responsible for providing young people with educational environments where such growth is possible.

### Education as Integral Experience

Finally, Roschelle and his reflections on Dewey suggest a vision of education as a cumulative experience that builds across a learner's school and life experiences. Roschelle cautions us to remain focused on the big picture, because if, "at a middle school level, you increase learning by 10 percent, but the kids never want to learn that subject again, you've blown it." While we design specific educational experiences, these are in the service of a larger progression toward productive adults in a democratic society.

## FOR FURTHER READING

Cohen, D. K., & Ball, D. L. (1999). *Instruction, capacity, and improvement* (CPRE Research Report No. RR-043). Philadelphia: University of Pennsylvania, Consortium for Policy Research in Education.

Rogoff, B. (1990). *Apprenticeship in thinking: Cognitive development in social context.* New York: Oxford University Press.

Roschelle, J., & Clancey, W. J. (1992). Learning as social and neural. *Educational Psychologist, 27*(4), 435–453.

Vygotsky, L. S. (1978). *The mind in society: Development of higher psychological processes.* Cambridge, MA: Harvard University Press.

# The Child and the Curriculum

JOHN DEWEY

P rofound differences in theory are never gratuitous or invented. They grow out of conflicting elements in a genuine problem—a problem which is genuine just because the elements, taken as they stand, are conflicting. Any significant problem involves conditions that for the moment contradict each other. Solution comes only by getting away from the meaning of terms that is already fixed upon and coming to see the conditions from another point of view, and hence in a fresh light. But this reconstruction means travail of thought. Easier than thinking with surrender of already formed ideas and detachment from facts already learned is just to stick by what is already said, looking about for something with which to buttress it against attack.

Thus sects arise: schools of opinion. Each selects that set of conditions that appeals to it; and then erects them into a complete and independent truth, instead of treating them as a factor in a problem, needing adjustment.

The fundamental factors in the educative process are an immature, undeveloped being; and certain social aims, meanings, values incarnate in the matured experience of the adult. The educative process is the due interaction of these forces. Such a conception of each in relation to the other as facilitates completest and freest interaction is the essence of educational theory.

But here comes the effort of thought. It is easier to see the conditions in their separateness, to insist upon one at the expense of the other, to make antagonists of them, than to discover a reality to which each belongs. The easy thing is to seize upon something in the nature of the child, or upon something in the developed consciousness of the adult, and insist upon that as the key to the whole problem. When this happens a really serious practical problem—that of interaction—is transformed into an unreal, and hence insoluble, theoretic problem. Instead of seeing the educative steadily and as a whole, we see conflicting terms. We get the case of the child vs. the curriculum; of the individual nature vs. social culture. Below all other divisions in pedagogic opinion lies this opposition.

The child lives in a somewhat narrow world of personal contacts. Things hardly come within his experience unless they touch, intimately and obviously, his own well-being, or that of his family and friends. His world is a world of persons with their personal interests, rather than a realm of facts and laws. Not truth, in the sense of conformity to external fact, but affection and sympathy, is its keynote. As against this, the course of study met in the school presents material stretching back indefinitely in time, and extending outward indefinitely into space. The child is taken out of his familiar physical environment, hardly more than a square mile or so in area, into the wide world—yes, and even to the bounds of the solar system. His little span of personal memory and tradition is overlaid with the long centuries of the history of all peoples.

Again, the child's life is an integral, a total one. He passes quickly and readily from one topic to another, as from one spot to another, but is not conscious of transition or break. There is no conscious isolation, hardly conscious distinction. The things that occupy him are held together by the unity of the personal and social interests which his life carries along. Whatever is uppermost in his mind constitutes to him, for the time being, the whole universe. That universe is fluid and fluent; its contents dissolve and re-form with amazing rapidity. But, after all, it is the child's own world. It has the unity and completeness of his own life. He goes to school, and various studies divide and fractionize the world for him. Geography selects, it abstracts and analyzes one set of facts, and from one particular point of view. Arithmetic is another division, grammar another department, and so on indefinitely.

Again, in school each of these subjects is classified. Facts are torn away from their original place in experience and rearranged with reference to some general principle. Classification is not a matter of child experience; things do not come to the individual pigeonholed. The vital ties of affection, the connecting bonds of activity, hold together the variety of his personal experiences. The adult mind is so familiar with the notion of logically ordered facts that it does not recognize—it cannot realize—the amount of separating and reformulating which the facts of direct experience have to undergo before they can appear as a "study," or branch of learning. A principle, for the intellect, has had to be distinguished and defined; facts have had to be interpreted in relation to this principle, not as they are in themselves. They have had to be regathered about a new center which is wholly abstract and ideal. All this means a development of a special intellectual interest. It means ability to view facts impartially and objectively; that is, without reference to their place and meaning in one's own experience. It means capacity to analyze and to synthesize. It means highly matured intellectual habits and the command of a definite technique and apparatus of scientific inquiry. The studies as classified are the product, in a word, of the science of the ages, not of the experience of the child.

These apparent deviations and differences between child and curriculum might be almost indefinitely widened. But we have here sufficiently fundamental divergences: first, the narrow but personal world of the child against the impersonal but infinitely extended world of space and time; second, the unity, the single wholeheartedness of the child's life, and the specializations and divisions of the curriculum; third, an abstract principle of logical classification and arrangement, and the practical and emotional bonds of child life.

From these elements of conflict grow up different educational sects. One school fixes its attention upon the importance of the subject-matter of the curriculum as compared with the contents of the child's own experience. It is as if they said: Is life petty, narrow, and crude? Then studies reveal the great, wide universe with all its fullness and complexity of meaning. Is the life of the child egoistic, self-centered, impulsive? Then in these studies is found an objective universe of truth, law, and order. Is his experience confused, vague, uncertain, at the mercy of the moment's caprice and circumstance? Then studies introduce a world arranged on the basis of eternal and general truth; a world where all is measured and defined. Hence the moral: ignore and minimize the child's individual peculiarities, whims, and experiences. They are what we need to get away from. They are to be obscured or eliminated. As educators our work is precisely to substitute for these superficial and casual affairs stable and well-ordered realities; and these are found in studies and lessons.

Subdivide each topic into studies; each study into lessons; each lesson into specific facts and formulae. Let the child proceed step by step to master each one of these separate parts, and at last he will have covered the entire ground. The road which looks so long when viewed in its entirety is easily traveled, considered as a series of particular steps. Thus emphasis is put upon the logical subdivisions and consecutions of the subject-matter. Problems of instruction are problems of procuring texts giving logical parts and sequences, and of presenting these portions in class in a similar definite and graded way. Subject-matter furnishes the end, and it determines method.

The child is simply the immature being who is to be matured; he is the superficial being who is to be deepened; his is narrow experience which is to be widened. It is his to receive, to accept. His part is fulfilled when he is ductile and docile.

Not so, says the other sect. The child is the starting-point, the center, and the end. His development, his growth, is the ideal. It alone furnishes the standard. To the growth of the child all studies are subservient; they are instruments valued as they serve the needs of growth. Personality, character, is more than subject-matter. Not knowledge or information, but self-realization, is the goal. To possess all the world of knowledge and lose one's own self is as awful a fate in education as in religion. Moreover, subject-matter never can be got into the child from without. Learning is active. It involves reaching out of the mind. It involves organic assimilation starting from within. Literally, we must take our stand with the child and our departure from him. It is he and not the subject-matter which determines both quality and quantity of learning.

The only significant method is the method of the mind as it reaches out and assimilates. Subject-matter is but spiritual food, possible nutritive material. It cannot digest itself; it cannot of its own accord turn into bone and muscle and blood. The source of whatever is dead, mechanical, and formal in schools is found precisely in the subordination of the life and experience of the child to the curriculum. It is because of this that "study" has become a synonym for what is irksome, and a lesson identical with a task.

This fundamental opposition of child and curriculum set up by these two modes of doctrine can be duplicated in a series of other terms. "Discipline" is the watchword of those who magnify the course of study; "interest" that of those who blazon "The Child" upon their banner. The standpoint of the former is logical; that of the latter psychological. The first emphasizes the necessity of adequate training and scholarship on the part of the teacher; the latter that of need of sympathy with the child, and knowledge of his natural instincts. "Guidance and control" are the catchwords of one school; "freedom and initiative" of the other. Law is asserted here; spontaneity proclaimed there. The old, the conservation of what has been achieved in the pain and toil of the ages, is dear to the one; the new, change, progress, wins the affection of the other. Inertness and routine, chaos and anarchism, are accusations bandied back and forth. Neglect of the sacred authority of duty is charged by one side, only to be met by counter-charges of suppression of individuality through tyrannical despotism.

Such oppositions are rarely carried to their logical conclusion. Common-sense recoils at the extreme character of these results. They are left to theorists, while common-sense vibrates back and forward in a maze of inconsistent compromise. The need of getting theory and practical common-sense into closer connection suggests a return to our original thesis: that we have here conditions which are necessarily related to each other in the educative process, since this is precisely one of interaction and adjustment.

What, then, is the problem? It is just to get rid of the prejudicial notion that there is some gap in kind (as distinct from degree) between the child's experience and the various forms of subject-matter that make up the course of study. From the side of the child, it is a question of seeing how his experience already contains within itself elements—facts and truths—of just the same sort as those entering into the formulated study; and, what is of more importance, of how it contains within itself the attitudes, the motives, and the interests which have operated in developing and organizing the subject-matter to the plane which it now occupies. From the side of the studies, it is a question of interpreting them as outgrowths of forces operating in the child's life, and of discovering the steps that intervene between the child's present experience and their richer maturity.

Abandon the notion of subject-matter as something fixed and ready-made in itself, outside the child's experience; cease thinking of the child's experience as also something hard and fast; see it as something fluent, embryonic, vital; and we realize that the child and the curriculum are simply two limits which define a single process. Just as two points define a straight line, so the present standpoint of the child and the facts and truths of studies define instruction. It is continuous reconstruction, moving from the child's present experience out into that represented by the organized bodies of truth that we call studies.

On the face of it, the various studies, arithmetic, geography, language, botany, etc., are themselves experience—they are that of the race. They embody the cumulative outcome of the efforts, the strivings, and the successes of the human race generation after generation. They present this, not as a mere accumulation, not as a miscellaneous heap of separate bits of experience, but in some organized and systematized way—that is, as reflectively formulated.

Hence, the facts and truths that enter into the child's present experience, and those contained in the subject-matter of studies, are the initial and final terms of one reality. To oppose one to the other is to oppose the infancy and maturity of the same growing life; it is to set the moving tendency and the final result of the same process over against each other; it is to hold that the nature and the destiny of the child war with each other.

If such be the case, the problem of the relation of the child and the curriculum presents itself in this guise: Of what use, educationally speaking, is it to be able to see the end in the beginning? How does it assist us in dealing with the early stages of growth to be able to anticipate its later phases? The studies, as we have agreed, represent the possibilities of development inherent in the child's immediate crude experience. But, after all, they are not parts of that present and immediate life. Why, then, or how, make account of them?

Asking such a question suggests its own answer. To see the outcome is to know in what direction the present experience is moving, provided it move normally and soundly. The far-away point, which is of no significance to us simply as far away, becomes of huge importance the moment we take it as defining a present direction of movement. Taken in this way it is no remote and distant result to be achieved, but a guiding method in dealing with the present. The systematized and defined experience of the adult mind, in other words, is of value to us in interpreting the child's life as it immediately shows itself, and in passing on to guidance or direction.

Let us look for a moment at these two ideas: interpretation and guidance. The child's present experience is in no way self-explanatory. It is not final, but transitional. It is nothing complete in itself, but just a sign or index of certain growth-tendencies. As long as we confine our gaze to what the child here and now puts forth, we are confused and misled. We cannot read its meaning. Extreme depreciations of the child morally and intellectually, and sentimental idealizations of him, have their root in a common fallacy. Both spring from taking stages of a growth or movement as something cut off and fixed. The first fails to see the promise contained in feelings and deeds which, taken by themselves, are uncompromising and repellent; the second fails to see that even the most pleasing and beautiful exhibitions are but signs, and that they begin to spoil and rot the moment they are treated as achievements.

What we need is something which will enable us to interpret, to appraise, the elements in the child's present puttings forth and fallings away, his exhibitions of power and weakness, in the light of some larger growth-process in which they have their place. Only in this way can we discriminate. If we isolate the child's present inclinations, purposes, and experiences from the place they occupy and the part they have to perform in a developing experience, all stand upon the same level; all alike are equally good and equally bad. But in the movement of life different elements stand upon different planes of value. Some of the child's deeds are symptoms of a waning tendency; they are survivals in functioning of an organ which has done its part and is passing out of vital use. To give positive attention to such qualities is to arrest development upon a lower level. It is systematically to maintain a rudimentary phase of growth. Other activities are signs of a culminating power and interest; to them applies the maxim of striking while the iron is hot. As regards them, it is perhaps a matter of now or never. Selected, utilized, emphasized, they may mark a turning-point for good in the child's whole career; neglected, an opportunity goes, never to be recalled. Other acts and feelings are prophetic; they represent the dawning of flickering light that will shine steadily only in the far future. As regards them there is little at present to do but give them fair and full chance, waiting for the future for definite direction.

Just as, upon the whole, it was the weakness of the "old education" that it made invidious comparisons between the immaturity of the child and the maturity of the adult, regarding the former as something to be got away from as soon as possible and as much as possible; so it is the danger of the "new education" that it regard the child's present powers and interests as something finally significant in themselves. In truth, his learnings and achievements are fluid and moving. They change from day to day and from hour to hour.

It will do harm if child-study leave in the popular mind the impression that a child of a given age has a positive equipment of purposes and interests to be cultivated just as they stand. Interests in reality are but attitudes toward possible experiences; they are not achievements; their worth is in the leverage they afford, not in the accomplishment they represent. To take the phenomena presented at a given age as in any way self-explanatory or self-contained is inevitably to result in indulgence and spoiling. Any power, whether of child or adult, is indulged when it is taken on its given and present level in consciousness. Its genuine meaning is in the propulsion it affords toward a higher level. It is just something to do with. Appealing to the interest upon the present plane means excitation; it means playing with a power so as continually to stir it up without directing it toward definite achievement. Continuous initiation, continuous starting of activities that do not arrive, is, for all practical purposes, as bad as the continual repression of initiative in conformity with supposed interests of some more perfect thought or will. It is as if the child were forever tasting and never eating; always having his palate tickled upon the emotional side, but never getting the organic satisfaction that comes only with digestion of food and transformation of it into working power.

As against such a view, the subject-matter of science and history and art serves to reveal the real child to us. We do not know the meaning either of his tendencies or of his performances excepting as we take them as germinating seed, or opening bud, of some fruit to be borne. The whole world of visual nature is all too small an answer to the problem of the meaning of the child's instinct for light and form. The entire science of physics is none too much to interpret adequately to us what is involved in some simple demand of the child for explanation of some casual change that has attracted his attention. The art of Raphael or of Corot is none too much to enable us to value the impulses stirring in the child when he draws and daubs.

So much for the use of the subject-matter in interpretation. Its further employment in direction or guidance is but an expansion of the same thought. To interpret the fact is to see it in its vital movement, to see it in its relation to growth. But to view it as a part of a normal growth is to secure the basis for guiding it. Guidance is not external imposition. It is freeing the life-process for its own most adequate fulfilment. What was said about disregard of the child's present experience because of its remoteness from mature experience; and of the sentimental idealization of the child's naïve caprices and performances, may be repeated here with slightly altered phrase. There are those who see no alternative between forcing the child from without, or leaving him entirely alone. Seeing no alternative, some choose one mode, some another. Both fall into the same fundamental error. Both fail to see that development is a definite process, having its own law which can be fulfilled only when adequate and normal conditions are provided. Really to interpret the child's present crude impulses in counting, measuring, and arranging things in rhythmic series involves mathematical scholarship—a knowledge of the mathematical formulae and relations which have, in the history of the race, grown out of just such crude beginnings. To see the whole history of development which intervenes between these two terms is simply to see what step the child needs to take just here and now; to what use he needs to put his blind impulse in order that it may get clarity and gain force.

If, once more, the "old education" tended to ignore the dynamic quality, the developing force inherent in the child's present experience, and therefore to assume that direction and control were just matters of arbitrarily putting the child in a given path and compelling him to walk there, the "new education" is in danger of taking the idea of development in altogether too formal and empty a way. The child is expected to "develop" this or that fact or truth out of his own mind. He is told to think things out, or work things out for himself, without being supplied any of the environing conditions which are requisite to start and guide thought. Nothing can be developed from nothing; nothing but the crude can be developed out of the crude—and this is what surely happens when we throw the child back upon his achieved self as a finality, and invite him to spin new truths of nature or of conduct out of that. It is certainly as futile to expect a child to evolve a universe out of his own mere mind as it is for a philosopher to attempt that task. Development does not mean just getting something out of the mind. It is a development of experience and into experience that is really wanted. And this is impossible save as just that educative medium is provided which will enable the powers and interests that have been selected as valuable to function. They must operate, and how they operate will depend almost entirely upon the stimuli which surround them and the material upon which they exercise themselves. The problem of direction is thus the problem of selecting appropriate stimuli for instincts and impulses which it is desired to employ in the gaining of new experience. What new experiences are desirable, and thus what stimuli are needed, it is impossible to tell except as there is some comprehension of the development which is aimed at; except, in a word, as the adult knowledge is drawn upon as revealing the possible career open to the child.

It may be of use to distinguish and to relate to each other the logical and the psychological aspects of experience—the former standing for subject-matter in itself, the latter for it in relation to the child. A psychological statement of experience follows its actual growth; it is historic; it notes steps actually taken, the uncertain and tortuous, as well as the efficient and successful. The logical point of view, on the other hand, assumes that the development has reached a certain positive stage of fulfilment. It neglects the process and considers the outcome. It summarizes and arranges, and thus separates the achieved results from the actual steps by which they were forthcoming in the first instance. We may compare the difference between the logical and the psychological to the difference between the notes which an explorer makes in a new country, blazing a trail and finding his way along as best he may, and the finished map that is constructed after the country has been thoroughly explored. The two are mutually dependent. Without the more or less accidental and devious paths traced by the explorer there would be no facts which could be utilized in the making of the complete and related chart. But no one would get the benefit of the explorer's trip if it was not compared and checked up with similar wanderings undertaken by others; unless the new geographical facts learned, the streams crossed, the mountains climbed, etc., were viewed, not as mere incidents in the journey of the particular traveler, but (quite apart from the individual explorer's life) in relation to other similar facts already known. The map orders individual experiences, connecting them with one another irrespective of the local and temporal circumstances and accidents of their original discovery.

Of what use is this formulated statement of experience? Of what use is the map?

Well, we may first tell what the map is not. The map is not a substitute for a personal experience. The map does not take the place of an actual journey. The logically formulated material of a science or branch of learning, of a study, is no substitute for the having of individual experiences. The mathematical formula for a falling body does not take the place of personal contact and immediate individual experience with the falling thing. But the map, a summary, an arranged and orderly view of previous experiences, serves as a guide to future experience; it gives direction; it facilitates control; it economizes effort, preventing useless wandering, and pointing out the paths which lead most quickly and most certainly to a desired result. Through the map every new traveler may get for his own journey the benefits of the results of others' explorations without the waste of energy and loss of time involved in their wanderings—wanderings which he himself would be obliged to repeat were it not for just the assistance of the objective and generalized record of their performances. That which we call a science or study puts the net product of past experience in the form which makes it most available for the future. It represents a capitalization which may at once be turned to interest. It economizes the workings of the mind in every way. Memory is less taxed because the facts are grouped together about some common principle, instead of being connected solely with the varying incidents of their original discovery. Observation is assisted; we know what to look for and where to look. It is the difference between looking for a needle in a haystack, and searching for a given paper in a well-arranged cabinet. Reasoning is directed, because there is a certain general path or line laid out along which ideas naturally march, instead of moving from one chance association to another.

There is, then, nothing final about a logical rendering of experience. Its value is not contained in itself; its significance is that of standpoint, outlook, method. It intervenes between the more casual, tentative, and roundabout experiences of the past, and more controlled and orderly experiences of the future. It gives past experience in that net form which renders it most available and most significant, most fecund for future experience. The abstractions, generalizations, and classifications which it introduces all have prospective meaning.

The formulated result is then not to be opposed to the process of growth. The logical is not set over against the psychological. The surveyed and arranged result occupies a critical position in the process of growth. It marks a turning-point. It shows how we may get the benefit of past effort in controlling future endeavor. In the largest sense the logical standpoint is itself psychological; it has its meaning as a point in the development of experience, and its justification is in its functioning in the future growth which it insures.

Hence the need of reinstating into experience the subject-matter of the studies, or branches of learning. It must be restored to the experience from which it has been abstracted. It needs to be psychologized; turned over, translated into the immediate and individual experiencing within which it has its origin and significance.

Every study or subject thus has two aspects: one for the scientist as a scientist; the other for the teacher as a teacher. These two aspects are in no sense opposed or conflicting. But neither are they immediately identical. For the scientist, the subject-matter represents simply a given body of truth to be employed in locating new problems, instituting new researches, and carrying them through to a verified outcome. To him the subject-matter of the science is self-contained. He refers various portions of it to each other; he connects new facts with it. He is not, as a scientist, called upon to travel outside its particular bounds; if he does, it is only to get more facts of the same general sort. The problem of the teacher is a different one. As a teacher he is not concerned with adding new facts to the science he teaches; in propounding new hypotheses or in verifying them. He is concerned with the subject-matter of the science as representing a given stage and phase of the development of experience. His problem is that of inducing a vital and personal experiencing. Hence, what concerns him, as teacher, is the ways in which that subject may become a part of experience; what there is in the child's present that is usable with reference to it; how such elements are to be used; how his own knowledge of the subject-matter may assist in interpreting the child's needs and doings, and determine the medium in which the child should be placed in order that his growth may be properly directed. He is concerned, not with the subject-matter as such, but with the subject-matter as a related factor in a total and growing experience. Thus to see it is to psychologize it.

It is the failure to keep in mind the double aspect of subject-matter which causes the curriculum and child to be set over against each other as described in our early pages. The subject-matter, just as it is for the scientist, has no direct relationship to the child's present experience. It stands outside of it. The danger here is not a merely theoretical one. We are practically threatened on all sides. Textbook and teacher vie with each other in presenting to the child the subject-matter as it stands to the specialist. Such modification and revision as it undergoes are a mere elimination of certain scientific difficulties, and the general reduction to a lower intellectual level. The material is not translated into life-terms, but is directly offered as a substitute for, or an external annex to, the child's present life.

Three typical evils result: In the first place, the lack of any organic connection with what the child has already seen and felt and loved makes the material purely formal and symbolic. There is a sense in which it is impossible to value too highly the formal and the symbolic. The genuine form, the real symbol, serve as methods in the holding and discovery of truth. They are tools by which the individual pushes out most surely and widely into unexplored areas. They are means by which he brings to bear whatever of reality he has succeeded in gaining in past searchings. But this happens only when the symbol really symbolizes—when it stands for and sums up in shorthand actual experiences which the individual has already gone through. A symbol which is induced from without, which has not been led up to in preliminary activities, is, as we say, a bare or mere symbol; it is dead and barren. Now, any fact, whether of arithmetic, or geography, or grammar, which is not led up to and into out of something which has previously occupied a significant position in the child's life for its own sake, is forced into this position. It is not a reality, but just the sign of a reality which might be experienced if certain conditions were fulfilled. But the abrupt presentation of the fact as something known by others, and requiring only to be studied and learned by the child, rules out such conditions of fulfilment. It condemns the fact to be a hieroglyph: it would mean something if one only had the key. The clue being lacking, it remains an idle curiosity, to fret and obstruct the mind, a dead weight to burden it.

The second evil in this external presentation is lack of motivation. There are not only no facts or truths which have been previously felt as such with which to appropriate and assimilate the new, but there is no craving, no need, no demand. When the subject-matter has been psychologized, that is, viewed as an out-growth of present tendencies and activities, it is easy to locate in the present some obstacle, intellectual, practical, or ethical, which can be handled more adequately if the truth in question be mastered. This need supplies motive for the learning. An end which is the child's own carries him on to possess the means of its accomplishment. But when material is directly supplied in the form of a lesson to be learned as a lesson, the connecting links of need and aim are conspicuous for their absence. What we mean by the mechanical and dead in instruction is a result of this lack of motivation. The organic and vital mean interaction—they mean play of mental demand and material supply.

The third evil is that even the most scientific matter, arranged in most logical fashion, loses this quality, when presented in external, ready-made fashion, by the time it gets to the child. It has to undergo some modification in order to shut out some phases too hard to grasp, and to reduce some of the attendant difficulties. What happens? Those things which are most significant to the scientific man, and most valuable in the logic of actual inquiry and classification, drop out. The really thought-provoking character is obscured, and the organizing function disappears. Or, as we commonly say, the child's reasoning powers, the faculty of abstraction and generalization, are not adequately developed. So the subject-matter is evacuated of its logical value, and, though it is what it is only from the logical standpoint, is presented as stuff only for "memory." This is the contradiction: the child gets the advantage neither of the adult logical formulation, nor of his own native competencies of apprehension and response. Hence the logic of the child is hampered and mortified, and we are almost fortunate if he does not get actual non-science, flat and common-place residua of what was gaining scientific vitality a generation or two ago—degenerate reminiscence of what someone else once formulated on the basis of the experience that some further person had, once upon a time, experienced.

The train of evils does not cease. It is all too common for opposed erroneous theories to play straight into each other's hands. Psychological considerations may be slurred or shoved one side; they cannot be crowded out. Put out of the door, they come back through the window. Somehow and somewhere motive must be appealed to, connection must be established between the mind and its material. There is no question of getting along without this bond of connection; the only question is whether it be such as grows out of the material itself in relation to the mind, or be imported and hitched on from some outside source. If the subject-matter of the lessons be such as to have an appropriate place within the expanding consciousness of the child, if it grows out of his own past doings, thinkings, and sufferings, and grows into application in further achievements and receptivities, then no device or trick of method has to be resorted to in order to enlist "interest." The psychologized is of interest—that is, it is placed in the whole of conscious life so that it shares the worth of that life. But the externally presented material, conceived and generated in standpoints and attitudes remote from the child, and developed in motives alien to him, has no such place of its own. Hence the recourse to adventitious leverage to push it in, to factitious drill to drive it in, to artificial bribe to lure it in.

Three aspects of this recourse to outside ways for giving the subject-matter some psychological meaning may be worth mentioning. Familiarity breeds contempt, but it also breeds something like affection. We get used to the chains we wear, and we miss them when removed. 'Tis an old story that through custom we finally embrace what at first wore a hideous mien. Unpleasant, because meaningless, activities may get agreeable if long enough persisted in. It is possible for the mind to develop interest in a routine or mechanical procedure if conditions are continually supplied which demand that mode of operation and preclude any other sort. I frequently hear dulling devices and empty exercises defended and extolled because "the children take such an 'interest' in them." Yes, that is the worst of it; the mind, shut out from worthy employ and missing the taste of adequate performance, comes down to the level of that which is left to it to know and do, and perforce takes an interest in a cabined and cramped experience. To find satisfaction in its own exercise is the normal law of mind, and if large and meaningful business for the mind be denied, it tries to content itself with the formal movements that remain to it—and too often succeeds, save in those cases of more intense activity which cannot accommodate themselves, and that make up the unruly and declassé of our school product. An interest in the formal apprehension of symbols and in their memorized reproduction becomes in many pupils a substitute for the original and vital interest in reality; and all because, the subject-matter of the course of study being out of relation to the concrete mind of the individual, some substitute bond to hold it in some kind of working relation to the mind must be discovered and elaborated.

The second substitute for living motivation in the subject-matter is that of contrast-effects; the material of the lesson is rendered interesting, if not in itself, at least in contrast with some alternative experience. To learn the lesson is more interesting than to take a scolding, be held up to general ridicule, stay after school, receive degradingly low marks, or fail to be promoted. And very much of what goes by the name of "discipline," and prides itself upon opposing the doctrines of a soft pedagogy and upon upholding the banner of effort and duty, is nothing more or less than just this appeal to "interest" in its obverse aspect—to fear, to dislike of various kinds of physical, social, and personal pain. The subject-matter does not appeal; it cannot appeal; it lacks origin and bearing in a growing experience. So the appeal is to the thousand and one outside and irrelevant agencies which may serve to throw, by sheer rebuff and rebound, the mind back upon the material from which it is constantly wandering.

Human nature being what it is, however, it tends to seek its motivation in the agreeable rather than in the disagreeable, in direct pleasure rather than in alternative pain. And so has come up the modern theory and practice of the "interesting," in the false sense of that term. The material is still left; so far as its own characteristics are concerned, just material externally selected and formulated. It is still just so much geography and arithmetic and grammar study; not so much potentiality of child-experience with regard to language, earth, and numbered and measured reality. Hence the difficulty of bringing the mind to bear upon it; hence its repulsiveness; the tendency for attention to wander; for other acts and images to crowd in and expel the lesson. The legitimate way out is to transform the material; to psychologize it—that is, once more, to take it and to develop it within the range and scope of the child's life. But it is easier and simpler to leave it as it is, and then by trick of method to arouse interest, to make it interesting; to cover it with sugar-coating; to conceal its barrenness by intermediate and unrelated material; and finally, as it were, to get the child to swallow and digest the unpalatable morsel while he is enjoying tasting something quite different. But alas for the analogy! Mental assimilation is a matter of consciousness; and if the attention has not been playing upon the actual material, that has not been apprehended, nor worked into faculty.

How, then, stands the case of Child vs. Curriculum? What shall the verdict be? The radical fallacy in the original pleadings with which we set out is the supposition that we have no choice save either to leave the child to his own unguided spontaneity or to inspire direction upon him from without. Action is response; it is adaptation, adjustment. There is no such thing as sheer self-activity possible—because all activity takes place in a medium, in a situation, and with reference to its conditions. But, again, no such thing as imposition of truth from without, as insertion of truth from without, is possible. All depends upon the activity which the mind itself undergoes in responding to what is presented from without. Now, the value of the formulated wealth of knowledge that makes up the course of study is that it may enable the educator to determine the environment of the child, and thus by indirection to direct. Its primary value, its primary indication, is for the teacher, not for the child. It says to the teacher: Such and such are the capacities, the fulfilments, in truth and beauty and behavior, open to these children. Now see to it that day by day the conditions are such that their own activities move inevitably in this direction, toward such culmination of themselves. Let the child's nature fulfil its own destiny, revealed to you in whatever of science and art and industry the world now holds as its own.

The case is of Child. It is his present powers which are to assert themselves; his present capacities which are to be exercised; his present attitudes which are to be realized. But save as the teacher knows, knows wisely and thoroughly, the race-expression which is embodied in that thing we call the Curriculum, the teacher knows neither what the present power, capacity, or attitude is, nor yet how it is to be asserted, exercised, and realized.

# CHAPTER TWO

# CONSTRUCTIVISM, WITH CONSTRAINTS

By definition, UDL education environments emphasize the provision of options. But this necessary flexibility must be applied thoughtfully and with careful attention to learning goals; openness is no more likely to promote deep learning than rigidity. A common concern about the Universal Design for Learning framework rests on the misconception that the goal is to remove all challenges in the process of learning, or to provide options in all aspects of a task such that learners are able to avoid struggle. In fact, education is not tractable without appropriate challenge. Learning relies on being confronted with, and working through, observations and ideas that challenge one's understandings, problems that push the edge of skills, and application of learning to novel, meaningful tasks. The flexibility inherent in UDL environments should be constrained so as to promote desirable difficulty. Students should struggle productively with construct-relevant ideas and activities while barriers to learning are systematically removed.

The featured article, "The Unschooled Mind: Why Even the Best Students in the Best Schools May Not Understand," which Howard Gardner originally gave as the International Baccalaureate Organization's annual Peterson Lecture, describes aspects of typical education that might interfere with learning and how educational experiences might instead be used to foster deep understanding. In a far-reaching discussion, Gardner begins by laying out three quarrels he has with the great developmental psychologist Jean Piaget and uses this as a springboard into an explanation of the concept of educating for understanding. As is typical in his writing, Gardner combines the use of familiar, accessible examples with insightful arguments about challenging topics—from what it means to be an expert (a person who can use knowledge in new situations), to the educational messages available from apprenticeships and children's museums, to how educators might rethink current approaches to assessment.

Gardner has spent decades developing a rich set of ideas about how learning is best fostered. The author of several best-selling and acclaimed books, Gardner is among the most influential public intellectuals in the United States. In his early years as a developmental psychologist, he trained with some of the giants of the field, forging personal connections with Erik A. Erikson, Jean Piaget, and Jerome Bruner. His work in neuropsychology focused on the impact of brain pathologies on artistic and other high-level skills. In the 1980s, he shifted the focus of his work to issues of teaching, learning, and school reform. He is best known for his theory of multiple intelligences, a critique of the notion that there exists but a single human intelligence that can be adequately assessed by standard psychometric instruments.

Gardner's insight into the balance between learners actively and somewhat freely developing their own understandings and educators purposefully guiding or limiting the bounds of this exploration in many ways elucidates how UDL defines the interaction among teaching, learning, and the environment in an inherently bidirectional (transactional), mutually supportive, and constructive manner. For this reason, we approached Gardner to share his perspective on the idea of what we call "constructivism, with constraints."

In our conversation with Gardner about "The Unschooled Mind," we were struck by his thoughts about how the UDL framework is *aligned with* a constructivist approach and yet clearly *distinguishable from* this type of overarching educational philosophy. Gardner emphasizes that UDL informs the development and "mindful" use of flexible materials, providing a practical approach to changing education. Our conversation focused on what the resulting approach to education might look like, marrying constructivism and constraints. Four key ideas emerged.

### Constructivism Is Not Intuitive

When you ask people how learning works best, the natural way to envision the learning process is to picture an expert imparting knowledge to a learner. Gardner suggests that everyone from children, to parents, to policy makers sees this approach as how learning works; they tend to see "knowledge, information existing outside of you, and the job of the teacher or the book is to give it to you as efficiently as possible, and, once you have it can give it back, that is what learning is all about." He suggests that this dominant view is the reason to demand constructivism, to clearly describe an alternative in which "the only way to make something your own is to wrestle with it in terms of your own understandings, see where your understandings are limited or not adequate . . . and, then try to figure out the best approach, the best strategy, the best method, the best experiment that will end up yielding an answer, or at least a better question." Knowledge building "involves active motivation and pursuit by the learner."

### Constraints Facilitate Learning

This process of wrestling to build one's own understanding fails to have optimal effects, however, unless guided in the appropriate places by a more skilled expert. For Gardner, the first category of constraints on learning is the natural constraints of humans as "not all-purpose learning systems": "There are certain things which we learn easily and don't even have to go to school, [and] there are other things which are quite difficult to learn, [so] if you want to understand human learning you have to understand as best you can what those biases, constraints, and inclinations are." This type of basic constraint or bias is backdrop to the purposeful type of constraints needed in educational settings.

Gardner argues that "naïve all-out constructivism, where you just give somebody a problem and you get out of the way" rarely succeeds in promoting deep understanding. Instead, learners need a frame that provides structure, and this frame can be withdrawn as it is less needed. Gardner makes clear that "no person ever created knowledge completely on his own, and all of the great discoveries, whether it's Darwin, or Galileo, or anybody, they were based on building on what other people did before, so why should we penalize young learners by saying, figure it out all by yourself?"

### "Individuate and Pluralize"

Being able to individually apply openness and constraints in the appropriate places during a learning experience for each unique learner poses an obvious challenge. Gardner's response is twofold. First, he suggests educators "individuate," or "learn as much about each person as possible to try to teach him or her in ways that are compatible." And while he recognizes that this may appear quixotic when thinking about the number of students educators often teach, he suggests that schools build up and leverage "individualized knowledge within the system"—including data from students and parents themselves—to provide a starting point for individualization.

Second, Gardner suggests that "pluralization" involves presenting key concepts and skills in multiple ways. This takes skill and is most successful when the educator possesses deep pedagogical and content knowledge so that she can "be shrewd about a particular idea or concept" in order to "use the very best entry points and modes of response and modes of presentation." In this respect, UDL echoes Gardner's work in calling for multiple means of representation as one of its three principles.

### Assessment as "Performance of Understanding"

Learners' progress in this approach to instruction will be best gauged when assessment is based on what Gardner calls "performances of understanding." Effective assessments investigate a learner's ability to apply the knowledge to an unexpected, complicated, new situation. Give a learner "something they couldn't have known about beforehand and ask them to mobilize their skills, knowledge, concepts, disciplines, and so on to make sense of it." This kind of performance should follow from a clear instructional goal guiding the learning experience, and it should have the potential to "expose the depth, and versatility, and subtlety of your thinking." Gardner suggests that researchers, even those who espouse a constructivist approach, are too quick to accept more typical assessments that rely on memorization and responses based on what was explicitly taught; he pushed us to instead ask "if somebody was a good student in our school, what should they be able to do that somebody in a direct instruction environment couldn't do?"

This last question pushes researchers towards an ambitious agenda that reflects the equally ambitious goals of the UDL framework. If UDL is intended to guide creation of learning environments in which all students are enabled and expected to demonstrate the kind of learning Gardner describes, then pursuing rich, meaningful questions may be the researcher's performance of understanding.

### FOR FURTHER READING

Carey, S. (1985). *Conceptual change in childhood.* Cambridge, MA: MIT Press.

Edelson, D. C., Gordin, D. N., & Pea, R. D. (1999). Addressing the challenges of inquiry based learning through technology and curriculum design. *Journal of the Learning Sciences, 8*(3/4), 391–450.

Gardner, H. (1981). *The quest for mind: Piaget, Levi-Strauss, and the structuralist movement.* New York: Knopf.

# The Unschooled Mind

## Why Even the Best Students in the Best Schools May Not Understand

HOWARD GARDNER

I'm trained in developmental psychology, a field in which the contributions of Jean Piaget are unequalled. I have had a very lively career during which I challenged Piaget on several issues. My three principal arguments with him are as follows.

First of all, Piaget believed that if you studied children, you had to know what they were going to become—what the end state of development is. Piaget thought it was to be a scientist; that's what Piaget was. However, in my own training I had spent a lot of time working in the arts. I felt that there was something wrong with a theory which only talked about the mind of the scientist as being the end-all of a child's development. So I began to explore what development would be like, if one thought of participation in the arts as an artist, or a critic, or a performer, or a connoisseur as being a viable end state. This is not to say that human beings should develop to become artists any more than they should develop to become scientists, but rather that we can develop many different kinds of human beings.

The second argument I had with Piaget, and the one that I gained recognition for, was with respect to the notion that there is a single thing called intelligence which can be measured by an intelligence test. Now it's not widely known that Piaget studied in Alfred Binet's laboratory, specifically with Théodore Simon who had worked with Binet. Piaget became interested in children's minds because of the mistakes the children made on the intelligence tests. Piaget explained the general intelligence that all human beings share.

I define intelligence as the ability to solve a problem, or to fashion a product which is valued in at least one culture or community. Psychologists of intelligence concede that solving problems is important, but they shy away from any concern about making something—like writing essays, staging plays, designing buildings, and other human feats. Moreover psychologists get upset when you talk about an ability being valued in a culture; that is because it suggests that, unless a culture provides certain opportunities, a person might not seem to be smart. Most psychologists believe that intelligence is completely in the brain . . . and if you know exactly where to stick the measurement device, you can figure out how smart that person is.

In my view intelligence is always an interaction between potentials and what's available in a culture. For example, Bobby Fischer was one of the greatest chess players in the history of the world. But if Bobby Fischer had been born in a culture where there was no chess, he would just have been an awkward geek; he had a brain that was perfectly matched to something in his culture, namely chess, but mismatched to just about everything else. It is worth pointing out that Piaget thought he was studying all of intelligence. But I believe he was studying logical mathematical intelligence (later in his life I think he came to the same conclusion about the focus of his own work). In contrast, I talk about intelligence which artists have as well as those intelligences which are crucial in the human sphere—something of great concern to educators as we begin to deal with global issues, moral issues, issues of value and the like.

My third argument with Piaget concerns the most interesting claim that he made. If you remember your studies of Piaget, you will remember that he maintained that children pass through stages of cognitive development. So infants "know" the world in one way, five-year-olds in another way, ten-year-olds in another way, and 15-year-olds in still another way. When you go from nine to 11 or from 13 to 16 years old, not only do you see the world in a very different way, but you can't even remember how you used to construe the world.

An example. At age seven you don't believe that you ever embraced certain ideas: if a ball of clay were squished, there would be less clay there; or that if water were poured into a different kind of vessel, there will be more or less water depending on the shape of the receiving vessel. Yet every four-year-old in the world believes those things. Where Piaget was wrong, I believe, was in his argument that when people get older, they see the world in a different way and they no longer have access to earlier ways of knowing. I argue that most of us, except in areas where we are expert, continue to think the way we did when we were five years of age. We continue to think the way we did before we went to school. That's a pretty radical thesis.

So my remarks focus on the subject of education for understanding. If I said to you, "What is understanding and how can we determine whether understanding has been achieved?"—Those are much more difficult questions.

I define understanding as the capacity to take knowledge, skills, concepts, facts learned in one context, usually the school context, and use that knowledge in a new context, in a place where you haven't been forewarned to make use of that knowledge. If you were only asked to use knowledge in the same situation in which it was introduced, you might understand, but you might not; we can't tell. But if something new happens out in the street or in the sky or in the newspaper, and you can draw on your earlier knowings, then I would infer that you understand. I'll introduce my "problématique" with three quite common-sense examples.

In the first five years of life children all over the world, with very little formal tutelage, learn to speak, to understand, to tell stories, to tell jokes, to draw, to sing, to invent new tunes, to engage in pretend play—all the things which Piaget and other psychologists demonstrated. Even though nobody knows how to teach these things, young people still learn them all. Then they go to school and suddenly, in the very place where we are supposed to know how to teach them, it's very hard and many of them don't do well. That's a paradox.

One more example. Students at the very best universities in the United States (places like MIT and Johns Hopkins), with very high grades in physics, ultimately leave their class and are given a problem to solve on the street, or a game to play, each of which involves various physical principles. Not only do the students use what they learned in school, but they actually answer in the same way that five-year-olds do.

Ask almost anybody what happens, what forces obtain, when you flip a coin. Most people will come up with the following answer (even people who have taken physics courses): you've got a certain amount of force in your hand and you transfer that force to the coin; for a while that force makes the coin go up and then, when the force kind of gets spent, the coin is tired and kind of flips to the ground. However, physics teaches us that the second you release the coin, the only force that obtains on the coin is gravity. That authoritative account goes against a very powerful intuition that you develop when you're young. And it's not the intuition that's abandoned. It's Newton's and Galileo's laws of motion that prove very difficult to master.

A third vignette is a personal one. My daughter, a very good student, telephoned me when she was a sophomore in college, crying. I said, "Why are you crying?" She said, "It's my physics; I don't understand it." I said, "Well, you know" (and I was telling the truth) "I really respect you for taking physics because it's difficult and I wouldn't have taken it in college." I then added, "I don't even care what grade you get, but it's really important that you understand your physics." So I said, "Go to your instructor and have him or her explain to you what it is you don't understand." And she said, "Dad, you don't get it! I've never understood."

This exchange had a profound impact on me. My daughter was not saying that she was a faker or a "poseur." What she was saying is what I think most of us experience: we know the moves to make in school, to get good grades and even to be successful, but we know that if people put the questions to us in another way, if they push to see how much we have really understood, the whole house of cards might fall.

At least in the United States, there are formidable obstacles to understanding.

1. Short-answer assessments, or what I call a "text/test context." You read a textbook. The test is based on the textbook, and the textbook tells you the answers you have to give.
2. The correct answer compromise is an "entente" between the teacher and the student. No matter how you respond, nobody should ask any further question. No one is made uncomfortable, but deeper understanding is avoided.
3. The pressure for coverage, which means: there are 37 chapters in the book and you must get through all 37 chapters by the end of the term.

So, three vignettes. The young child learns so easily; the school child has difficulty. The students who get A's at the best universities in the world are still Aristotelians in their models of the physical world. And then, of course, the most powerful evidence from my own daughter. What's going on here? I call it cognitive Freudianism.

Freud convinced people that, as adults, we continue to have the same personality traits as we did when we were children. We fight the same battles we fought in the nursery with our parents and our siblings. Most people who live in a modern Western society believe this. (If you don't believe it and you pay me $100 an hour, I will convince you that it's true.) That's what psychoanalysis is all about. I'm making the claim that Freud was correct in an area that he wasn't expert in, and where Piaget was allegedly the authority. Namely, except in areas where we are experts, most of us continue to think the way we did when we were five years old.

An expert is a person who comes to understand the world differently. But that is very difficult to do and I'm going to argue today that it's not done very often. This is the thesis of my remarks. I'm going to provide evidence that no matter where you look in the curriculum, you will find students who don't understand: physics, mathematics, biology, literature, art. It's ubiquitous. Later I will chronicle things we can do about this situation. It is possible to educate for understanding.

My analysis of the potency of the five-year-old mind has three foci, which I have introduced to you already. There is the young natural learner: the three, four or five-year-old who absorbs and constructs so much about the world without formal tutelage. There is the student in most schools who basically masters what school requires so that he or she can get to the next level. But I will argue he doesn't really understand. Then there's the individual we want: the person who can use knowledge in new situations. That's my definition of an expert.

A form of knowing (a theory of knowledge) goes with each of these three foci. The expert is a person who can use the skills that are valued in his or her culture. So when an historical example comes up, he can draw on history; when a physical example comes up, he can draw from physics, and so on. That's what we want; that's why we go to school. If people are not going to be able to use the knowledge acquired, then we may as well close schools down. Scholastic knowledge is what we are very good at doing in school; but unless that scholastic knowledge can be activated in new circumstances, it remains inert and essentially useless.

We teach people notations, squiggles on a paper, formal concepts—what is gravity, what is density, what is force. People who have no sense of what it's like in the world can nonetheless give you a formula and a definition if that's what is called for in class. Then, if you're lucky and you attend an excellent college preparatory school, you get epistemic forms. Epistemic forms constitute the ways in which people think in the different disciplines. To think like a historian is not the same as to think like a literary critic or a biologist.

In the first years of life a natural learner benefits from what Piaget so brilliantly described: sensory motor knowledge, learning about the world, using your hands and your eyes, exploring the world of objects, the world of liquids poured from one container to another, and what I call first-order symbolic competence. People use words, pictures, gestures to communicate meanings. That's what every five-year-old can do.

That's the good news. However, five-year-olds do one thing which is troublesome: they form intuitive conceptions or theories—theory of matter, theories of mind, theories of life. Every normal five-year-old develops these theories. And those theories can prove serviceable for getting along in the world. However, all too often the theories are wrong. School is supposed to replace the erroneous theories with better theories.

So what's a theory of matter? A theory of matter is: if I have a heavy object in this hand, a light object in this hand and I release them at the same time, the heavier one will fall more quickly. That's what you learn intuitively. Heavy things fall more quickly. However, Galileo went to the top of the tower of Pisa, dropped two objects, and since then informed individuals understand that that's not in fact what happens. We understand that the laws of acceleration are independent of weight (density). But as children we develop a very powerful theory of matter, and that's very hard to shake.

Here's a theory of life: every five-year-old believes if it's moving, it's alive; if it's not moving, it's dead. This is a very useful theory. However, it doesn't help for sleeping dogs, and computers pose a real problem. Are computers which display moving images alive or dead? It's very hard to say.

Here's a theory of mind. I've got a mind; you've got a mind. If we look the same, our minds are the same. If we look different, our minds are different. If you look like me, you've got a good mind; if you look different, you've got a bad mind. This is a very powerful theory which is very entrenched. It shows up in all kinds of places. Just turn on the television for evidence. It's a conception like this that education is supposed to deal with, and it's this, I maintain, that education has, by and large, failed to deal with.

Why do these misconceptions arise and endure? I claim it happens because there are different kinds of constraints operating on us.

The first constraint has to do with the kind of species we are. We learn certain things very easily. We develop certain theories very readily, and other ones prove very hard for us to acquire. It's a whole interesting evolutionary question why that should be the case.

There are institutional constraints. If you put 30 to 50 people in a room like this and one person in front of them, it's very hard to explain things so that all who are present can understand. For every person who is nodding, three are nodding off.

There are also disciplinary constraints. The moves that have been developed over the centuries for analysis in one discipline are very different from the moves in other disciplines. Physical causality is not like historical causality or literary causality.

Anticipating what we might do, there is some hope. The hope lies in two institutions. One of them is very old: the apprenticeship. There are many powerful clues about how to educate for understanding contained in the apprenticeship. The other is a new institution, more familiar in the United States than in most other countries, but it is spreading rapidly: the children's museum, the science museum, the discovery museum, or the San Francisco Exploratorium. Very powerful education implications lurk in those two institutions.

Let me try to summarize this argument.

The natural learner displays what I call intuitive understanding. He or she is very promiscuous with the theories already developed in the young mind. Whenever anything happens, the young child draws on the theories of mind, matter, and life to explain them, whether or not those theories are appropriate at all.

In contrast, the scholastic learner never tries to apply the theory any-where, except where he or she is told to. So, the scholastic learner gives a ritualized performance. The teacher asks the question, the student gives the prescribed answer or is told that she is wrong, and you go on to the next student.

The disciplined learner, the expert, produces a discipline of understand-ing, which means that not only can he or she draw on knowledge when it's appropriate but, equally importantly, doesn't draw on that knowledge when it's not appropriate. The five-year-old is too promiscuous and uses it always. The ten-year-old is repressed (the opposite of being promiscuous) and never uses it. But the person with disciplined understanding has good taste and uses the knowledge just when it's appropriate.

I've argued that there are some deep, if you will some epistemological, reasons why it's very difficult to teach for understanding. These limitations cover every discipline. I've already mentioned physics. Most people remain five-year-olds or Aristotelians even though they studied physics. Here is a wonderful example, actually from astronomy. Twenty-five Harvard stu-dents have just graduated, all wearing their gowns and their mortar boards. An interviewer says to the students: "Tell me, why is the earth warmer in the summer than it is in the winter?" Twenty-three out of the 25 students imme-diately came up with the same answer, the answer which you would come up with if you didn't know what I was speaking about, namely the answer that the earth is closer to the sun in the summer than it is in the winter. Now if we think about it, that doesn't make any sense because it wouldn't account for the seasons in different parts of the earth. The right explanation has to do with the angle of the earth on its axis as it spins around. But 23 out of 25 students forget to apply what they have learned in their astronomy classes and give the same five-year-old kind of answer.

You might say physics is hard. How about biology? Research shows that students who have taken not one but two or three courses in biology focusing on the topic of evolution still do not understand the basics of evolution. They still believe that something in one generation can be passed on to the next, even if it was acquired in the former generation. They are also still perfectionists. They think that each organism is trying to get more perfect, and that there is an unseen hand that's guiding that perfection rather than simply variation and selection within a particular ecological niche. So problems encountered in physics extend to biology and to the other sciences as well.

What about mathematics? Mathematics is all abstract. It has nothing to do with the real world. So maybe people don't have misconceptions in the area of mathematics. What they have instead is what I call rigid algorithms. They learn to fill in numbers into a formula.

Consider this problem. There are six times as many students as professors. If there are ten professors, how many students are there? Anyway, that is quite a simple problem. The answer is 60. If I ask you to capture the above information in a written equation where S stands for students and P stands for professors, most people will write the following equation: $6S = P$. This is because if you parse the sentence it says there are six times as many students as there are professors. However, what they are actually writing is "six times sixty equals ten," which is clearly an absurd result.

What happens in mathematics is that students learn how to plug numbers into formulas, how to solve equations. As long as the information is presented to them in a certain canonical order, they will get the answer right. If, however, the problem is presented in a new way, in a way which actually requires understanding of the formalism, most people will not get it right because they will not understand the formalism.

I think back to my own education. I studied the quadratic equation, and I must have solved 500 problems with the quadratic equation. I'm sure by the time I finished school, I could do the quadratic equation in my sleep. Never did anybody give me any education of what a quadratic equation stood for. Nowadays if I ran into a problem, I wouldn't have a clue that it involved the quadratic equation, even though I might, on a dark and stormy night, remember what a quadratic equation was. But I got very good grades in mathematics because I wasn't expected to know where to use this kind of formalism.

So, the problem in science is misconceptions. The problem in mathematics is rigidly applied algorithms. How about in the arts, in the humanities?

In the arts and the humanities the problem is different. It's what I call scripts or stereotypes. Early in life children develop very powerful theories about the world. A favorite script is the restaurant script. Every four-year-old knows that if you go to a restaurant, somebody comes and seats you. You are given the menu; you order. Food comes. You eat it and then you call for the check, and you leave.

If you go to McDonald's, you pay first but that's an exception to the script. Every four-year-old also knows about birthday parties: who comes, what you serve, that kind of thing. The rules are different in different cultures, but everybody knows about birthday parties or analogous celebrations in their vicinity.

Another script which you develop when you are very young is the Star Wars script—named both after the movie of that name and after President Reagan's strategic defense initiative. Star Wars says: "it's good to be big; you should be big yourself; if you're not big, align yourself with somebody who is big." If you look like that person, you will be good and people who look different will be bad. That's the Star Wars script and it's very powerful!

You can have people who've studied world history, and you ask them about the causes of the First World War. They say: "Oh, it's very complicated. There was colonialism, imperialism, ethnic strife and long-term rivalries," and they give you a very nuanced response. Then you say to them: "Well, what's happening in the Gulf war of 2003?" They will say: "Well, there was this bad guy named Saddam Hussein and if we got rid of him, everything would be OK." Now, that's a Star Wars type of explanation.

Perhaps the best example of the unschooled mind in the arts comes out of the University of Cambridge in the UK. In the 1920s a literary critic and poet named I. A. Richards did a study of Cambridge undergraduates. He reported it in a book called *Practical Criticism* (1929). He took Cambridge undergraduates who were the best and brightest literary students. He gave them poems and he asked two questions about the poems:

- What do they mean?
- Are they any good?

He performed one manipulation on the poems. He removed the names of the poets. (It's like touring the Louvre without the labels.)

What did Richards find? He found that the students didn't have a clue about which poems were good (according to the critics) and which were bad. They rejected John Donne. They rejected Gerald Manley Hopkins. They embraced a Sunday poet who couldn't get into the *Cambridge Chronicle* and, when they were asked what accounted for the quality, they replied: if a poem rhymed, scanned, dealt with a pleasant subject, but was not too sentimental, it was good. But if it dealt with philosophy or anything tragic or anything abstract, it was bad. So, here you have good students who have studied literature. When the authorial clue is removed (namely this is by a good poet, this is by a bad poet or by a non-poet), these elite students display the same taste that someone with no education in literature would exhibit.

I've argued that in every area of the curriculum you have real problems, revealing how difficult it is to educate for understanding. You have misconceptions in the sciences, rigidly applied algorithms in mathematics, and scripts and stereotypes in social studies, humanities, and the arts. I'm going to argue that there is some hope after all. One source of hope entails taking some lessons from the old institution of apprenticeships and the new institution of children's museums.

Now I want to be very clear about this point. People misunderstand me to say that we should institute seven-year agreements between the apprentice and the master, where the apprentice is indentured and has to sweep the floor and that kind of thing. Or that we should close schools down and put everybody in children's museums. That's not what I mean.

I contend that there are very powerful educational messages in these two institutions. In the case of the apprenticeship, a young person works for someone who is the master of his or her discipline or craft, and who uses that discipline or craft every day in the course of genuine problem-solving. The master poses the problems and requires products from the apprentice at his or her level of competence; when the apprentice becomes more competent, the standards are raised accordingly. The master never has to take kids and test them at the end of the week, or the end of the year, because essentially he and the student are assessing every day. Moreover the master embodies the learning that he or she wants the child to acquire.

In the United States every teacher can read and write but very few of our elementary school teachers actually do read and write regularly. In fact, the average American schoolteacher reads one book a year. People who live in a literate world who read and write and talk about what they are reading and writing will have youngsters who do the same. People who simply say you should read but turn on the TV for seven hours give a very different message.

Until 25 years ago there were almost no children's museums. These locales contain very lively demonstrations of many of the principles that students learn about in school. Museums allow children to explore those principles, those ideas, at their own pace and in ways that are comfortable for that child. Frank Oppenheimer, who founded the Exploratorium in San Francisco, said: "Nobody flunks museum."

I became a devotee of children's museums because when I took kids to children's museums, I sometimes found that kids who were called bright in school could not engage with the "hands-on" opportunities. They were very unschooled. But kids who were not considered bright in school could often learn very well in those contexts.

For each of the areas of the curriculum in which I have diagnosed a problem, there is a move that we can make as educators that can be helpful.

In the case of misconceptions I recommend Christopherian encounters, named after Christopher Columbus. If you believe the world is flat, but every month or every year you travel around the world and you come back to where you started, that tends to belie the notion that the world is flat. In a Christopherian encounter, you expose your theories to disconfirmation. If your theories are consistently dis-confirmed, you will slowly abandon them and hopefully construct better theories.

Most schoolkids believe that the reason that you are warm when you put on a sweater is because that sweater has warmth in it. If every year in school during the winter you put a sweater outside and you come in the morning and find it is freezing cold, that tends to disconfirm the notion that warmth inheres in the sweater.

Christopherian encounters have to happen over and over again. Think about the brain/mind as a surface which, earlier in life, becomes engraved with these primitive theories. What school usually does is simply to put some powder over that engraving so you can't see it any longer. And as long as you're in school, the powder is what the observer notices. When you leave school, and you slam the door, the powder disperses and the engraving is still there, the early theory. What happens in the Christopherian encounter is that you slowly abrade that early engraving and you put a new and better one in its place.

But note that it doesn't happen in one time. Let me tell you what's wrong with the "one time" thing. If you ask my son Benjamin, at age seven, what's the shape of the world, he will tell you it's round. This makes you think he's very smart. But if you asked Benjamin where he is standing, he will say:

"That's easy. I'm on the flat part underneath." His theory has been totally unaffected but he has absorbed the powder that is required: namely, if you want to shut up your father, you say that the world is round because that's what grownups say, but who could believe it?

Thus Christopherian encounters challenge those notions every day.

In mathematics the cure for a rigidly applied algorithm is what I call rich exploration of the relevant semantic domain. You must know what the equation stands for. You have to understand the formalism. So if you are going to do distance, rate and time problems—a common algebra exercise—you do a lot of experimenting. You try to predict how long it will take for something to get from one point to the other. You develop an intuition for the formalism so that when you learn the formalism, it actually refers to something that you already have an intuition for, that you already have an understanding for.

This has been done quite brilliantly with calculus. Before any of the formalism is introduced, students learn to make predictions about their bodies moving at various speeds, and the kind of graphs that would be produced over the course of time, and procedures like that.

A mathematician is not somebody who remembers all the formalisms. A mathematician is somebody who doesn't care if he/she remembers because, if necessary, he/she can derive it again because he/she understands what it stands for. That's why most of us are not mathematicians.

In the case of the humanities, the cure for stereotypes is the regular adoption of multiple stances. If it becomes a regular habit of mind to look at things from many different points of view, you will gradually abandon stereotypical thinking.

During the 1991 Gulf War, one of my sons went to school where there were youngsters from many different countries. The teacher had a very good idea. Rather than everybody just affirming what the cable news network reported, he had a student from Iran and a student from Kuwait and a student from Israel, etc., each convey his understanding of what was happening every day. Then, a few weeks after that, the teacher asked the kids in the school: "What do you think Moshe will think about this and what do you think Omar will think about this?" That's giving students the opportunity to put themselves into other people's minds.

If you study any revolution from the point of view of the vanquished as well as the victors, you get a very different story. If you study the American Revolution from the point of view of the British, where it was seen as a colonial uprising, and from the point of view of the French, where it was seen as a good opportunity to get at the British, it's a very different story than if you just read the average triumphant American textbook. That's how you break down stereotypical thinking, but it has to become a regular habit of mind, otherwise it won't work at all.

Let me, in conclusion, describe a project that I'm involved in to educate for understanding. It is based upon three core ideas which I have worked out in conjunction with colleagues at Harvard:

1. The identification of rich, generative ideas—nutritious topics on which it's worth spending a lot of time;
2. The development of different kinds of teaching languages—multiple ways to approach those topics, so we can be sure that students have maximum access to those ideas; and
3. What I now call "ongoing assessment."

"Ongoing assessment" means assessment is taking place all the time by students and by peers as well as by the teacher.

We believe that if you can identify rich ideas, explore them in multiple ways, and give students much opportunity to assess their own learning, there is a chance for education for understanding.

I now want to flesh out those ideas.

First of all, the greatest enemy of understanding is coverage. If you are determined to cover everything in the book, you virtually guarantee that very few students will understand. So, if you want to educate for understanding, you've got to make tough choices about what to focus on. And obviously you should focus on those things which have the biggest payoff. If you're teaching a course in history or social studies and you decide, say, to focus on democracy, or if you're teaching a course in biology and you choose to focus on evolution, you can cover a lot of the important material in those subjects by focusing on those topics. It will mean, however, if you're doing history, you're not going to get through every decade. If you're doing biology, you're not going to get through every cycle or through every part of the cell, or every part of the tree. It's a hard choice, but it's a choice worth making. If you have rich concepts and you spend time on them, you can approach them in different ways.

Growing out of my theory of MI [multiple intelligences], I claim that almost any topic which is worth spending time on can be approached from at least six different "windows" into the same room:

1. Narrational: the story mode.
2. A quantitative, logical rational way of dealing with numbers, principles, causality.
3. A foundational way, asking basic kinds of questions such as: Why is this important? How does it relate to what came before? How is it related to our lives today?
4. Aesthetic: What does it look like? What does it sound like? What appearance does it make? What patterns and configurations? How does it impress you?
5. Hands on: What is it actually like to be this thing, to do this thing? If you're studying evolution, what is it like to breed Drosophila? If you're studying democracy, what's it like to be in a group that decides by consensus as opposed to one that decides by autocracy, oligarchy or some other political principle?
6. Personal: Can you integrate this topic through debate, role play, projects, jigsaw participation and other joint interactions?

There are two advantages of using these multiple entry points. First of all, you're more likely to reach every child, because not every child learns most readily in the same way. That's one of the burdens of the theory of MI. Second of all, and equally important, if you approach a topic from many different vantage points, you're modeling for a student what it is like to be an expert. Because an expert is somebody who can always represent knowledge in more than one way. No expert can think about his or her topic in only one way. Experts have very flexible ways of thinking about their topics. You're modeling as a master to your apprentices if you approach a topic in a number of different ways.

That leaves assessment.

In authentic assessments we get far away from short answer examinations. We move toward what I call performance-based exams, where you actually demonstrate what it is that you're supposed to be able to do. Projects, exhibitions, portfolios, and "process folios" provide good ways of assessing whether the students are really understanding.

In work with teachers in local schools we ask them first to define "understanding goals"—these are the broad things that we want to achieve in a course. They will be very familiar things to you, like having a sense of the scientific method or understanding something about the nature of revolution.

What we then do, which may not be so familiar to you, is define a whole family of "performances of understanding"—these are performances which, if a student can carry them out, will count as evidence for understanding.

This entails a play with language, but I think it's an important play, because people tend to think of understanding as something that happens in the head. Perhaps it does, but we don't know you understand unless you can perform your understanding publicly. So, your performance involves analyses, critiques, debates, projects that you create, exhibitions that you put on, things like that.

Finally, given the "understanding goals" and the "performances of understanding," how are those performances going to be assessed? You make the assessment criteria absolutely clear. People know exactly what they are going to have to be able to do in order to perform an understanding. There are no surprises, no mysteries, no key to the answers, but rather examples all around of what a good performance is and what are not such good performances, from apprentice level all the way to that of a master.

I'm going to finish with a number of thoughts that I have had.

- After working for decades in psychology and education, I realized that I've been interested primarily in two things. One is how to observe students carefully, and MI theory is a way to look at students more carefully. The other is how to observe student work more carefully—and that is done by having assessment that looks at student performances very carefully.
- In most of the schools that I visit, not much time is spent watching the students and developing a model of how particular students learn; not nearly enough time is spent looking at student work. This is what I call the teacher's fallacy. I taught a great class, therefore the students understood. I teach, therefore you understand. The only way you can find out if students are understanding is to have them actually do some work and then examine it correctly.
- One technique that has become very popular in the U.S. is the minute paper. At the end of a topic, and sometimes at the end of every session, you ask the student to write down one thing that he or she learned in the period and one question that he or she still has. It's a revelation! I never cease to learn when I do the minute paper. And the misconceptions are revealing. But unless misconceptions get out in the open, they sit there underneath accumulating that powder.

- Portfolios are great—but I don't have time to look at my students' work! I'm too busy, too much pressure for coverage, too many faculty meetings. I've a second job. If you don't have time to look at students' work, you shouldn't teach. Because if you don't look at your students' work, you have no idea whether they are learning anything.
- I used to think that if we simply change the assessment, everything else will be fine. But if the curriculum isn't good, the assessment is worthless. You can have wonderful assessment and curriculum, but if the staff isn't well instructed, teachers aren't educated even before or during the experience, the assessment and curricula are worthless.
- Finally, "school doesn't have to be the way you remember it." Unfortunately, the unschooled mind even applies to parents and teachers; we have a stereotype formed by the age of five about what school is like. Namely, somebody at the front of the room is talking just as I am, and you're sitting in your seat, trying to be quiet, and all the knowledge is in the teacher's head and the purpose is to put it into your head. That's a very powerful idea. Whether people love school or hate school, most have that stereotype.

Unless we can help people think differently about what school can be like, what can be studied, how it can be taught, how it can be learned, then the opportunity for education for understanding is not going to be seized.

Now Piaget said one valuable thing which I didn't adhere to. He said that developmental psychologists should not try to be educators. And he steered clear of proposing educational theory. I have stepped into the lion's den today and offered you an educational theory that comes out of developmental psychology. Only time will tell whether I should have adhered to Piaget's admonition.

*This chapter was first presented as the Peterson Lecture to the International Baccalaureate Organization. The transcript of the talk was published in* IBWorld *in April 2003. An edited version of this talk was published as chapter 2 of Howard Gardner's* Development and Education of the Mind *(Routledge, 2006), which appears here with some further revision by the author.* © *Howard Gardner. Reprinted with the author's permission.*

# CHAPTER THREE

# EMOTION AND COGNITION ARE CO-REGULATED

For centuries, philosophers and scientists have been trying to understand and touting perspectives on the relationship between emotion and cognition. Some of these positions are value laden, elevating logical and rational thought as the ideal and treating emotion as an obstruction to reason. Modern research provides a more complex view, where emotion and cognition are fundamentally co-regulated and interdependent.

Taken together, the Universal Design for Learning principles recognize that learning is at once both emotional and cognitive. The relationship between emotion and cognition is complex. Based in social interaction, emotions are biological processes that organize human behavior by constraining thought and action as the environment is appraised as either beneficial or detrimental, or a complex mix of the two. The accuracy and efficiency of thinking processes, perceptions, and effort are influenced by affective states, while motivation and emotion substantially predict learning behavior and outcomes. Positive and negative emotion can, each on its own accord, activate or deactivate motivation states and enhance or detract from productive learning. Even moderate fluctuations in emotion can systematically affect cognitive processing, and vice versa.

Justin Storbeck and Gerald L. Clore's "On the Interdependence of Cognition and Emotion" offers a strong and systematic exploration of the relationship between emotion and cognition in thinking and learning through a thorough analysis of the most relevant research literature. In the essay the authors describe the long-held view that emotion and cognition are independent entities and then systematically debunk this idea through logical argument drawing on several decades of research. Specifically, they suggest, like others (e.g., Immordino-Yang & Damasio, 2007; Duncan & Barrett, 2007), that emotion and cognition are interrelated in a complex, rich mental life and that divorcing them is neither desirable nor warranted based on the research.

Storbeck and Clore describe an "affect-as-information" view in which emotion modulates cognition, perception, and an array of thought processes. From specific experiments showing that positive moods are associated with processing that is generative and that negative moods restrict cognition, to neuroscience evidence that emotion and cognition are not processed in distinct brain regions, the clear message is that emotion and cognition are "inherently integrated."

The authors' view on the interdependence of emotion and cognition is strongly reflected in the UDL framework and guidelines and in Mary Helen Immordino-Yang's work—a view that is still unique within Western education (with the obvious exception of programs in social and emotional learning) and rarely systematically reflected in the pedagogy of day-to-day classroom practice or instructional design.

Though UDL explicitly describes Multiple Means of Engagement as one of its three principles, it would be wrong to assume that engagement is the only area of the UDL guidelines where emotion, or affect more generally, is considered. In fact, the framework assumes the interdependence of emotion and cognition in learning and thinking; and, as such, the successful application of the guidelines will require that practitioners and education developers think extensively about how a student's emotion and cognition will relate dynamically in the context of the UDL-designed lesson, tool, curriculum, or educational environment more broadly conceived.

An affective neuroscientist and human development psychologist, Immordino-Yang studies the neural, psychophysiological, and psychological bases of social emotion, self-awareness, and culture and their implications for social and moral development, intrinsic motivation, learning, and schools. She uses an interdisciplinary, developmental approach that combines affective and social neuroscience, human development psychology, and educational psychology. We spoke with Immordino-Yang about the co-regulation of emotion and cognition because she has had success in using her research in affective neuroscience to inform education. She also has a long relationship with CAST and substantial experience with the UDL framework.

Through her research, Immordino-Yang provides many strong examples of problem-centered thinking around emotion in learning. She was drawn to pursue her doctorate when, as a teacher, she noticed differences in the ways that her immigrant and second language learner students were grappling with challenging concepts: "I could see their understanding of the science was . . . pervaded by their cultural meaning making about their experiences." Her experiences with these students affected the course of her career; she became deeply interested in understanding how cultural and emotional ways of knowing organize thinking and learning. Cognition and emotion feed "back and forth on one another," she says. "Watching that happen, studying that relationship gives us a view into the interdependence of our social lives and out intellectual lives with all the cognitive and emotional information and processing that implies."

In our conversation with Immordino-Yang about Storbeck and Clore's article and her own work, three themes emerged.

### Emotion and Cognition, or "Thinking in Real Life"

Research typically fragments or splits the human organism into "investigatable" units—biology, behavior, culture, emotion, cognition, etc.—resulting in the inevitable loss of the person as an integrated whole. This is problematic when trying to generate knowledge that is usable in education, because in practice the unit of analysis is the full complexity of the whole person in context. Based on her work, Immordino-Yang is very clear about the interdependence of emotion and cognition. She sees emotion and cognition as "two different ways to examine the thinking that we do . . . thinking is at once emotional and cognitive."

To make her point, Immordino-Yang suggested a real-world example: a child trying to understand a story about another person's life. The child's ability to appreciate that story for, say, its inspirational quality depends on both her cognitive abilities (to represent and interrelate information) and her emotional ability to grasp the implications, "to notice the important parts and the things that are relevant, and to bring [her] attention to bear on these."

Thinking and learning in real life require both emotion and cognition, at once, all the time.

### Perception and Processing Are Everything

With the ebb and flow of daily life, emotions change with broad variability both within and between individuals. Emotions change as people experience and appraise their environment as beneficial or threatening, malignant or benign; appraisal is the driving force that shapes affective response and cognitive engagement. Perception is everything in this regard, but what about other forms of processing?

Some of Immordino-Yang's most recent work has focused on this question. In particular, she points out, practitioners often talk about the benefits of downtime and reflection for students. Introspection, mindfulness, and sense making are important components of many intervention models, including many programs classified under the social and emotional learning frame. Now neuroscience is beginning to provide insight into the importance of downtime processing in supporting the ultimate efficacy of other time spent in focused attention. Specifically, as Immordino-Yang explains, the neural networks responsible for maintaining focused attention seem to toggle with the "default mode" of brain function that is active during rest, daydreaming, and other nonattentive but awake mental states. "There seem to be two broad systems. One is what I call 'looking out.' It's looking into the world and perceiving things and getting information and attending to tasks in the moment," which she sees as "extremely important for all kinds of academic learning." The other system, which Immordino-Yang says "has been mostly neglected so far," is the "default mode," what she calls "looking in" and which includes "processes of letting down your outer vigilance and letting behaviors in the world become sort of automated and functional rather than high level and instead focusing your mental energy into reflecting on meaning, consolidating information and connecting into previous memories and possible future outcomes and imaginary scenarios."

### *Learning from Difference and Variability*

Individual differences in the processes by which people construct new and subjective understandings of the world are striking and systematic, involving both cognitive and emotional processes in complex ways. In the process of meaning making, emotion and cognition are remarkably variable across individuals, but this variability seems to systematically organize around constructs like culture. Immordino-Yang notes that cognitive and emotional subjectivity and variability in meaning making "can be tracked scientifically using multimethod designs where we use qualitative interviews combined with psychophysiological recording and with neuroimaging to build profiles for individuals and within a cultural group." She finds that it is possible to define commonalities and differences, and by examining such variability and systematic differences we can come to define the fundamental dimensions on which people interact with others to build a sense of self. "We find . . . there are cultural ways of shaping the thinking that we do, and those influence biological processes, as well as the other way around . . . We can build really complex profiles of people that relate their subjective experience of their own selves and the world and their learning to their underlying biology." This work should provide new insight to the way biology works and is affected by culture both between and within individuals, with the potential to inform the way education environments and curricula are designed to be more flexible and culturally relevant.

## FOR FURTHER READING

Csikszentmihalyi, M. (1991). *Flow: The psychology of optimal experience.* New York: Harper & Row.

Duncan, S., & Barrett, L. F. (2007). Affect is a form of cognition: A neurobiological analysis. *Cognition and Emotion, 21*(6), 1184–1211.

Immordino-Yang, M., & Damasio, A. (2007). We feel, therefore we learn: The relevance of affective and social neuroscience to education. *Mind, Brain, and Education, 1*(1), 3–10.

Lazarus, R. (1991). *Emotion and adaptation.* New York: Oxford University Press.

Stipek, D. (1996). Motivation and instruction. In D. C. Berliner & R. C. Calfee (Eds.), *Handbook of educational psychology* (pp. 85–113). New York: Macmillan.

Zajonc, R. B. (1980). Feeling and thinking: Preferences need no inferences. *American Psychologist, 35*(2), 151–175.

# On the Interdependence of Cognition and Emotion

JUSTIN STORBECK AND GERALD L. CLORE

*Author's Abstract:* Affect and cognition have long been treated as independent entities, but in the current review we suggest that affect and cognition are in fact highly interdependent. We open the article by discussing three classic views for the independence of affect. These are (i) the affective independence hypothesis, that emotion is processed independently from cognition, (ii) the affective primacy hypothesis, that evaluative processing precedes semantic processing, and (iii) the affective automaticity hypothesis, that affectively potent stimuli commandeer attention and evaluation is automatic. We argue that affect is not independent from cognition, that affect is not primary to cognition, nor is affect automatically elicited. The second half of the paper discusses several instances of how affect influences cognition. We review experiments showing affective involvement in perception, semantic activation, and attitude activation. We conclude that one function of affect is to regulate cognitive processing.

Different views of the relationship between cognition and emotion can be seen in the comments of two prominent psychologists upon receipt of distinguished scientist awards. Robert Zajonc (1980, p. 151) in a paper titled "Preferences Need No Inferences," proclaimed: "Affect and cognition . . . constitute independent sources of effects in information processing." A year later, upon receipt of the same award, Gordon Bower (1981, p. 147), in a paper on "Mood and Memory," stated, "I am a cognitive psychologist, and . . . the emotional effects we have found so far seem understandable to me in terms of ideas that are standard fare in cognitive psychology." These two pivotal papers both argued for the importance of studying emotion, but they proposed different meta-theories. Zajonc argued that affect and cognition are processed independently and that affect has temporal priority over even basic cognitive processes. In contrast, Bower argued that cognitive processing could be used to understand emotional phenomena. We agree with Bower's conception, and we extend it to suggest that cognitive processes are necessary for the processing, elicitation, and experience of emotions. The concepts of "cognition" and "emotion" are, after all, simply abstractions for two aspects of one brain in the service of action. Zajonc believed that emotion is independent from cognition. Our own view is that the study of emotion and cognition should be integrated, because the phenomena themselves are integrated (Dewey, 1894; Parrott & Sabini, 1989). We argue against the notion that discrete emotions have separate and distinct areas in the brain (Duncan & Barrett, 2007). Rather, emotions emerge from a combination of affective and cognitive processes (see Moors, 2007).[1] Moreover, in agreement with Bower (1981), we suggest that emotion can be studied using cognitive paradigms. Both laboratory findings and everyday observation suggest a unity and interrelatedness of cognitive and affective processes, and that trying to dissect them into separate faculties would neglect the richness of mental life (Roediger, Gallo, & Geraci, 2002, p. 319). We suggest, like others, that the interconnections found within the brain provide no obvious basis for divorcing emotion from cognition (Erickson & Schulkin, 2003; Halgren, 1992; Lane & Nadel, 2000; Phelps, 2004).

This article has two parts. The first part is a critical review of what recent neuroscience and social psychological research tells us about three popular ideas about cognition and emotion.[2] These include the affective independence hypothesis, that emotion is processed independently of cognition via a subcortical "low route," the affective primacy hypothesis, that affective and evaluative processing takes precedence over semantic processing, as evident in the mere exposure effect and affective priming, and the affective automaticity hypothesis, that affectively potent stimuli commandeer attention and that affective processes are especially likely to be automatic. In the second part, we suggest that rather than being processed independently, affect modifies and regulates cognitive processing, as illustrated in a review of some recent research from our own lab.

## I. ASSESSING THREE HYPOTHESES ABOUT AFFECT AND COGNITION

### A. The Affective Independence Hypothesis: The Low Route

Zajonc (2000) lists ten ways in which affect and cognition differ and suggests that they arise from separate systems. Papers in this tradition sometimes cite LeDoux's (1996) proposal that the amygdala can elicit emotion before information reaches the cortex. In this section, we suggest (a) that the low route does not play a role in processing the complex stimuli typically used in social and emotional research (e.g., faces, ideographs, objects), and (b) that the amygdala, and emotion in general, does not function independently of perceptual and cognitive processes.

The "low route" (LeDoux, 1996; LeDoux, Romanski, & Xagoraris, 1989) is a pathway that allows stimulus processing without cortical influence as studied in rats. When light hits the retina, the signal is relayed to the amygdala through the thalamus without going first to the visual cortex. The pathway is adequate to support fear conditioning between illumination changes and fear-invoking events (e.g., shock). Based on studies with the auditory cortex, which have similar relay pathways as the visual cortex, information can reach the amygdala within 20 ms (Quirk, Armony, & LeDoux, 1997; Quirk, Repa, & LeDoux, 1995).

LeDoux and colleagues used rat models to examine the low route to emotion, and the question remains whether a similar pathway exists in humans. First, comparative anatomical studies (Linke, De Lima, Schwegler, & Pape, 1999) and behavioural studies (Shi & Davis, 2001) using rat-based models suggest that this pathway may be functionally relevant only when cortical areas have been lesioned or damaged. In humans, converging evidence suggests that the low route may not be functionally important for emotion processing (Halgren, 1992; Kudo, Glendenning, Frost, & Masterson, 1986; Rolls, 1999; Shi & Davis, 2001; Storbeck, Robinson, & McCourt, 2006). However, the existence of the low route in humans is still debated (see LeDoux, 2001).[3]

Can the low route discriminate emotional vs. non-emotional stimuli without cortical involvement? That is, can the low route sufficiently discriminate a snake from a bunny without cortical involvement? We say No. The low route has limited capacity for stimulus discrimination. Fear conditioning studies that find support for the low route typically require only detection of the presence or absence of a stimulus (Duvel, Smith, Talk, & Gabriel, 2001; LeDoux et al., 1989; Shi & Davis, 2001). When the task requires discriminating one stimulus from another (e.g., CS += high freq. tone, CS -= low freq. tone), then cortical analysis appears to be necessary (Butler, Diamond, & Neff, 1957; Duvel et al., 2001; Komura et al., 2001; McCabe, McEchron, Green, & Schneiderman, 1993; Nicholson & Freeman, 2000; Thompson, 1962).

One way to test the affective independence hypothesis is to temporarily inactivate the visual cortex to determine whether it is necessary for the amygdala to determine affective significance of stimuli. Fukuda, Ono, and Nakamura (1987) did just that in awake, behaving monkeys. They observed that when the visual cortex (representing early cognitive processing) was temporarily inactivated, monkeys failed to learn and failed to demonstrate appropriate affective associations to visual cues of edible vs. inedible objects. But, the amygdala was still intact, because the monkeys could determine the affective significance of the same stimuli based on taste. This study suggests that in order to determine whether a peanut or a baseball is edible based on visual properties and prior experience, the visual cortex is necessary.

Another way to determine whether the amygdala is independent of initial cognitive processing is to record single-cell activity within the visual cortex and the amygdala. Again, if the amygdala can process visual stimuli independent of cortical input, then amygdala neurons should still remain active to visually presented objects that have affective significance when the visual cortex is temporarily inactivated. Nishijo, Ono, Tamura, and Nakamura (1993) recorded such vision-relevant neurons in the amygdala of monkeys. They discovered that these neurons failed to respond to affectively significant visual stimuli when the visual cortex was temporarily inactivated. They suggested that amygdala activity is not related directly to sensory inputs, but rather it relies on view-invariant representations of objects from the visual cortex. That is, the goal of the visual cortex is to create unique neural signatures for unique objects regardless of its orientation, background lighting, etc. Therefore, the same affective significance can be retrieved regardless of the visual state the object is in. Halgren offers similar conclusions as Nishijo et al. by suggesting that when "the amygdala performs emotional evaluation, it does so within the cognitive system. This could explain why it has been so difficult to dissociate emotional from cognitive processing in humans" (Halgren, 1992, p. 212).

Faces have always received special attention in the study of emotion due to their possible evolutionary connection to survival (Davey, 1995; Öhman, 1997). Adolphs (2002) suggested that processing and recognising a fear face requires a network of various structures and that the low route alone is incapable of such processing. He proposed that the visual cortex first grossly identifies the face, and in particular determines whether the face contains an expression or not. Support for this model comes from the fact that there are two areas in the monkey visual cortex dedicated to face processing, areas STS and IT. Area STS (superior temporal sulcus) is involved in encoding facial expressions, while the IT (inferotemporal cortex) is involved in encoding facial identity (see Allison, Puce, & McCarthy, 2000; Kanwisher, McDermott, & Chun, 1997; Narumoto, Okada, Sadato, Fukui, & Yonekura, 2001; Rotshtein, Malach, Hadar, Graif, & Hendler, 2001, for related literature on humans). Both areas, STS and IT, have strong reciprocal connections to the amygdala, suggesting the amygdala receives highly processed facial information pertaining to both facial identity and facial expression (Baylis, Rolls, & Leonard, 1987; Fukuda et al., 1987; Nishijo, Ono, & Nishino, 1988b; Rolls, 1992). For example, Rotshtein et al. (2001) found that lateral occipital cortex in humans, which processes facial expressions, is concerned with the configuration for each expression, rather than with its affective value. That is, the visual cortex does not code for affective significance (Rolls, 1999; Rotshtein et al., 2001), but rather codes for facial configurations and these configurations are sent to the amygdala for affective processing. Thus, the visual cortex is needed for the amygdala to correctly identify and respond to emotional stimuli.

For emotional stimuli used by psychologists (e.g., snakes; emotional faces) the processing capacities of the low route would appear to be inadequate (see Rolls, 1999; Smith, Cacioppo, Larsen, & Chartrand, 2003, for similar concerns). But, the low route is still cited to help explain particular affective phenomena (e.g., Bargh, 1997; Berkowitz & Harmon-Jones, 2004; Zajonc, 2000). However, we suggest that the fact that the amygdala relies on cortical input to make an evaluation requires reconsideration of whether emotion at initial levels of processing can be dissociated from cognitive processing. We should also note that the same processes occur regardless of whether stimuli are presented subliminally or supraliminally (Rolls & Tovee, 1994; Rolls, Tovee, Purcell, Stewart, & Azzopardi, 2004; Storbeck et al., 2006).

*Conclusions.* Davidson (2003) claimed that one of seven deadly sins of cognitive neuroscience is to assume that affect is independent from cognition. We and several others agree that emotion should not be divorced from cognition (Adolphs & Damasio, 2001; Barnard, Duke, Byrne, & Davidson, 2007; Davidson, 2003; Duncan & Barrett, 2007; Eder & Klauer, 2007; Erickson & Schulkin, 2003; Lane & Nadel, 2000; Lavender & Hommel, 2007; Lazarus, 1995; Parrott & Sabini, 1989; Phelps, 2004; Storbeck et al., 2006). For instance, based on anatomical connections alone (Ghashghaei & Barbas, 2002) areas necessary for cognition and emotion are highly interconnected, and these connections are bidirectional, suggesting integrated processing of emotion and cognition. Halgren (1992) suggests that emotion and cognition are so interconnected that it is not practical to try to disentangle the temporal and casual relations of emotion and cognition.

### B. The Affective Primacy Hypothesis

In addition to the idea that affect and cognition are independent sources of influence, is the allied idea of affective primacy (Zajonc, 1980, 2000). The mere exposure phenomenon (Zajonc, 1968) was an important source of evidence for the hypothesis, because mere exposure involves an affective reaction that is not dependent on conscious categorisation or identification of the liked stimulus.

One problem with accepting the grand conclusions, that affective processing occurs without cognitive processing, drawn from mere exposure research is that they rest on an equation of consciousness with cognition (Lazarus, 1995). However, single-cell recording shows that the visual cortex can readily identify stimuli presented below subjective thresholds. Therefore, lack of conscious awareness has no bearing on whether the visual cortex categorises and identifies a stimulus. In fact, studies have demonstrated that the only difference between a stimulus presented for 30 ms as opposed to 1000 ms is the strength at which a neural population fires (Rolls, 1999; Rolls & Tovee, 1994; Rolls et al., 1994). But the response pattern output remains the same, which is thought to reflect a unique neural signature for a given stimulus type. That is, the neural population identifies X whether presented for 30 ms or 1000 ms, but the firing is stronger so that the system is more confident for 1000 ms presentations than for 30 ms presentations.

Another problem is that the mere exposure effect gets weaker the longer stimuli are presented, as respondents have time to process the identity of the stimulus and to realise that they have seen it before. The mere exposure effect is, therefore, a mistake based on a misattribution of fluency as liking instead of as familiarity (Winkielman, Schwarz, Fazendeiro, & Reber, 2003). Of course, most real-world emotional reactions are not errors of this kind, so that its appeal as a model of how affect is related to cognition is limited.

More importantly, Zajonc (2000) assumed that the mere exposure effect does not rely on cognitive or cortical involvement, suggesting the effect may rely on the low route to emotion. The low route to emotion would allow for affective processing without cortical or cognitive input. However, available evidence suggests that the effect does not rely on processing by the amygdala. For example, Greve and Bauer (1990) report the case of a patient, GY, who had an accident that severed the connection between the visual cortex and the amygdala. They found that GY showed the mere exposure effect even though visual information was not getting to the amygdala. Elliott and Dolan (1998) also report that the mere exposure effect relies more on frontal cortical networks. They failed to observe any relevant amygdala activation. These data suggest that the mere exposure effect is not a phenomenon that requires the amygdala, let alone one that could be based in the low route to the amygdala.

*Affective priming as evidence for affective primacy.* Another phenomenon that has been interpreted as demonstrating a special status for affect is affective priming. Research suggests that people routinely evaluate objects in their environment (Murphy & Zajonc, 1993; Niedenthal, 1990). For example, in sequential priming studies, briefly presented prime words are followed by target words that participants categorise (e.g., as positive or negative) as quickly as possible (Bargh, Chaiken, Govender, & Pratto, 1992; Bargh, Chaiken, Raymond, & Hymes, 1996; Fazio, Sanbonmatsu, Powell, & Kardes, 1986). Priming is then seen when, for example, positive primes facilitate responses to positive targets and interfere with responses to negative targets. Such affective priming suggests that people may automatically evaluate stimuli without an intention to do so.

In an effort to rule out the possibility that the response facilitation is really due to some semantic dimension, investigators typically choose primes and targets that have no association other than being similar or dissimilar in evaluative meaning. However, Storbeck and Robinson (2004) point out that this practice of limiting the relationship between primes and targets to evaluation may force respondents into evaluative priming. If so, it would lose its value as evidence that affect is independent of cognition or has primacy over semantic meaning.

To test this hypothesis, Storbeck and Robinson (2004) used "a comparative priming method" in which words were selected to vary not only evaluatively but also categorically. For example, primes or targets might be positively or negative valenced animals (e.g., puppies, snakes) or positive or negatively valenced texture words (smooth, rough). Thus, prime-target pairs were related evaluatively (good vs. bad), but also descriptively (animals vs. textures).

Two tasks were used, an evaluation task and a lexical decision task, and both revealed semantic but not affective priming. In addition, the same result was found when they used pictures instead of words. To verify that the practice of artificially limiting the relationship between primes and targets to evaluation had promoted affective priming in prior studies, Storbeck and Robinson (2004) then repeated their experiment but removed any systematic descriptive relationship between primes and targets, such that all words were now animal exemplars. As expected, the usual affective priming results reappear when participants are given only evaluation as a possible basis for relating primes and targets.

Another comparative priming study was performed by Klauer and Musch (2002). They used primes and targets that could be categorised based on affect or another non-affective dimension, and manipulated only the task demand (i.e., to evaluate or categorise). They concluded that affective priming is not based on a special evaluation system. Rather, affective priming relies on the same mechanisms responsible for semantic priming.

These experiments suggest that affective priming is not obligatory. The evaluative meaning on which affective priming is based is represented within a larger semantic network in which it is not the dominant mode of semantic categorisation. Evaluation is doubtlessly a very basic level of analysis, but evaluative meaning is not processed apart from other dimensions of semantic meaning, nor does it invoke a special automatic evaluator.

The Storbeck and Robinson experiments used supraliminal exposures of primes, but Erdley and D'Agostino (1988) used subliminal exposures. In a very different paradigm, they too found that when both affective and descriptive features were present, priming occurred along semantic rather than evaluative lines, suggesting that categorisation may often have priority over evaluation.

One might hypothesize that affect is elicited automatically at the onset of a stimulus and degrades from that point. If so, the use of a relatively long Stimulus Onset Asynchrony (SOA) (300 ms) by Storbeck and Robinson (2004) might conceivably have prevented detection of affective priming. To assess this possibility, studies might again use the comparative-priming approach and shorten either stimulus durations or response times, either of which might allow early components of the priming process to be visible. A study by Klinger, Burton, and Pitts (2000) satisfied these two requirements, and concluded that when primes are presented subliminally and response-window procedures are used, finding semantic or affective priming depends mainly on task requirements and response competition.

The Klinger et al. study is unique in the use of the response-window procedure. Since spreading activation builds up over hundreds of milliseconds (Perea & Rosa, 2002), such procedures tend to reduce any effects due to spreading activation within the semantic network, making it likely that any priming effects obtained are due to response compatibility, rather than spreading activation. It is interesting to note, though, that both semantic and affective priming were sensitive to similar task constraints, suggesting that both result from similar mechanisms. Other studies using similar comparative methods and response-window procedures also found both affective and categorical priming (Klauer & Musch, 2002; Klinger et al., 2000). However, crucially, these studies failed to equate semantic and affective features, and in each, affect was the most salient feature. Together these studies suggest that with response-window procedures, regardless of prime duration, priming is driven by response compatibility.

Since the use of a response window shortens the time available for effects due to spreading activation, what happens when spreading activation is allowed to build up over time, by presenting primes subliminally without a response window. Kemp-Wheeler and Hill (1992) performed such a study with a lexical decision task, and found both affective and semantic priming. But they also found that affective priming occurred mostly when people could detect the prime. Such detection did not facilitate semantic priming. They argued that affective priming is a subform of semantic priming and occurs when more time is given to revealing the affective significance of primes and targets.

Moving away from the priming procedure, Storbeck, Robinson, Ram, Meier, and Clore (2004) examined evaluations and categorisations of single target words using a response-window procedure. The window of response varied from 100 ms to 2000 ms and the dependent measure was accuracy. The experiment included nine participants over five days with over 500 trials per day. This allowed us to produce predictive models for the rise of semantic and affective accuracy. The results revealed that in shorter response windows, participants were more accurate in detecting semantic information than affective information. Other studies have found that semantic distinctions can occur as early as 80 ms, while evaluative distinctions start around 100 ms (Van Rullen & Thorpe, 2001).

EEG measures can also be used to discriminate semantic and affective aspects of processing without involving motor output processes. Cacioppo, Crites, and Gardner (1996) and Ito and Cacioppo (2001) found that ERP potentials always tracked semantic relations, even when semantic analysis was not the focus of the task. ERPs also tracked affective features, but only when the task had an explicitly evaluative focus, unless the evaluative components were quite potent. More critically, evidence suggests that the same discriminative processing based on semantic features performed by the visual cortex occurs whether stimuli are presented subliminally or supra-liminally, regardless of conscious experience (Dehaene et al., 2001; Rolls & Tovee, 1994; Rolls et al., 1994; Stenberg, Lindgren, & Johansson, 2000). ERP and single-cell recordings both demonstrate that semantic information appears to be represented regardless of the task at hand and whether or not there is conscious perception of the stimuli. That is, semantic information always gets activated, regardless of the explicit task, whereas affective infor-mation is processed mainly when evaluation is an explicit part of the task or a highly salient aspect of the stimulus.

To be clear, in this view, the system needs an identification stage before an evaluation stage, and identification occurs in later stages of processing in the visual cortex. Even in classical conditioning, some kind of identification is required by the cortex (e.g., visual cortex) to discriminate a conditioned stimulus from all other stimuli. By "identification stage" we mean simply that a view invariant, neural signature of an object is activated in the visual cortex. Only then can the object activate affective and other associations.

*Conclusions.* These studies suggest that both semantic[4] and affective features are represented in a single semantic network, and that semantic information (which is not to say lexical information, see footnote 3) has a necessary priority. That is, we feel that affective priming is a special case of semantic priming and can be obtained when affect is part of the task demand, the salient feature of the stimuli, or the focus of attention (Storbeck & Robinson, 2004). Under the right set of circumstances, affective relations can be made more accessible than semantic relations (e.g., Bargh et al., 1992, 1996; Klinger et al., 2000; Storbeck & Robinson, 2004). For example, Stor-beck and Robinson (2004) found that when they crossed descriptive and evaluative features of stimuli in an evaluative priming task, semantic but not affective priming was observed. But when the relations between primes and targets stimuli were limited to their evaluative features, then affective prim-ing was observed. Thus, under the right set of conditions, affective priming can readily be observed, but such evaluative priming is in no way obligatory. Thus, the fact that evaluative priming can be found when evaluative mean-ing is made salient, provides little support for ideas about affective primacy or about the separate nature of affective and cognitive processing.

### C. The Affective Automaticity Hypothesis

Although the automatic-controlled distinction arose in cognitive psychology (Shiffrin & Schneider, 1977), a special association is often assumed between affect and automaticity. Perhaps the idea was that thoughts can be more easily controlled than feelings has made affect seem to have a life of its own. One can decide to think about one particular topic rather than another, but one cannot decide to feel one way or another, except by guiding thoughts. Is automaticity a key distinction that makes affect and emotion separate from cognition?

Cognitive psychologists have recently become critical of the term "automaticity." Recent reviews have concluded that the initial demonstrations of what was purported to be automaticity may actually have required attention after all (see, Lavie & De Fockert, 2003; Logan, 2002; Pashler, Johnston, & Ruthruff, 2001; Stolz & Besner, 1999). For example, Pashler et al. (2001, p. 648) stated that, "A variety of proposals for 'wired-in' attention capture by particular stimulus attributes have been effectively challenged; attention, it turns out, is subject to a far greater degree of top-down control than was suspected 10 years ago." Generally, the relevant data have come from studies of cognition rather than affect. In this section, we suggest that the same conclusion applies in the case of affective stimuli.

Harris, Pashler, and Coburn (2004) examined whether affective words could be processed automatically. Their data indicated that affective words can slow responses down on a primary task, suggesting that affect may capture attention. However, when the primary task was made difficult, thus reducing attentional resources, affective words failed to slow responses, suggesting that affect did not capture attention. These results suggest that under high-load conditions, when attention is occupied, affective words should not be expected to "grab" attention in a bottom-up manner. Instead, affect appears to be processed by top-down networks. Similar results have been found when emotional faces were used in a modified Posner cueing paradigm (Fox, Russo, Bowles, & Dutton, 2001) and when threat-related words and faces were used in a variation of the Stroop task (White, 1996). Moreover, examining the affective pronunciation priming task, De Houwer and Randell (2002) observed affective priming only when attention was focused on the primes. When attention was not focused on the primes, affective priming was not observed in the pronunciation paradigm.

These studies all presented evidence to suggest that affective stimuli require attention and that they do not grab attention in a bottom-up manner. However, Lundqvist and Öhman (2005) have argued that evolutionarily relevant threat stimuli (e.g., snakes, spiders, faces) should be especially likely to be processed pre-attentively (see Davey, 1995, for a relevant criticism to evolutionary preparedness account).

Relevant data are limited, but, the data available would suggest that even faces require attention in order to be processed. As discussed above, Fox et al. (2001) found that angry, happy, and neutral faces failed to capture attention when the effects of attention capture versus disengagement were disentangled. Narumoto et al. (2001) found that when faces were presented, area STS, which processes facial expressions, was significantly activated only when the task required facial expression discrimination, but not when identity or gender discriminations were required for the emotional faces (see also Critchley et al., 2000). Pessoa, Kastner, and Ungerleider (2002) performed a study similar to the Harris et al. study, but they used pictures with facial expressions and collected neuroimaging data. They observed that under low-load conditions, amygdala activation was observed to task-irrelevant fear faces. But, under high-load conditions, when processing resources were limited, the amygdala failed to show significant activation to task-irrelevant fear faces, suggesting that attention was driven by top-down influences. These findings suggest that even the amygdala needs attentional resources in order to process fear faces and that fear faces can fail to capture attention.

*Amygdala evaluation requires attention.* It has been suggested that emotional stimuli are processed automatically, namely, without attention (LeDoux, 1996; Öhman, Esteves, & Soares, 1995; Vuilleumier, Armony, Driver, & Dolan, 2003), and that the amygdala plays a key role in automatic stimulus evaluation (Morris, Öhman, Dolan, 1998; Whalen et al., 1998). This process is often cited as the basis of affective primacy (e.g., Bargh & Chartrand, 1999; Zajonc, 2000). However, cortical input appears to be more important in amygdala processing than has sometimes been emphasised (as discussed earlier), and the data reviewed below suggest that the amygdala requires attention to process threatening and novel stimuli.

Several studies have tested the hypothesis that exposure to affective words should elicit amygdala activation, reflecting the automatic evaluation process (Beauregard et al., 1997; Canli, Desmond, Zhao, Glover, & Gabrieli, 1998). No evidence was found of the hypothesised amygdala activation unless attention was explicitly drawn to the affective content of words by asking participants to evaluate them. Such results suggest that the amygdala does not continuously evaluate all incoming stimuli.

These studies involved lexical stimuli, but the same turns out to be true for the evaluation of pictures.[5] When presented with affective pictures, Keightley et al. (2003) found no amygdala activation. When participants were explicitly asked to evaluate affective stimuli, amygdala activation was found only for negative information (Keightley et al., 2003; Lane, Chua, & Dolan, 1999). For fearful faces, however, even passive viewing showed amygdala activation (Critchley et al., 2000; Morris et al., 1998; Vuilleumier et al., 2003; Whalen et al., 1998). However, with other face stimuli there was no amygdala activation even when participants explicitly evaluated them (Critchley et al., 2000; Keightley et al., 2003). Happy and angry faces also showed no amygdala activation for either passive viewing or active evaluation (Blair, Morris, Frith, Perrett, & Dolan, 1999; Morris et al., 1998; Surguladze et al., 2003).

*Conclusions.* These results suggest that valence is not automatically processed by the amygdala, but the amygdala may be sensitive to arousing stimuli such as fearful faces. Other research groups have also suggested that the amygdala is important for encoding arousal, but not the valence, dimension of stimuli (Adolphs & Damasio, 2001; Adolphs, Russell, & Tranel, 1999; Cahill et al., 1996; Lane et al., 1999; McGaugh, 2004; Morris et al., 1998; Surguladze et al., 2003). Moreover, the evidence suggests that when affect is salient and processing demands are relatively low, emotional information may engage attention. But when processing demands are high and affective stimuli are not of attention, affect will not "capture" attention. Such findings limit the conditions for automaticity, and, as cognitive psychology has already discovered, processing relies on attention, even for affective stimuli.

## II. THE AFFECT-COGNITION CONNECTION

Throughout history, people's optimism or pessimism about the human condition has often turned on their beliefs about the possibility of rational thought unsullied by emotion. Gradually, however, cognition and emotion are coming to be viewed as complementary rather than antagonistic processes. Our current research is informed by an affect-as-information approach (Schwarz & Clore, 1983; Clore & Storbeck, 2006), which assumes that affective reactions provide useful feedback both explicitly and implicitly from emotional appraisal processes. Evidence in support of such a view comes from observations that the inability to use affective feedback as a result of brain damage has profoundly negative consequences for judgement and decision making (Damasio, 1994). Conversely, expertise at using affective information seems to be associated with effective personal and social functioning (Mayer, Salovey, & Caruso, 2004).

### A. Emotion Modulates Cognition[6]

In Part I, we argued against the idea that cognition and emotion involved distinct brain areas or that they operate independently. The strongest claim for independence relied on the "low route" to emotion (LeDoux, 1996), a direct pathway from the sensory thalamus to the amygdala. However, by all available evidence, the low route does not appear to be a candidate for explaining any instance of human emotion. If it operates at all in humans, it appears incapable of even basic affective discriminations without cognitive input. Rather, the evidence from neuroscience suggests that evaluations of the amygdala are dependent upon input from the visual cortex. We suggested that affect probably does not proceed independently of cognition, nor precede cognition in time.

How, then, do we see the relationship between emotion and cognition? At the most general level, emotion modulates and mediates basic cognitive processes. The brain, of course, accomplishes numerous tasks all at once, including automatic processes (Barnard et al., 2007; Robinson, 1998). As the sensory cortex identifies stimuli in the environment, the visual cortex processes it in a view-invariant manner, allowing it to determine attributes of the object, including its affective significance, regardless of the position the object happens to be in. Once the visual cortex creates a view-invariant code for the object, it projects that information to other areas in the brain.

One of the primary pathways of the visual cortex is to the amygdala, and the role of the amygdala is in part to determine the urgency of the stimulus, which eventuates in the marking of apparently important experiences hormonally and in terms of experienced arousal. The amygdala retrieves the affective value of the stimulus or determines that it is novel and guides subsequent cognitive processing. The amygdala has extensive back projections to all areas of the visual cortex, which we believe modulate visual perception, attention, and memory for affectively significant stimuli. Note that the amygdala is probably not the only area involved in emotional processing that can modulate cognition. The visual cortex also has extensive projections to areas such as the orbitofrontal cortex, prefrontal cortex, and cingulate cortex, all of which can guide cognitive processing based on affective value.

In this section, we illustrate how we believe affect regulates cognition by briefly reviewing several recent studies from our lab. The studies discussed focus on two problems—the role of affect in perception and the affective regulation of styles of information processing. We note that in performance situations, emotional cues regulate cognitive processing, serving to adjust the mix of cognition and perception. Of special interest are several recent experiments that ask about affective consequences for implicit processes of learning, memory, priming, and attitude.

### B. The Affective Regulation of Perception

The "New Look" in perception, a movement in the 1950s (Bruner, 1957), maintained that rather than being a passive registration of reality, perception reflected internal expectations and motivations as part of an adaptive process. That movement quickly ran its course without having much impact, but, today, research again suggests that perception of the physical world is influenced by emotion and other internal factors. For example, Proffitt and colleagues (e.g., Bhalla & Proffitt, 1999; Proffitt, Stefanucci, Banton & Epstein, 2003; Witt, Proffitt, & Epstein, 2004) have found that hills appear steeper and distances farther to people with reduced physical resources, either from wearing a heavy backpack, being physically tired, or being elderly. Recent research shows that emotion can have similar effects. In one study (Riener, Stefanucci, Proffitt, & Clore, 2003) participants listened to happy or sad music as they stood at the bottom of a hill. The results showed that sadness can make mountains out of molehills. Sad mood led to overestimation of the incline on verbal and visual measures, but not on a haptic measure. That is, the sad individuals were more likely to say that the hill was steeper compared to happy individuals, but both groups provided similar haptic responses.

Affective feelings thus appear to inform explicit, but not implicit measures of perception. That is, when asked to estimate the incline verbally in degrees (i.e., verbal measure) and when indicating the incline analogically with a sort of protractor (i.e., visual measure), individuals feeling sad estimated the hill to be significantly steeper than individuals who were feeling happy or who had not heard any music. Such perceptual measures are thought to reflect conscious visual perception that relies on processing in the ventral visual stream, or "what" system, concerned with visual identification (Milner & Goodale, 1995). A reasonable argument can be made for why this system might be sensitive to resources for coping with inclines and distances (Proffitt, 2006). The third, haptic measure involved tilting a palm board (without looking at it) to match the incline of the hill. This haptic measure of incline is generally found to be quite accurate and to be immune from the influence of resource depletion such as physical exhaustion. It was also unaffected by sad mood. The measure is thought to reflect unconscious visual perception and relies on processing in the dorsal visual stream, or "how" system, engaged in the visual control of motor behaviour. Whereas it might be adaptive for one's perception of a hill to reflect one's resources, as decisions on whether to take action or not might hinge on such information, but for regulation of one's actual foot placement, such overestimations might be disastrous.

In extensions of this work, Stefanucci, Proffitt, and Clore (2005) also examined the effect of fear on hill estimates. They had individuals on top of the hill and to manipulate fear, some individuals stood on a skateboard, whereas others stood on a stable platform. They found that individuals on the skateboard provided steeper verbal hill estimates again on both the verbal and visual measures when compared to individuals standing on the stable platform. As expected, the haptic measure was again unaffected by the manipulation of emotion.

### C. Affective Regulation of Processing

At the beginning of the cognitive revolution, Jerome Bruner (1957) famously concluded that people are active processors who typically "go beyond the information given." A number of experiments have been conducted in our lab over the past five years in which emotions and moods were added to classic experiments in cognitive psychology. One way to summarise our results is to say that happy affect appears to promote this "going beyond" through its influence on "relational processing." In contrast, negative affect leads to more item-specific processing. Such results lead us to conclude that Bruner's dictum, and all that it implies, may not be applicable when emotional cues of sadness are present. The experiments from our lab suggest (perhaps ironically) that the cognitive revolution had a hidden emotional trigger.

Many of the classic phenomena on which cognitive psychology was founded turn out to depend on affect. For instance, we observed that individuals in happy moods, but not those in sad moods, demonstrate schema effects on constructive memory of the kind introduced by Bartlett in 1932 (Gasper & Clore, 2002). Other classic phenomena also turn out to be more pronounced in happy moods than in sad moods. These include semantic priming (Storbeck & Clore, 2006), script processing (Bless et al., 1996), schema-guided memory (Gasper & Clore, 2002), stereotype use (Isbell, 2004), heuristic reasoning (Gasper, 2000), the global superiority effect (Gasper & Clore, 2002), and false memory generation (Storbeck & Clore, 2005).

These results do not arise from general performance deficits caused by sad mood. On the contrary, general reaction times, overall memory accuracy, and basic performance levels often show no mood-based differences. Moreover, since the classic paradigms often rely on particular errors to show the mediating role of knowledge structures, individuals in sad moods may perform better in certain ways than those in happy moods.

These observations are compatible with findings demonstrating that positive moods are associated with processing that is generative (e.g., Erez & Isen, 2002), constructive (e.g., Fiedler, 2001), and broad (e.g., Fredrickson & Branigan, 2005). Our own account of these effects emphasises the informational properties of affect. For example, during task performance, positive affect may be experienced as efficacy and negative affect as difficulty. Feeling that one is effective confers value on one's own generative thoughts and goals resulting in the reliance on them to process incoming information (relational processing). On the other hand, experiences of difficulty and lack of efficacy reduce the apparent value of one's own cognitions and goals, leading to a focus on more-specific, literal aspects of stimuli.

### D. Affective Regulation of Implicit Processes

*Priming.* In other research, Storbeck and Clore (2006) tested whether this relational processing of associations can carry over to semantic knowledge. They observed that happy individuals were more likely to relate primes and targets together, demonstrating both category and evaluative priming, depending on the nature of the task. However, sad individuals failed to demonstrate priming on the same tasks, suggesting they were impaired in relating the descriptive meaning from primes to targets. Again, the results suggest that negative affective cues act as though they undermine confidence in using accessible cognitions. In the implicit learning situation, it prevented expression of what had been learned, and in the priming situation, it allowed sad participants to respond to target stimuli independently from the descriptive meaning of the primes.

*False memory effects.* To investigate further the hypothesis that negative affect impairs the formation and use of implicit associations, Storbeck and Clore (2005) induced positive and negative moods before a false-memory task. The task produces false memories by presenting word lists in which the lists are composed of words that are highly associated to a non-presented word, referred to as the critical lure. False memories are engendered because as individuals are relating the words from the list together, the critical lures should come to mind and are then likely to be falsely recalled. We observed that, in fact, negative moods led to a decrease in activation and subsequent recall of critical lures compared to the positive mood group and the control group. In addition, no differences were observed for the recall of presented items between the three groups. Ironically, the observed effect demonstrated that negative affect can improve memory performance by inhibiting the use of lexical associations during learning. Such findings suggest that affect from mood can influence the expression of implicit associations (Storbeck & Clore, 2005, 2006).

*Affective involvement in implicit attitudes.* The previous experiments show that affective states modulate the use of implicit associations in cognitive performance situations. Extensive prior research has already shown that affective states can influence evaluative judgements or attitudes expressed in self-report measures. But the intense interest in implicit attitude measurement raises the question of whether or not affect influences attitudes when assessed on implicit measures such as the Implicit Association Test or IAT (Greenwald, McGhee, & Schwartz, 1998).

Several experiments (Huntsinger, Sinclair, Dunn, & Clore, 2006) tested the hypothesis that positive affect would serve as a "go" sign and negative affect as a "stop" sign for acting on goals that were either chronically or temporarily activated. The goal in one experiment concerned taking an egalitarian stance regarding sexist attitudes, and in the other experiment the goal was either to adopt or not to adopt the racial attitudes held by an experimenter. Implicit measures of attitude were employed (a lexical decision task and an IAT). An elaborate set of effects neatly confirmed the predictions, showing that in each case, happy moods prompted participants to act on their chronic or temporarily activated goals, whereas sad moods interfered with goal expression. Importantly, the goals had been activated implicitly as a subtle part of the social situation, and the attitudes were measured implicitly using two different measures—see also DeSteno, Dasgupta, Bartlett, and Cajdric (2004) for a demonstration of the effects of anger on implicitly measured prejudice toward an outgroup. Thus, affective states appear to regulate not only the expression of implicit learning and implicit lexical associations, but also the expression of implicitly measured attitudes.

In summary, our main goal of this section was to demonstrate that affect and cognition should be thought of as fundamentally interactive. In this view, affect is [a] potential moderator of all kinds of cognitive operations from perception and attention to implicit learning and implicit associations (see also, Duncan & Barrett). We have argued against conceptualising emotion as a separate force in opposition to cognition in favour of viewing cognition and emotion as inherently integrated. We included examples of recent research in our own lab showing affective moderation of basic cognitive processes.

### NOTES

1. That is, we, along with others (e.g., Barrett, 2006), suggest that there is not a brain centre dedicated to specific emotions such as fear, happiness, etc. But, there are specific areas critically involved in emotion processing. For instance, the amygdala is critically involved in the emotion of fear, but is not specifically dedicated to fear.
2. The conception of emotion we raise, affective independence and affective primacy, comes mainly from Zajonc (1980, 2000). The affective automaticity derives from arguments made by Bargh and colleagues (Bargh, 1997; Ferguson & Bargh, 2003).
3. In particular, the strongest evidence for such a route comes from affective blindsight individuals. Individuals have damage to area V1 of the visual cortex and as a result have no conscious perception of the world. However, these individuals still demonstrate affective reactions to fear-inducing visual stimuli. In the literature though, this is still a debated issue. First, the pathways involved are unclear. That is, although information may not be visually conscious to blindsight individuals, areas of the visual cortex still receive visual information (area V4 and extrastriate) from subcortical structures such as the pulvinar and superior collicolus. Therefore, although the area V1 is damaged, areas of the visual cortex still receive the same visual information. Storbeck, Robinson, and McCourtt (2006) examine this issue more extensively.
4. We will use the term "semantic" to describe the meaning analysis that we propose precedes affective analysis. What we have in mind specifically are at least three achievements: (1) the integration of multiple features of the object into a single "object" code; (2) the identification of this object; and (3) the categorisation of the object (e.g., as animate or not). The term semantic, then, refers somewhat more directly to the achievements of area IT (especially invariance, identification, and categorisation) that seem to occur in order for a person to retrieve affective associations.
5. A host of fMRI studies have demonstrated the activation of the amygdala to masked fear faces and other emotional stimuli. Such studies are interesting because individuals do not have a conscious perception of the image. However, the amygdala only shows enhanced activation to arousing images (e.g., fear faces), but not to non-arousing faces (e.g., houses). Although such evidence suggests that amygdala activation can occur without perceptual awareness, we still suggest that the visual system still codes that image and sends its input forward to the amygdala in the same manner as if the stimulus was presented supraliminally. Moreover, imaging studies have a weakness of comparative activity. Therefore, it is difficult to gage how much processing is done between masked and non-masked fear faces. In addition, there is plenty of evidence to suggest that the visual cortex processes masked and non-masked images in a similar manner.

    Moreover, evidence from single-cell recording suggests that the visual system can still determine whether a face or a house was presented regardless of whether each image was presented with a mask and subliminally. Therefore, studies demonstrating that the amygdala activates for a subliminal, but not a supraliminal picture does not mean that the visual cortex did not send the same information. There is no reason to believe that the categorisation processes performed by area IT are conscious. Indeed, on the basis of ERP data, we might conclude that unconscious categorisation routinely precedes conscious categorisation. Furthermore, unconscious categorisation by the visual system may occur extremely quickly after stimulus exposure, in as little as 48 ms for "global templates" (Sugase, Yamane, Ueno, & Kawano, 1999) and 70-80 ms for classes of stimuli (Van Rullen & Thorpe, 2001). Interestingly, Van Rullen and Thorpe (2001) also found that the initial (70-80) categorisation-related ERP component was not highly correlated with a participant's response to the task at hand, whereas an ERP component that occurred at 190 ms post-stimulus onset was. Thus, categorisation appears to occur quite rapidly and seems to occur independently of later, possibly more conscious, categorisation processes. Relatedly, people can classify objects on the basis of category membership even with no awareness of the distinct categories guiding their response (e.g., Reed, Squire, Patalano, Smith, & Jonides, 1999). In summary, we conclude that categorisation occurs within later stages of the visual cortex, specifically area IT. Moreover, other data suggest that these same visual areas are not sensitive to the affective significance of objects (Iwai et al., 1990; Nishijo, Ono, & Nishino, 1988a; Rolls, 1999; Rolls, Judge, & Sanghera, 1977). Thus, within area IT and other later stages of the visual cortex we appear to have considerable evidence for categorisation prior to affect retrieval. Recall that studies have found distinct category-related ERPs within 70-80 ms post-stimulus onset (e.g., Van Rullen & Thorpe, 2001). Object identification also appears to occur (continued) rapidly, perhaps within 100 ms of stimulus onset (Lehky, 2000; Rolls & Tovee, 1994). These findings suggest that categorisation tends to occur prior to identification. Nevertheless, studies that present masked stimuli have demonstrated that even stimuli presented as briefly as 20-60 ms with pre-and postmasks are still sufficiently processed by area IT to support object identification (Dehaene et al., 2001; Rolls, 1999; Vogels & Orban, 1996). In the latter connection, Rolls, Tovee, Purcell, Stewart, and Azzopardi (1994) argued that such subliminal presentations reduce the amplitude of neural responses to stimuli, but do not change fundamental neural identification processes (see also Kovacs, Vogels, & Orban, 1995, for similar results). Thus, the primary difference between subliminal and optimal viewing conditions pertains to the amplitude of the neuronal responses within area IT, but sufficient processing still occurs to produce an invariant neural code (i.e., identification). From this perspective, demonstrations of "unconscious" cognition or affect are not particularly special from a neurological point of view.

6. The section title implies that cognition does not modulate emotion. We would suggest, like others have, that in fact cognition does modulate emotion (e.g., Ochsner & Gross, 2005), but such a discussion is beyond the scope of this article.

## REFERENCES

Adolphs, R. (2002). Recognizing emotion from facial expressions: Psychological and neurological mechanisms. *Behavioral and Cognitive Neuroscience Reviews, 1*, 21–62.

Adolphs, R., & Damasio, A. (2001). The interaction of affect and cognition: A neuro-biological perspective. In J. P. Forgas (Ed.), *Handbook of affect and social cognition* (pp. 27–49). Mahwah, NJ: Lawrence Erlbaum Associates, Inc.

Adolphs, R., Russell, J., & Tranel, D. (1999). A role for the human amygdala in recognizing emotional arousal from unpleasant stimuli. *Psychological Science, 10,* 167–171.

Allison, T., Puce, A., & McCarthy, G. (2000). Social perception from visual cues: Role of the STS region. *Trends in Cognitive Sciences, 4,* 267–278.

Bargh, J. (1997). The automaticity of everyday life. In R. S. Wyer Jr. (Ed.), *The automaticity of everyday life: Advances in social cognition* (Vol. 10, pp. 1–61). Mahwah, NJ: Lawrence Erlbaum Associates, Inc.

Bargh, J., Chaiken, S., Govender, R., & Pratto, F. (1992). The generality of the automatic attitude activation effect. *Journal of Personality and Social Psychology, 62,* 893–912.

Bargh, J., Chaiken, S., Raymond, P., & Hymes, C. (1996). The automatic evaluation effect: Unconditional automatic attitude activation with a pronunciation task. *Journal of Experimental Social Psychology, 32,* 104–128.

Bargh, J., & Chartrand, T. (1999). The unbearable automaticity of being. *American Psychologist, 54,* 462–479.

Barnard, P. J., Duke, D. J., Byrne, R. W., & Davidson, I. (2007). Differentiation in cognitive and emotional meanings: An evolutionary analysis. *Cognition and Emotion, 21,* 1155–1183.

Barrett, L. F. (2006). Emotions as natural kinds? Perspectives on *Psychological Science, 1,* 28–58.

Bartlett, F. C. (1932). Remembering: *A study in experimental and social psychology.* Cambridge: Cambridge University Press.

Baylis, G., Rolls, E. T., & Leonard, C. (1987). Functional subdivisions of the temporal lobe neocortex. *Journal of Neuroscience, 7,* 330–342.

Beauregard, M., Chertkow, H., Bub, D., Murtha, S., Dixon, R., & Evans, A. (1997). The neural substrate for concrete, abstract, and emotional word lexica: A positron emission tomography study. *Journal of Cognitive Neuroscience, 9,* 441–461.

Berkowitz, L., & Harmon-Jones, E. (2004). More thoughts about anger determinants. *Emotion, 4,* 107–130.

Bhalla, M., & Proffitt, D. (1999). Visual-motor recalibration in geographical slant perception. *Journal of Experimental Psychology: Human Perception and Performance, 25,* 1076–1096.

Blair, R., Morris, J., Frith, C., Perrett, D., & Dolan, R. (1999). Dissociable neural responses to facial expressions of sadness and anger. *Brain, 122,* 883–893.

Bless, H., Clore, G. L., Schwarz, N., Golisano, V., Rabe, C., & Wolk, M. (1996). Mood and the use of scripts: Does a happy mood really lead to mindlessness? *Journal of Personality & Social Psychology, 71,* 665–679.

Bower, G. H. (1981). Mood and memory. *American Psychologist, 36,* 129–148.

Bruner, J. S. (1957). Going beyond the information given. In J. S. Bruner et al. (Eds.), *Contemporary approaches to cognition* (pp. 41–69). Cambridge, MA: Harvard University Press.

Butler, R., Diamond, I., & Neff, W. (1957). Role of auditory cortex in discrimination of changes in frequency. *Journal of Neurophysiology, 20,* 108–120.

Cacioppo, J., Crites, S., & Gardner, W. (1996). Attitudes to the right: Evaluative processing is associated with lateralized late positive event-related brain potentials. *Personality & Social Psychology Bulletin, 22*, 1205–1219.

Cahill, L., Haier, R., Fallon, J., Alkire, M., Tang, C., Keator, D., et al. (1996). Amygdala activity at encoding correlated with long-term, free recall of emotional information. *Proceedings of the National Academy of Sciences, 93*, 8016–8021.

Canli, T., Desmond, J., Zhao, Z., Glover, G., & Gabrieli, J. (1998). Hemispheric asymmetry for emotional stimuli detected with fMRI. *Neuroreport, 9*, 3233–3239.

Chaiken, S., & Trope, Y. (1999). *Dual-process theories in social psychology.* New York: Guilford Press.

Clore, G. L., & Storbeck, J. (2006). Affect as information about liking, efficacy, and importance. In J. P. Forgas (Ed.), *Hearts and minds: Affective influences on social cognition and behaviour.* New York: Psychology Press.

Critchley, H., Daly, E., Phillips, M., Brammer, M., Bullmore, E., Williams, S., et al. (2000). Explicit and implicit neural mechanisms for processing of social information from facial expressions: A functional magnetic resonance imaging study. *Human Brain Mapping, 9*, 93–105.

Damasio, A. (1994). *Descartes' error: Emotions, reason, and the human brain.* New York: Avon Books.

Davey, G. C. L. (1995). Preparedness and phobias: Specific evolved associations or a generalized expectancy bias? *Behavioral and Brain Sciences, 18*, 289–325.

Davidson, R. J. (2003). Seven sins in the study of emotion: Correctives from affective neuroscience. *Brain and Cognition, 52*, 129–132.

De Houwer, J., & Randell, T. (2002). Attention to primes modulates affective priming of pronunciation responses. *Experimental Psychology, 49*, 163–170.

Dehaene, S., Naccache, L., Cohen, L., Bihan, D., Mangin, J., Poline, J., et al. (2001). Cerebral mechanisms of word masking and unconscious repetition priming. *Nature Neuroscience, 4*, 752–758.

DeSteno, D., Dasgupta, N., Bartlett, M. Y., & Cajdric, A. (2004). Prejudice from thin air: The effect of emotion on automatic intergroup attitudes. *Psychological Science, 15*, 319–324.

Dewey, J. (1894). The ego as cause. *Philosophical Review, 3*, 337–341.

Duncan, S., & Barrett, L. F. (2007). Affect is a form of cognition: A neurobiological analysis. *Cognition and Emotion, 21*, 1184–1211.

Duvel, A., Smith, D., Talk, A., & Gabriel, M. (2001). Medial geniculate, amygdalar and cingulate cortical training-induced neuronal activity during discriminative avoidance learning in rabbits with auditory cortical lesions. *Journal of Neuroscience, 21*, 3271–3281.

Elliott, R., & Dolan, R. J. (1998). Neural response during preference and memory judgments for subliminally presented stimuli: A functional imaging study. *Journal of Neuroscience, 18*, 4697–4704.

Erdley, C., & D'Agostino, P. (1988). Cognitive and affective components of automatic priming effects. *Journal of Personality & Social Psychology, 54*, 741–747.

Erez, A., & Isen, A. (2002). The influence of positive affect on the components of expectancy motivation. *Journal of Applied Psychology, 87*, 1055–1067.

Erickson, K., & Schulkin, J. (2003). Facial expressions of emotion: A cognitive neuroscience perspective. *Brain and Cognition, 52,* 52–60.

Fazio, R., Sanbonmatsu, D., Powell, M., & Kardes, F. (1986). On the automatic activation of attitudes. *Journal of Personality and Social Psychology, 50,* 229–238.

Ferguson, M., & Bargh, J. (2003). The constructive nature of automatic evaluation. In J. Musch & K. Klauer (Eds.), *The psychology of evaluation: Affective processes in cognition and emotion* (pp. 169–188). Mahwah, NJ: Lawrence Erlbaum Associates, Inc.

Fiedler, K. (2001). Affective states trigger processes of assimilation and accommodation. In L. Martin & G. Clore (Eds.), *Theories of mood and cognition: A user's guidebook* (pp. 86–98). Mahwah, NJ: Lawrence Erlbaum Associates, Inc.

Fox, E., Russo, R., Bowles, R., & Dutton, K. (2001). Do threatening stimuli draw or hold visual attention in subclinical anxiety? *Journal of Experimental Psychology: General, 130,* 681–700.

Fredrickson, B., & Branigan, C. (2005). Positive emotions broaden the scope of attention and thought-action repertoires. *Cognition and Emotion, 19,* 313–332.

Fukuda, M., Ono, T., & Nakamura, K. (1987). Functional relations among inferior temporal cortex, amygdala, and lateral hypothalamus in monkey operant feeding behavior. *Journal of Neurophysiology, 57,* 1060–1077.

Gasper, K. (2000). How thought and differences in emotional attention influence the role of affect in processing and judgment: When attempts to be reasonable fail. *Dissertation Abstracts International: Section B: the Sciences & Engineering, 60,* 5834.

Gasper, K., & Clore, G. L. (2002). Attending to the big picture: Mood and global versus local processing of visual information. *Psychological Science, 13,* 34–40.

Ghashghaei, H. T., & Barbas, H. (2002). Pathways for emotion: Interactions of prefrontal and anterior temporal pathways in the amygdala of the rhesus monkey. *Neuroscience, 115,* 1261–1279.

Greenwald, A. G., McGhee, D. E., & Schwartz, J. L. K. (1998). Measuring individual differences in implicit cognition: The implicit association task. *Journal of Personality and Social Psychology, 74,* 1464–1480.

Greve, K., & Bauer, R. (1990). Implicit learning of new faces in prosopagnosia: An application of the mere-exposure paradigm. *Neuropsychologia, 28,* 1035–1041.

Halgren, E. (1992). Emotional neurophysiology of the amygdala within the context of human cognition. In J. Aggleton (Ed.), *The amygdala: Neurobiological aspects of emotion, memory, and mental dysfunction* (pp. 191–228). New York: Wiley-Liss.

Harris, C., Pashler, H., & Coburn, N. (2004). Moray revisited: High-priority affective stimuli and visual search. *The Quarterly Journal of Experimental Psychology, 57A,* 1–31.

Huntsinger, J. R., Sinclair, S., Dunn, E., & Clore, G. L. (2006). If it feels good, just do it: Mood shapes conscious and unconscious goal pursuit. Unpublished Manuscript, University of Virginia.

Isbell, L. (2004). Not all happy people are lazy or stupid: Evidence of systematic processing in happy moods. *Journal of Experimental Social Psychology, 40,* 341–349.

Ito, T., & Cacioppo, J. (2001). Electrophysiological evidence of implicit and explicit categorization processes. *Journal of Experimental Social Psychology, 36,* 660–676.

Iwai, E., Yukie, M., Watanabe, J., Hikosaka, K., Suyama, H., & Ishikawa, S. (1990). A role of amygdala in visual perception and cognition in Macaque monkeys (macaca fuscata and macaca mulatta). *Tohoku Journal of Experimental Medicine, 161,* 95–120.

Kanwisher, N., McDermott, J., & Chun, M. (1997). The fusiform face area: A module in human extrastriate cortex specialized for face perception. *Journal of Neuroscience, 17,* 4302–4311.

Keightley, M., Winocur, G., Graham, S., Mayberg, H., Hevenor, S., & Grady, C. (2003). An fMRI study investigating cognitive modulation of brain regions associated with emotional processing of visual stimuli. *Neuropsychologia, 41,* 585–596.

Kemp-Wheeler, S., & Hill, A. (1992). Semantic and emotional priming below objective detection threshold. *Cognition and Emotion, 6,* 113–128.

Klauer, K., & Musch, J. (2002). Goal-dependent and goal-independent effects of irrelevant evaluations. *Personality and Social Psychology Bulletin, 28,* 802–814.

Klinger, M., Burton, P., & Pitts, S. (2000). Mechanisms of unconscious priming: I. Response competition, not spreading activation. *Journal of Experimental Psychology: Learning, Memory, and Cognition, 26,* 441–455.

Komura, Y., Tamura, R., Uwano, T., Nishijo, H., Kaga, K., & Ono, T. (2001). Retrospective and prospective coding for predicted reward in the sensory thalamus. *Nature, 412,* 546–549.

Kovacs, G., Vogels, R., & Orban, G. (1995). Cortical correlate of pattern backward masking. *Proceedings of the National Academy of Sciences of the USA, 92,* 5587–5591.

Kudo, M., Glendenning, K., Frost, S., & Masterson, R. (1986). Origin of mammalian thalamocortical projections. I. Telencephalic projection of the medial geniculate body in the opossum (Didelphis virginiana). *Journal of Comparative Neurology, 245,* 176–197.

Lane, R. D., & Nadel, L. (Eds.). (2000). *Cognitive neuroscience of emotion: Series in affective science.* New York: Oxford University Press.

Lane, R., Chua, P., & Dolan, R. (1999). Common effects of emotional valence, arousal and attention on neural activation during visual processing of pictures. *Neuropsychologia, 37,* 989–997.

Lavie, N., & De Fockert, J. (2003). Contrasting effects of sensory limits and capacity limits in visual selective attention. *Perception & Psychophysics, 65,* 202–212.

Lazarus, R. (1995). Vexing research problems inherent in cognitive-mediational theories of emotion and some solutions. *Psychological Inquiry, 6,* 183–196.

LeDoux, J. (1996). *The emotional brain: The mysterious underpinnings of emotional life.* New York: Simon & Schuster.

LeDoux, J. (2001). *Synaptic self: How our brain becomes who we are.* New York: Viking Publishing.

LeDoux, J., Romanski, L., & Xagoraris, A. (1989). Indelibility of subcortical emotional memories. *Journal of Cognitive Neuroscience, 1,* 238–243.

Lehky, S. (2000). Fine discrimination of faces can be performed rapidly. *Journal of Cognitive Neuroscience, 12,* 848–855.

Linke, R., De Lima, A., Schwegler, H., & Pape, H. (1999). Direct synaptic connections of axons from superior colliculus with identified thalamo-amygdaloid projection neurons in the rat: Possible substrates of a subcortical visual pathway to the amygdala. *Journal of Comparative Neurology, 403*, 158–170.

Logan, G. (2002). An instance theory of attention and memory. *Psychological Review, 109*, 376–400.

Lundqvist, D., & Öhman, A. (2005). Caught by the evil eye: Nonconscious information processing, emotion, and attention to facial stimuli. In L. F. Barrett, P. Niedenthal, & P. Winkielman (Eds.), *Emotion and consciousness* (pp. 97–122). New York: Guilford Press.

Mayer, J., Salovey, P., & Caruso, D. (2004). Emotional intelligence: Theory, findings, and implications. *Psychological Inquiry, 15*, 197–215.

McCabe, P., McEchron, M., Green, E., & Schneiderman, N. (1993). Electrolytic and ibotenic acid lesions of the medial subnucleus of the medial geniculate prevent the acquisition of classically conditioned heart rate to a single acoustic stimulus in rabbits. *Brain Research, 619*, 291–298.

McGaugh, J. L. (2004). The amygdala modulates the consolidation of memories of emotionally arousing experiences. *Annual Reviews in Neuroscience, 27*, 1–28.

Milner, A., & Goodale, M. (1995). *The visual brain in action.* Oxford, UK: Oxford University Press.

Morris, J., Öhman, A., & Dolan, R. (1998). Conscious and unconscious emotional learning in the human amygdala. *Nature, 393*, 467–470.

Murphy, S., & Zajonc, R. (1993). Affect, cognition, and awareness: Affective priming with optimal and suboptimal stimulus exposure. *Journal of Personality and Social Psychology, 64*, 723–739.

Narumoto, J., Okada, T., Sadato, N., Fukui, K., & Yonekura, Y. (2001). Attention to emotion modulates fMRI activity in human right superior temporal sulcus. *Cognitive Brain Research, 12*, 225–231.

Nicholson, D., & Freeman, J. (2000). Lesions of the perirhinal cortex impair sensory preconditioning in rats. *Behavioural Brain Research, 112*, 69–75.

Niedenthal, P. (1990). Implicit perception of affective information. *Journal of Experimental Social Psychology, 26*, 505–527.

Nishijo, H., Ono, T., & Nishino, H. (1988a). Single neuron response in amygdala of alert monkey during complex sensory stimulation with affective significance. *Journal of Neuroscience, 8*, 3570–3583.

Nishijo, H., Ono, T., & Nishino, H. (1988b). Topographic distribution of modality-specific amygdalar neurons in alert monkey. *Journal of Neuroscience, 8*, 3556–3569.

Nishijo, H., Ono, T., Tamura, R., & Nakamura, K. (1993). Amygdalar and hippocampal neuron responses related to recognition and memory in monkey. *Progress in Brain Research, 95*, 339–357.

Ochsner, K., & Gross, J. (2005). The cognitive control of emotion. *Trends in Cognitive Sciences, 9*, 242–249.

Öhman, A. (1997). As fast as the blink of an eye: Evolutionary preparedness for preattentive processing of threat. In P. J. Lang, et al. (Eds.), *Attention and orienting: Sensory and motivational processes* (pp. 165–184). Mahwah, NJ: Lawrence Erlbaum Associates, Inc.

Öhman, A., Esteves, F., & Soares, J. (1995). Preparedness and preattentive associative learning: Electrodermal conditioning to masked stimuli. *Journal of Psychophysiology, 9*, 99–108.

Parrott, G., & Sabini, J. (1989). On the "emotional" qualities of certain types of cognition: A reply to arguments for the independence of cognition and affect. *Cognitive Therapy and Research, 13*, 49–65.

Pashler, H., Johnston, J., & Ruthruff, E. (2001). Attention and performance. *Annual Review of Psychology, 52*, 629–651.

Perea, M., & Rosa, E. (2002). Does the proportion of associatively related pairs modulate the associative priming effect at very brief stimulus-onset asynchronies? *Acta Psychologica, 110*, 103–124.

Pessoa, L., Kastner, S., & Ungerleider, L. (2002). Attentional control of the processing of neutral and emotional stimuli. *Cognitive Brain Research, 15*, 31–45.

Phelps, E. (2004). The human amygdala and awareness: Interactions between emotion and cognition. In M. Gazzaniga (Ed.), *The cognitive neurosciences* (3rd ed., pp. 1005–1015). Cambridge, MA: MIT Press.

Proffitt, D. R. (2006). Embodied perception and the economy of action. *Perspectives on Psychological Science, 1*, 110–122.

Proffitt, D., Stefanucci, J., Banton, T., & Epstein, W. (2003). The role of effort in perceiving distance. *Psychological Science, 14*, 106–112.

Quirk, G., Armony, J., & LeDoux, J. E. (1997). Fear conditioning enhances different temporal components of toned-evoked spike trains in auditory cortex and lateral amygdala. *Neuron, 19*, 613–624.

Quirk, G., Repa, J., & LeDoux, J. E. (1995). Fear conditioning enhances short-latency auditory responses of lateral amygdala neurons: Parallel recordings in the freely behaving rat. *Neuron, 15*, 1029–1039.

Reed, J., Squire, L., Patalano, A., Smith, E., & Jonides, J. (1999). Learning about categories that are defined by object-like stimuli despite impaired declarative memory. *Behavioral Neuroscience, 113*, 411–419.

Riener, C., Stefanucci, J. K., Proffitt, D., & Clore, G. L. (2003). Mood and the perception of spatial layout. Poster presented at the 44th Annual Meeting of the Psychonomic Society, Vancouver, BC, Canada.

Robinson, M. D. (1998). Running from William James' bear: A review of preattentive mechanisms and their contributions to emotional experience. *Cognition and Emotion, 12*, 667–696.

Roediger, H. L., Gallo, D., & Geraci, L. (2002). Processing approaches to cognition: The impetus from the levels-of-processing framework. *Memory, 10*, 319–332.

Rolls, E. T. (1992). Neurophysiological mechanisms underlying face processing within and beyond the temporal cortical visual areas. *Philosophical Transactions of the Royal Society of London, Series B: Biological Sciences, 335*, 11–21.

Rolls, E. T. (1999). *The brain and emotion*. Oxford, UK: Oxford University Press.

Rolls, E. T., Judge, S., & Sanghera, M. (1977). Activity of neurons in the inferotemporal cortex of the alert monkey. *Brain Research, 130*, 229–238.

Rolls, E. T., & Tovee, M. (1994). Processing speed in the cerebral cortex and the neurophysiology of visual masking. *Proceedings of the Royal Society of London, Series B: Biological Sciences, 257*, 9–15.

Rolls, E. T., Tovee, M., Purcell, D., Stewart, A., & Azzopardi, P. (1994). The responses of neurons in the temporal cortex of primates, and face identification and detection. *Experimental Brain Research, 101,* 473–484.

Rothstein, P., Malach, R., Hadar, U., Graif, M., & Hendler, T. (2001). Feeling or features: Different sensitivity to emotion in high-order visual cortex and amygdala. *Neuron, 32,* 747–757.

Schwarz, N., & Clore, G. L. (1983). Mood, misattribution, and judgments of well-being: Informative and directive functions of affective states. *Journal of Personality and Social Psychology, 45,* 513–523.

Shi, C., & Davis, M. (2001). Visual pathways involved in fear conditioning measured with fear-potentiated startle: Behavioral and anatomic studies. *Journal of Neuroscience, 21,* 9844–9855.

Shiffrin, R., & Schneider, W. (1977). Controlled and automatic human information processing: II. Perceptual learning, automatic attending and a general theory. *Psychological Review, 84,* 127–190.

Smith, N., Cacioppo, J., Larsen, J., & Chartrand, T. (2003). May I have your attention, please: Electrocortical responses to positive and negative stimuli. *Neuropsychologia, 41,* 171–183.

Stefanucci, J. K., Proffitt, D. R., & Clore, G. (2005, May). Skating down a steeper slope: The effect of fear on geographical slant perception. Poster presented at the 5th Annual Meeting of the Society for Vision Sciences, Sarasota, FL, USA.

Stenberg, G., Lindgren, M., & Johansson, M. (2000). Semantic processing without conscious identification: Evidence from event-related potentials. *Journal of Experimental Psychology: Learning, Memory, and Cognition, 26,* 973–1004.

Stolz, J., & Besner, D. (1999). On the myth of automatic semantic activation in reading. *Current Directions in Psychological Science, 8,* 61–65.

Storbeck, J., & Clore, G. L. (2005). With sadness come accuracy, with happiness, false memory: Mood and the false memory effect. *Psychological Science, 16,* 785–791.

Storbeck, J., & Clore, G. L. (2006). Turning on and off affective and categorical priming with mood. Manuscript submitted for publication.

Storbeck, J., & Robinson, M. D. (2004). Preferences and inferences in encoding visual objects: A systematic comparison of semantic and affective priming. *Personality and Social Psychology Bulletin, 30,* 81–93.

Storbeck, J., Robinson, M. D., & McCourt, M. E. (2006). Semantic processing precedes affect retrieval: The neurological case for cognitive primacy in visual processing. *Review of General Psychology, 10,* 41–55.

Storbeck, J., Robinson, M. D., Ram, N., Meier, B., & Clore, G. L. (2004). [Unpublished raw data]. University of Virginia.

Sugase, Y., Yamane, S., Ueno, S., & Kawano, K. (1999). Global and fine information coded by single neurons in the temporal visual cortex. *Nature, 400,* 869–873.

Surguladze, S., Brammer, M., Young, A., Andrew, C., Travis, M., Williams, S., et al. (2003). A preferential increase in the extrastriate response to signals of danger. *NeuroImage, 19,* 1317–1328.

Thompson, R. (1962). The role of the cerebral cortex in stimulus generalization. *Journal of Comparative and Physiology Psychology, 55,* 279–287.

Van Rullen, R., & Thorpe, S. (2001). The time course of visual processing: From early perception to decision-making. Journal of *Cognitive Neuroscience, 13*, 454–461.

Vogels, R., & Orban, G. (1996). Coding of stimulus invariance temporal neurons. *Progress in Brain Research, 112*, 195–211.

Vuilleumier, P., Armony, J., Driver, J., & Dolan, R. J. (2003). Distinct spatial frequency sensitivities for processing faces and emotional expressions. *Nature Neuroscience, 6*, 624–631.

Whalen, P., Rauch, S., Etcoff, N., McInerney, S., Lee, M., & Jenike, M. (1998). Masked presentations of emotional facial expressions modulate amygdala activity without explicit knowledge. *Journal of Neuroscience, 18*, 411–418.

White, M. (1996). Automatic affective appraisal of words. *Cognition and Emotion, 10*, 199–211.

Winkielman, P., Schwarz, N., Fazendeiro, T., & Reber, R. (2003). The hedonic marking of processing fluency: Implications for evaluative judgment. In J. Musch & K. Klauer (Eds.), *The psychology of evaluation: Affective processes in cognition and emotion* (pp. 189–217). Mahwah, NJ: Lawrence Erlbaum Associates, Inc.

Witt, J. K., Proffitt, D. R., & Epstein, W. (2004). Perceiving distance: A role of effort and intent. *Perception, 33*, 577–590.

Zajonc, R. (1968). Attitudinal effects of mere exposure. *Journal of Personality and Social Psychology, 9*, 1–27.

Zajonc, R. (1980). Feeling and thinking: Preferences need no inferences. *American Psychologist, 35*, 151–175.

Zajonc, R. (2000). Feeling and thinking: Closing the debate over the independence of affect. In J. P. Forgas (Ed.), *Feeling and thinking: The role of affect in social cognition. Studies in emotion and social interaction* (Vol. 2., pp. 31–58). New York: Cambridge University Press.

# CHAPTER FOUR

# THE DYNAMICS OF SCAFFOLDING

From the perspective of UDL, learning occurs in the transaction between the person and the environment, which means many factors influence the process and outcome of learning. One factor that Universal Design for Learning holds as axiomatic is the notion of scaffolding. In its original use, the term *scaffolding* (as introduced by Wood, Bruner, and Ross in 1976) describes clinical-like interactions between a parent and child or a tutor and student. In modern terms, scaffolding is the use of systematic and customized contextual support applied as students struggle with new ideas and phenomena and discarded after the learning process is complete and a concept is robust. Under scaffolding:

1. The expert and novice co-participate in the task
2. The task is beyond the current understanding of the novice
3. The expert levies contextual supports (e.g., models, prompts, hints) to bolster the novice learner while completing the task and tailors supports to the specific needs of the novice
4. The expert makes constant assessments of the novice's understanding during the task
5. The scaffold is faded as the novice's knowledge becomes robust

From the beginning, the notion of scaffolding has been closely linked to developmental theory, most notably the pioneering work of Lev Vygotsky (1978). Vygotsky's framework, which emphasized the social nature of learning, has profoundly influenced both developmental theory and educational practice, although in very different ways. Educators have largely adopted what has been called *the metaphor of scaffolding* (Stone, 1998), an approach where teachers use intuition and craft knowledge to inform how and when they apply contextual support and scaffold student learning. While the concept of scaffolding is hugely important in the process of teaching and learning, there is very little empirical knowledge about the dynamic ways students' concepts shift and change over time in the context of scaffolding. This lack of systematic knowledge is hugely problematic given the explosion of computer-based and online learning, where curriculum designers attempt to leverage technology to "build" contextual supports and scaffolding into classroom materials. The technology enables previously unimaginable capacities for moment-to-moment, precisely calibrated scaffolding of learning, but the current state of the research leaves instructional designers to rely on intuition about how to put into practice the scaffolding concept.

In the featured essay, "The Dynamics of Competence: How Context Contributes Directly to Skill," authors Kurt W. Fischer, Daniel H. Bullock, Elaine J. Rotenberg, and Pamela Raya describe a body of research that makes clear the "collaboration between person and context" that necessarily characterizes development and learning. This move beyond the dichotomy of considering only the learner or the environment reflects the UDL perspective on how learning happens. Further, this perspective sets the stage for an educational research agenda that recognizes that competence is not fixed or static at any point in time but, instead, is always reflective of a range, is always dependent on a varying, dynamic system.

Fischer and colleagues place a premium on the *dynamic* nature of learning and change. They assume that people do not have a specific level of knowledge that is fixed; instead, knowledge and performance vary between two stable states: optimal and functional levels. For example, in baseball, a pitcher will be more likely to perform at an optimal level with a catcher who is skilled at offering support and guidance than with an inexperienced catcher who offers minimal support. The less-skilled pitching performance with the unsupportive catcher is not an illusory departure from the pitcher's real ability but instead represents a real change based on the effects of the catcher's activities, such as the prompts given and the ways his actions mesh with the needs of the pitcher. Such variation in performance is hypothesized to occur in a range where competence is low (i.e., functional level) without support and high (i.e., optimal level) with support.

The dynamic variability between what Fischer and coauthors refer to as functional and optimal understanding is ultimately very useful in practice and in research, as this range enables students to see what they are capable of and it gives them information about what they know and what they need to learn.

In this essay, the authors suggest that this range is a "property of the way the human nervous system operates" and show how the neural substrates reflect the development of skills as they move through levels of complexity, all in hopes of developing "autonomous control."

In his research, Fischer, who directs the Mind, Brain, and Education Program at the Harvard Graduate School of Education, focuses on the dynamic organization of behavior and the way it changes, especially cognitive development, social behavior, emotions, and brain bases. In his approach, called dynamic skill theory, he aims to integrate organismic and environmental factors.

We reached out to Fischer to help us consider issues of contextual support and scaffolding because of his expertise as a developmental theorist and his microdevelopmental studies that capture, in detail, the effects of such supports. Fischer spoke of his early work with colleague Mac Watson, when they discovered with infants the effects of support from parents in completing tasks in the laboratory— work that took place before Vygotsky's seminal work *Mind in Society* (1978) had even been translated into English.

Fischer's work aligns with and goes beyond the original conception of scaffolding, arriving at a point of great interest for UDL: how novice learners can become expert learners when they become aware of and assume responsibility for their own learning. In his research, he attempts to capture the essential characteristics of scaffolds in learning and to move beyond vague metaphors by leveraging the power of dynamic systems methods and models to pin down the *process* of scaffolding.

Fischer's dynamic perspective on scaffolding has important implications for UDL as he works to better understand on an empirical level how children learn and the ways in which we conceptualize learning ability and disability (Fischer, Rose, & Rose, 2007). Four key themes emerged from our conversation with Fischer.

### Contextual Support Is Fundamental to Learning and Development

While the provision of contextual supports could be thought of as primarily occurring in purposeful instruction, Fischer makes clear that social support for learning is a foundational element in human culture. Referencing Vygotsky, he says that "one of the things we do in human cultures is to teach our children the kind of fundamental knowledge of the culture. And in that process, there's a whole lot of activities that you're going to participate in where they're . . . getting help from other members of the culture, often older people who are really familiar with cultural practices." This help could be in the form of support from other people, such as parents, teachers, and siblings, as well as through cultural tools, such as books and computers. Fischer suggests that the details of this cultural transmission process have been surprisingly understudied, though the existence of this kind of support is robustly demonstrated.

### Variability Within a Developmental Range

The provision and removal of social, contextual support provides a dimension through which to consider variability within an individual learner. Fischer provides several examples of learners showing high levels of skills or knowledge when provided with, or shortly after receiving, contextual support, but this performance degrades after the support is removed. The difference between the high-support performance, or optimal level, and the low- or no-support performance, or functional level, is termed the *developmental range*.

Fischer describes, for example, a set of experiments in which children were asked to tell stories, and these stories were evaluated in terms of complexity levels. The finding of fluctuations between levels in the developmental range is robust: "If you provide support, you get a high-level story. Ten minutes later, the story is gone, the high-level story is gone. You reinstitute the support; it comes back. Ten minutes later, it's gone, and you can do that over and over and over. We've done it as many as six or seven times for a given kid, and every time it falls apart again, for most of the kids. So, it's a really powerful phenomenon, and a whole lot of people, especially teachers, know about it implicitly, but hardly anybody talks about it explicitly."

### Learners Develop Initial Understandings That Guide Their Learning

At the high end of the developmental range, the learner's understanding may only be at a surface, or tentative, level, but this initial understanding can serve a critical role in allowing the learner to guide his or her own learning. Fischer notes that "one of the things I think that happens is that when kids function at a higher level, they get a kind of general idea about what it means to be more sophisticated in what they can do in their skill. And then they use that to guide their own learning." As an example, Fischer cited his study with Nira Granott and James Parziale (Granott, Fischer, & Parziale, 2002) in which young adults were asked to figure out how Lego robots move. The participants showed a new kind of understanding based on a reaction they observed and used this observation to lead to a robust idea of input-output models to guide their continued learning. An initial, tentative idea can be built on to develop a richer understanding; learners, in essence, scaffold themselves.

### Dynamics in Assessment and Research

Developmental range (optimal to functional) and, thus, the variability in thinking during the process of concept development should be of central importance in the design of educational assessments and research in the learning sciences. Ability fluctuates routinely over time in response to different contexts, people, and problems. This variability is not error. Rather, such variability comprises essential information about student understanding and knowledge development in the process of learning. What does it mean to measure performance where there is a systematic effect of contextual support? Fischer suggests that structuring assessments based on this knowledge would make them capable of better informing instruction, as the educator would have a more robust picture of how the learner's understanding varies with different contextual conditions.

Similarly, the variability caused by differences in contextual support, and the wide fluctuations in learner ability, suggests that many of our traditional research and modeling approaches do not adequately capture the learning process. Fischer suggests that dynamic systems approaches "started out with the idea that growth is not a linear process, growth is logistic, and that is a basic principle that comes out of biology that, you know, virtually all life grows in logistic curves. You know, if you look at an S-shaped growth curve, you can take one part of it and say that's linear, but it's really not." He is encouraged by the increased attention to dynamic systems models but points out that few researchers "studying learning and teaching in development, educationally" are using these models even though they better reflect the learning process.

## FOR FURTHER READING

Fischer, K. W., Rose, L. T., & Rose, S. (2007). Growth cycles of mind and brain: Analyzing developmental pathways of learning disorders. In K. W. Fischer, J. H. Bernstein, & M. H. Immordino-Yang (Eds.), *Mind, brain, and education in reading disorders.* Cambridge: Cambridge University Press.

Granott, N., Fischer, K. W., & Parziale, J. (2002). Bridging to the unknown: A transition mechanism in learning and development. In N. Granott & J. Parziale (Eds.), *Microdevelopment: Transition processes in development and learning* (pp. 131–156). Cambridge: Cambridge University Press.

Palincsar, A. S. (1998). Keeping the metaphor of scaffolding fresh: A response to C. Addison Stone's "The metaphor of scaffolding: Its utility for the field of learning disabilities." *Journal of Learning Disabilities, 31*(4), 370–373.

Rappolt-Schlichtmann, G., Tenenbaum, H. R., Koepke, M. F., & Fischer, K. W. (2007). Transient and robust knowledge: Contextual support and the dynamics of children's reasoning about density. *Mind, Brain, and Education, 1*(2), 98–108.

Stone, A. (1998). The metaphor of scaffolding: Its utility for the field of learning disabilities. *Journal of Learning Disabilities, 3*(4), 344–364.

Vygotsky, L. S. (1978). *Mind in Society: The development of higher psychological processes.* Cambridge, MA: Harvard University Press.

Wood, D., Bruner, J., & Ross, G. (1976). The role of tutoring in problem solving. *Journal of Child Psychology and Psychiatry and Allied Disciplines, 17*(2), 89–100.

# The Dynamics of Competence
## How Context Contributes Directly to Skill

KURT W. FISCHER, DANIEL H. BULLOCK, ELAINE J. ROTENBERG,
AND PAMELA RAYA

In psychological development, person and context collaborate to produce action and thought. Although this statement or something close to it is now generally accepted by many developmental scholars, the full implications of the contributions of context are still not widely appreciated. Context does not merely influence behavior. It is literally part of the behavior, participating with the person to produce an action or thought.

Psychological systems in general arise from the collaboration of person and context. Most theories of psychological systems treat the person as the source of the systems and relegate the context to a minor role. An especially clear case of this mistake is the concept of competence, which characterizes a person's best knowledge—the upper limit of what he or she can say or do. A person is typically said to possess a certain competence, independent of its use in any context.

In this chapter we show that competence is an emergent characteristic of a person-in-a-context, not of the person alone. Competence arises from the collaboration between person and context, with competence changing when context changes. People are especially important in this collaboration, molding the context to support particular kinds of actions and thoughts in those they interact with. The effects of this sort of social support are dramatic, producing sharp shifts in competence level in individual children.

Competence rises abruptly with the provision of support and drops dramatically when the support is removed.

Theories of mind have generally suffered from the fundamental mistake of focusing explanation primarily on either the organism or the environment as the primary source of knowledge or intelligence (Fischer & Bullock,

1984). Theories of competence have been fundamentally flawed by their focus on the organism and their failure to recognize the contributions of context to competence. We suggest a different approach that grounds competence in the concept of skill, starting with the assumption that all behavior arises from collaboration of person and context. The dynamics of changes in competence are explained by analysis of developmental levels of skills as well as a neural network model.

## THE FAILURE OF COMPETENCE THEORIES

Cognitive scientists and psychometricians often speak of a person's competence, or ability, as if the person possessed a fixed capacity analogous to the amount of liquid that can be placed in a glass. Whatever context the child is in, the competence remains the same, according to this view. Variations in performance across context and age provide a serious problem for such theories.

The most extreme versions of such competence theories have proved untenable. Chomsky (1965) treated the child's language competence as fixed from early infancy through the operation of an innate language acquisition device. To explain the vast developmental changes that researchers have documented in language and cognition, he and his students impute biological constraints to the child that somehow interfere with the Chomskian competence, preventing it from becoming fully evident in behavior until later years. Building on this analysis, neonativists have repeatedly searched for some early behavior that relates to a "competence" and then neglected to analyze how the purported competence develops or how it is affected by context (Fischer & Bidell, 1991).

Another example of an extreme competence theory is Piaget's hypothesized epistemic subject, defined as a knower uninfluenced by context, analogous to a moving object in a perfect vacuum, where there is no resistance from other objects, events, or energy fields. Although Piaget (1936/1952) was one of the early voices calling for an approach integrating organismic and environmental influences, he built a theory that focused primarily on the child and neglected the environment and the bothersome developmental decalage that it produced (Beilin, 1971; Broughton, 1981; Piaget, 1971). In the last years of his life, however, Piaget recognized the problems with his earlier view and outlined a different view giving a more important role to context (Piaget 1981–1983/ 1987).

As developmentalists, most of us have taken a path similar to Piaget's, rejecting extreme competence theories. In their place, competence/ performance models have been proposed, providing more moderate characterizations of competence (e.g., Flavell & Wohlwill, 1969; Klahr & Wallace, 1976; Overton & Newman, 1982; Pascual-Leone, 1970). For a given domain and age, the child is considered to have a fixed competence, as reflected in his or her highest stage of performance. Variation below this highest stage occurs commonly and is attributed to factors like effort and task difficulty that impede demonstration of the true competence. As in the extreme competence theories, the person's competence is fixed at any one time, like the capacity of a glass to hold water. But unlike in the extreme theories, a set of processes are specified by which the competence eventuates in performance—ways that the person activates and utilizes the competence. Just as the glass can be half empty, people may only use a portion of their competence at any moment. When all the performance factors are controlled, people will show their true competence, the real upper limit on their performance.

Like their predecessors, these theories fail because they segregate the organism from the environment, locating most organismic factors in competence and most environmental ones in performance. This fundamental error not only fails to recognize the collaboration of person with context, but it also insulates the theory from test. The performance factors in the theory interfere both with the expression of competence and with the testing of the theory of competence. When findings do not support a prediction, they are interpreted as reflecting some performance factor rather than requiring a revision of the theory of competence. Like the Ptolemaic view that the stars and planets circle the earth, the competence theory is saved by post hoc epicycles in the performance component to maintain the perfect spheres of competence. The framework proposed in this chapter eliminates the segregation of organism from environment and makes competence a directly observable characteristic of individual people in-context.

## TAKING CONTEXT SERIOUSLY: THE ECOLOGY OF MIND

In recent years, there have been many calls for giving environment or context a more active role in explaining cognition and development. Bronfenbrenner (1979), Neisser (1976), J. J. Gibson (1979), and others have called for an ecological approach. For cognitive development, the works of Vygotsky and Gibson have been especially powerful in leading investigators to analyze the contribution of environment. Vygotsky (1978) focused on the social environment—how other people contribute to children's cognitive development and how children internalize these social influences. Gibson (1979) emphasized that the perceptual inputs for people in specific environments, called affordances, are richly structured and that people can detect and use them without the need for complex internal, mental construction. Many voices argue currently that context is actually a part of people's action, perception, thought, and knowledge (e.g., Cole & Scribner, 1974; Magnusson, 1988; Rogoff & Lave, 1984; chapters by Bronfenbrenner, Meacham, Reed, Rogoff, Wozniak, this volume).

These views require a radical restructuring of developmental theories. It is not enough to recognize the importance of experience in cognitive functioning. Of course, people need to experience a specific context to master skills in it or to detect affordances in it. A mechanic who has mastered the repair of a Toyota four-cylinder engine will typically have difficulty when first faced with the fancy engine of a Porsche. Likewise, a person who has grown up in Peoria will often have difficulty making sense of a myth told by African hunter-gatherers. Examples like the auto mechanic and the person from Peoria are frequently cited to support contextualism, but they are not convincing to skeptics because they are too obvious, showing only a global effect of experience. Virtually any framework that allows for the effects of experience will predict effects like these, including competence/performance theories.

What is needed instead is analysis of the dynamic effects of context on skill. For competence in development, this analysis predicts that *context affects the developmental level or stage of a person's competence even when the effects of experience and domain are controlled for.* We describe research that shows powerful effects in which for a narrowly specified domain, a person's developmental level varies dramatically as a function of contextual support. This effect is so powerful that a person's competence or ability can no longer be treated as a fixed characteristic of the person independent of context.

## SKILL: COLLABORATION BETWEEN PERSON AND CONTEXT

The concept of *skill* is a good starting point for the integration of person with context (Bruner, 1982; Fischer, 1980). In ordinary English usage, it implies both person and context simultaneously. People have a skill for riding a bicycle, a skill for listening to their friends, a skill for repairing Toyota engines, a skill for doing analysis of variance. A person cannot have a skill independent of a context. Skill requires a *collaboration* between person and context.

This conception means that skills vary not only between people but also across contexts for a given person (Fischer & Farrar, 1987). When a man borrows someone else's bicycle and rides it or rides his familiar bicycle on an unfamiliar kind of terrain (say, across a grassy field instead of on a road or sidewalk), he must adapt his skill to the context of the new bicycle or terrain. He cannot immediately ride skillfully by using the skill he possesses from before. He initially rides awkwardly, working to adapt the old skill to the new bicycle or terrain. Similarly, when a woman attempts to perform analysis of variance with a difference computer program or when she tries to analyze the data in a study with an unfamiliar design, she has to work to adapt her skill. It can take days or weeks of hard work to generalize the skill to the new context.

Notice that the skill concept includes the person as well as the context. It is as much a mistake to leave out the person as to leave out the context (Fischer & Bullock, 1984). Skills are characteristics of persons-in-contexts.

The concept of skill provides a foundation for building a theory of how person and environment collaborate to produce competence. Skill replaces the organismic definition of competence with the radical idea that capacities literally arise from the collaboration of person with context. A major goal of theory and research then becomes finding principles that specify how person and context collaborate to produce competences. Empirically, competence is defined most simply as an upper limit on the developmental level of behavior. Our research shows that behavior shows not one upper limit but different limits as a function of context.

## HOW CONTEXTUAL SUPPORT DIRECTLY AFFECTS DEVELOPMENTAL LEVEL

A person does not have a single developmental level, even when assessment is limited to a specific domain. Level varies systematically both across people and across contexts within the domain. For example, within a few minutes a 7-year-old child will demonstrate, in Piagetian terminology, concrete operational thinking as his or her best performance in one context and then preoperational thinking as his or her best performance in a slightly different context.

The domains in our research were highly specific. In one series of studies, we assessed individual children acting out and telling pretend stories in which they made realistic dolls act nice and/or mean with each other. All assessment contexts involved the same setting, toys, and contents, the same experimenter, and similar procedures. Another domain involved individual children sorting blocks into boxes forming classification matrices based on color, shape, and size, again with each context involving the same setting, toys, contents, experimenter, and procedures. Yet another domain (described in a later section) involved adolescents and adults explaining how they made decisions about complex knowledge dilemmas.

Within each domain, the contexts varied primarily in terms of the degree and type of social support that the experimenter provided for the task. In low support contexts, he or she simply asked a child to act out some mean and nice stories or to sort some blocks into boxes. In high support contexts, he or she provided explicit support for a particular behavior—for example, modeling a specific story or a way of sorting blocks.

The understanding of mean and nice social interactions was measured on the multistep developmental sequence shown in Table 4.1, which captures development between approximately 2 and 15 years of age. For example, for Step 3, the story involved one-dimensional social influence or reciprocity: One doll acted mean (or nice) to a second, and the second one acted mean (or nice) in return because of the first one's meanness (or niceness). The steps in Table 4.1 were specified in terms of the cognitive developmental levels and transformations of skill theory, which was used to predict the sequence (Fischer, Hand, Watson, Van Parys, & Tucker, 1984; Hand, 1982; Rotenberg, 1988). The sequence was tested via the statistics of scalogram analysis, and in several studies it formed a virtually perfect Guttman scale.

Despite the narrowness of the domain, the individual child's competence varied dramatically with assessment context. Competence was defined as the upper limit on the child's performance, his or her highest step. In one type of context, as shown in Fig. 4.1, a typical 7-year-old produced stories at the upper limit of Step 3, as well as at lower steps. In another type of context, that same child produced a story at the upper limit of Step 6, as well as at lower steps. For both types of contexts, the data fit the basic empirical criterion for competence: Behavior often varied below the highest step (3 and 6, respectively), but it did not exceed that step.

We have replicated this phenomenon across a score of studies of stories and classification involving hundreds of middle-class U.S. girls and boys between 3 and 18 years of age (Elmendorf, 1992; Fischer & Elmendorf, 1986; Fischer et al., 1984; Fischer, Shaver, & Carnochan, 1990; Lamborn

**FIGURE 4.1   Developmental range of a 7-year-old**

| Level | Step | |
|---|---|---|
| Rp1 | 1 | |
| | 2 | |
| Rp2 | 3 | FUNCTIONAL LEVEL (low support) |
| | 4 | |
| | 5 | |
| Rp3 | 6 | OPTIMAL LEVEL (high support) |
| | 7 | |
| Rp4/A1 | 8 | |
| A2 | 9 | |

& Fischer, 1988; Rose, 1990; Woo, 1990). The stories have included not only the domain of nice and mean interactions, but also various other social domains, including social roles (such as doctor-patient, mother-father-child, boy-girl, and child-adult), attributions about aggression, and perspective taking. The phenomenon has also replicated for several nonstory tasks, including classification of blocks.

In the classification research, a developmental scale for classification that was generally similar to that in Table 4.1 was used with children between 1 and 7 years of age (Fischer & Bidell, 1991; Fischer & Roberts, 1991). When children were repeatedly tested in low and high support contexts over a 2-month period, they showed different competences (upper limits), with the low support context consistently evoking a competence several steps lower than the high support context.

In summary, the research showed that in diverse domains, children demonstrated two very different competences, which we have called their *functional* and *optimal* levels. These two competences were tied to different kinds of social-contextual support: Low support contexts allowing relatively spontaneous behavior produced functional-level competence, whereas high support contexts priming more complex behavior produced optimal-level competence. The interval between the two levels is called a child's developmental range (Lamborn & Fischer, 1988).

### Spontaneous Contexts and Functional Level

In several kinds of spontaneous contexts, children showed the same upper limit—their functional level. For the mean and nice story tasks, individual children acted out or told stories spontaneously in two different contexts after they had seen an adult act out a series of stories about mean and nice interactions. In one context, called *free play*, the adult asked the child to make up some stories of her own while the adult went away to do something else for several minutes. In the other context, called best story, the adult returned and asked the child to show the *best story* she could.

Children's upper limit was the same in both spontaneous contexts. During free play, they produced several stories that ranged from the upper limit down to lower steps in the sequence. The 7-year-old in Fig. 4.1 showed at least one story at Step 3 and several other stories at Steps 1 and/or 2. In the best-story context, children produced a single story, and it was almost always at the highest step shown in free play. For the 7-year-old in Fig. 4.1, the best story was at Step 3.

To test whether the children were indeed showing a true upper limit, we introduced several procedures that could reasonably be expected to induce higher performance. The best-story context itself was one such check, and it supported the competence hypothesis: When asked to give the best story they could, 80%–100% of the children produced the same highest step as in free play, and most of the remaining children were within one step of that limit. When there was a difference between the two contexts, best story was usually one step lower than free play. This difference is predictable from measurement error, because the child had only one chance to show the highest step in the best-story context but multiple chances in the free-play context.

Other checks of the common limit in the two contexts included practice with the stories and instruction. Under both circumstances, the phenomenon replicated, with the same highest step continuing to obtain for both free play and best story. When practice or instruction produced a change in functional level in free play, it typically produced the same change in best story. Overall, however, the effects of practice and instruction were only modest. Average functional level improved at most one step when children were given both instruction and practice (Rotenberg, 1988).

Taken alone, these results would seem to support a simple competence view, because free-play and best-story contexts produced the same upper limit even with repeated assessment. However, the results for the second type of assessment context were dramatically different: The children's competence increased substantially in high support contexts.

**TABLE 4.1    A developmental sequence for understanding mean and nice social interactions**

| Level | Step | Skill | Examples |
|---|---|---|---|
| Rp1: Single representations | 1 | Active agent: A person performs at least one behavior fitting a social-interaction category of mean or nice. | Child pretends that one doll hits another doll ("mean") or gives another doll candy ("nice"). |
| | 2 | Behavioral category: A person performs at least two behaviors fitting an interaction category of mean or nice. | Child has one doll act nice to another doll, giving it candy and saying, "I like you." The second doll can be passive. |
| Rp2: Representational mappings | 3 | One-dimensional social influence: The mean behaviors of one person produce reciprocal mean behaviors in a second person. The same contingency can occur for nice behaviors. | Child has one doll say mean things and hit another doll, who responds by hitting and stating dislike for the first one. The second one's behavior is clearly produced by the first one's behavior. |
| | 4 | One-dimensional social influence with three characters behaving in similar ways: Same as Step 3, but with three people interacting reciprocally in a mean way (or a nice way). | With three dolls, child has one tease the others, while a second one hits the others. The third doll rejects both of the first two because they are mean. |
| | 5* | One-dimensional social influence with three characters behaving in opposite ways: The nice behaviors of one person and the mean behaviors of a second person produce reciprocal nice and mean behaviors in the third person. | With three dolls, child has one act friendly to others, while a second one hits others. The third doll responds nicely to the first doll and meanly to the second. |
| Rp3: Representational systems | 6 | Two-dimensional social influence: Two people interact in ways fitting opposite categories, such that the first one acts both nice and mean, and the second one responds with reciprocal behaviors in the same categories. | Child has one doll initiate friendship with a second doll but in a mean way. The second one, confused about the discrepancy, declines the friendship because of the meanness. The first then apologizes and makes another friendly gesture, which the second one responds to accordingly. |

| Level | Step | Skill | Examples |
|---|---|---|---|
| | 7 | Two-dimensional social influence with three characters: Same as Step 6 but with three people interacting reciprocally according to opposite categories. | With three dolls, child has one doll act friendly to a second one, while a third initiates play in a mean way. The second doll acts friendly to the first one and rejects the third, pointing out the latter's meanness. The third then apologizes for being mean, while the first one does something new that is mean. The second doll accepts the third one's apology and rejects the first one, pointing out the change in his or her behavior. |
| Rp4/A1: Single abstractions | 8 | Single abstraction integrating opposite behaviors: Two instances of interactions involving opposite behaviors take place as in Step 6, and the relations between the two interactions are explained in terms of some general abstraction, such as that intentions matter more actions. | With three characters, child has one act friendly to a second, while a third initiates play in a mean way. The second character responds to each accordingly, but then learns that the nice one had mean intentions while the mean one had nice intentions. The second character then changes his or her behavior to each to match their intentions and explains that he or she cares more about people's intentions than their actions. |
| A2: Abstract mappings | 9 | Relation of two abstractions integrating opposite behaviors: Two instances of interactions involving opposite behaviors are explained in terms of the relation of two abstractions, such as intention and responsibility: People who have a deceitful intention can be forgiven if they take responsibility in a way that undoes the deceit. | With three dolls, child has two of them act nice on the surface to a third, both with the intention of deceiving him or her into doing their homework. When the deceit is discovered by the third character, the first one takes responsibility for the deceit by admitting the intention and re-establishing his or her honesty. But the second one does not show such responsibility. The third character forgives the first one, but not the second, because he or she cares about people taking responsibility for their deceitful intention and undoing the deceit. |

*Step 5 is transitional between Levels Rp2 and Rp3. Apparently it can be mastered at Level Rp2, but it is much easier to do at Level Rp3.

### Supportive Contexts and Optimal Level

The type of context that evoked a higher level involved immediate contextual support for performance: An adult presented key information to the child about a story, and then the child acted out or told a story based on that information. Across two different contexts providing such contextual support, children showed the same optimal level. In one, called *elicited imitation*, the adult acted out and explained the story in detail and then asked the child to make up a similar story. In the other, called *memory prompt*, the adult reminded the child of the gist and key elements of an earlier story and then asked the child to show that story. Both of these contexts prompted key elements in the story.

Children showed the same upper limit in both contexts—their optimal level. In both elicited-imitation and memory-prompt contexts, they correctly produced all stories presented up to the upper limit and failed all stories beyond the limit. For the 7-year-old in Fig. 4.1, the limit was Step 6—a jump of three steps above the functional level. This level is called optimal because it is hypothesized to reflect the best performance that children can produce on their own. We have argued elsewhere that it also shows stagelike discontinuities in development, whereas the functional level shows nonstagelike continuous change (Fischer & Pipp, 1984). But that issue is not essential to this argument.

Children showed consistent optimal levels across repeated trials. In studies where children practiced the stories repeatedly, there was only a modest increase in step, averaging at most one step in Table 4.1 (Rotenberg, 1988). Individual differences were consistent from trial to trial. Instruction also caused a small increase in performance beyond that of practice, and it was similarly reliable. The occurrence of optimal level was thus a stable, replicable phenomenon in individual children.

Figure 4.2 shows results of one of the studies of practice and instruction, in which children performed under four contexts—two supportive contexts (elicited imitation and memory prompt) and two spontaneous contexts (free play and best story; Rotenberg, 1988). Eight 7-year-olds, instructed in how to recall the gist of the story to help their performance, were tested on the stories for Steps 3, 5, 6, and 7 in Table 4.1. They were assessed three times with the elicited-imitation, free-play, and best-story conditions and once with the memory-prompt condition. In the latter, memory prompts were given for each story, with the prompt providing the gist of the story, including a few key actions and objects. In Fig. 4.2 the upper limit is shown for the

**FIGURE 4.2**   **Reliability of highest step for understanding nice and mean under high and low support conditions with repeated assessments**

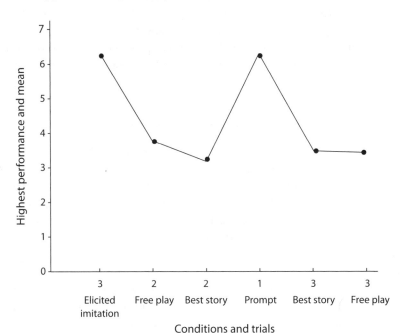

*Note:* Elicited imitation and prompt conditions provided high support. Free play and best story conditions provided low support. Numbers on x-axis indicate the repetition of the condition that is graphed.

third elicited-imitation assessment, the second and third free-play and best-story assessments, and the single memory-prompt assessment.

The highest steps elicited by the two supportive contexts were virtually identical, and those elicited by the two spontaneous contexts were lower and virtually identical. In elicited imitation, the stories were at Step 6. In free play and best story, they dropped precipitously to Step 3. Then, the memory prompts were given, and the stories again rose to Step 6, which was identical to the results for elicited imitation. Free-play and best-story contexts were repeated, and the stories again fell to Step 3. Every child showed the same general pattern of change, with some variation in the individual child's optimal and functional levels.

Clearly, the optimal-and functional-level results are highly replicable. In these studies children showed distinct competences for spontaneous and supportive contexts. Their competences arose from the dynamic interplay of person with context, changing in a matter of minutes as the context changed. A child participates in one context, producing a specific level, and then the child changes to participate in a different context, producing a different specific level. Return to the first context produces a return to the initial level, and so forth. This kind of effect can be repeated trial after trial for each individual child.

## DEVELOPMENTAL RANGE—WHERE COMPETENCES GROW

We propose that functional and optimal levels define the developmental range of a domain for a child—from skills that the child can produce easily on his or her own to skills that the child can produce only with strong contextual support (Bidell & Fischer, 1991). It is primarily within this range that short-term growth in skill occurs and that practice, instruction, and contextual variation have their effects.

Researchers or educators wanting to assess a child's understanding need to think in terms of a range, not a point on a scale. And they need to always consider context as an integral part of any competence they assess. Context includes not only the dimension of social support but also issues of domain. Children's functional and optimal levels vary substantially across domains. Failure to consider range and context leads to major errors of assessment.

The developmental range is related to Vygotsky's (1978) concept of the zone of proximal development as well as the associated concept of scaffolding (Bruner, 1982; Wood, 1980). Like developmental range, these Vygotskian concepts emphasize that the child's actions vary over a range closely tied to development and are strongly affected by the behaviors of other people.

There is at least one important difference between developmental range and zone of proximal development, however. In most of the studies of the zone, the adult actually intervenes in the task and performs part of it for the child. In our research, on the contrary, the adult does not directly intervene in the performance of the task. It is no surprise that a child and an adult together can perform a task better than a child alone. It is more surprising that the mere provision of social contextual support strongly affects the child's solo performance. In the supportive context, an adult prompts a skill in the child and then does nothing more: The child has no direct aid from the adult. But even with the adult not doing any of the task, the child and the supportive context collaborate to produce optimal performance.

The child truly demonstrates a competence to act on his or her own with support.

In addition, the research results show what appears to be a contradiction of the Vygotskian analysis. The zone of proximal development involves the child's gradual internalization of interactions between two people, one of whom is an adult or an accomplished peer (Vygotsky, 1978). As the child becomes adult, he or she becomes able to control the structures individually, without scaffolding. Thus, the zone gradually decreases or even disappears with age. On the other hand, the developmental range does not shrink with age but grows larger, as shown in Fig. 4.3, for the mean and nice stories (Hand, 1982). In infancy and early childhood, children's functional level seems to be close to their optimal level, at least for familiar domains (Fischer & Hogan, 1989; Watson & Fischer, 1980). Starting at about 3½ years, the gap between functional and optimal level becomes strong, and thereafter it seems to grow ever larger with age.

**FIGURE 4.3   Highest step for understanding nice and mean under three conditions as a function of age**

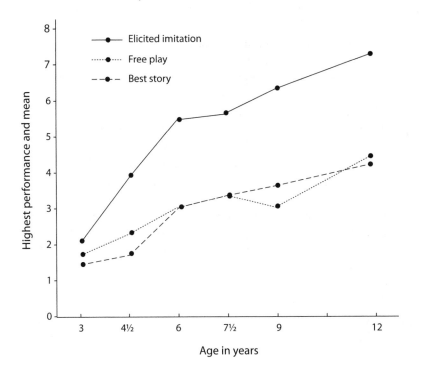

## CONTEXTUAL SUPPORT OF HIGHER REASONING: REFLECTIVE JUDGMENT

The developmental range does not end with childhood but extends into adulthood. A study of the developmental range for reflective judgment shows that developmental range grows larger at least through the late 20s, as people construct high-level abstract reasoning about the bases of knowledge. Optimal and functional levels occur at these ages too, and the distance between them grows with age.

Reflective judgment is reasoning about the bases for knowing, especially when dealing with conflicting arguments about a complex issue. Kitchener and King (1981) devised an interview for assessing reflective judgment by asking people to deal with dilemmas in which at least two opposing opinions are stated about an issue. For example, one of the dilemmas deals with the health effects of chemical additives to food: Do these additives promote health or cause disease?

Longitudinal research has shown that people's judgments develop through the seven stages shown in Table 4.2. Children start out with the view that knowing is a concrete state based on direct experience. At the middle stages, they come to understand that knowledge depends on one's viewpoint and is therefore uncertain. In the later stages, they move beyond the focus on uncertainty and consider the justification and evidence for a conclusion and the process of inquiry by which it was reached. Kitchener and Fischer (1990) presented a skill analysis of the stages of reflective judgment.

To assess optimal and functional levels of reflective judgment, we asked students to reason about knowledge dilemmas in two contexts (Kitchener, Lynch, Fischer, & Wood, 1993). The low support context was the traditional Reflective Judgment Interview (RJI), in which the person is presented with a series of dilemmas and for each dilemma is asked to state a position and to explain the bases for it. The high support context was a new assessment interview, the Prototypic Reflective Judgment Interview (Kitchener & Fischer, 1990). People were presented with the same dilemmas as in the RJI, but contextual support was provided by presentation of a prototypic answer for each stage of each dilemma. (These prototypes were based on answers given by people in earlier studies using the RJI.) After a student read one of the prototypes, he or she was asked to explain it in his or her own words.

Subjects were 104 students between 14 and 28 years of age, half male and half female. Students were tested individually in two sessions, with each session including first the spontaneous context (RJI) and then the supportive context (Prototypic Reflective Judgment Interview). After the first session,

**TABLE 4.2   Stages of development of reflective judgment**

| Skill Level | Stage of Reflective Judgment |
|---|---|
| Level Rp1: Single representations | Stage 1: Single category for knowing: To know means to observe directly without evaluation. |
| Level Rp2: Representational mappings | Stage 2: Two categories for knowing: People can be right about what they know, or they can be wrong. |
| Level Rp3: Representational systems | Stage 3: Three categories for knowing: People can be right about what they know, or they can be wrong, or knowledge may be incomplete or temporarily unavailable. The status of knowledge may differ in different areas. |
| Level Rp4/A1: Systems of representational systems, which are single abstractions | Stage 4: Knowledge is uncertain: The fact that knowledge is unknown in several instances leads to understanding knowledge as an abstract process that is uncertain. |
| Level A2: Abstract mappings | Stage 5: Knowledge is relative to a context or viewpoint; it is subject to interpretation. Thus it is uncertain in science, history, philosophy, etc. Conclusions must be justified. |
| Level A3: Abstract systems | Stage 6: Knowledge is uncertain and subject to interpretation, but it is possible to abstract some justified conclusions across domains or viewpoints. Knowledge is an outcome of these processes. |
| Level A4: Systems of abstract systems, which are principles | Stage 7: Knowledge occurs probabilistically via inquiry, which unifies concepts of knowledge. Knowledge can be reached with various degrees of certainty depending on justifications and evidence. |

*Note:* Descriptions are adapted from Kitchener and Fischer (1990) and Kitchener and King (1981).

students were also given a series of questions and guidelines to help them think about drawing conclusions about complex issues before the second session; these materials did not include direct statements about the actual dilemmas.

The results showed a clear separation of functional and optimal levels, with students performing approximately a stage higher in the supportive context than in the spontaneous one. These results held over both sessions. That is, producing higher stage responses in the supportive context in the first session and having 2 weeks to think about the dilemmas did not reduce the difference between optimal and functional levels, although there was a small overall increase in level between sessions.

Consistent with the previous finding that developmental range increased with age in childhood, the distance between functional and optimal levels of reflective judgment grew with age during adolescence and adulthood too. In the teenage years, the mean difference was about .6 stages, but by the late 20s it had grown to twice as much, 1.2 stages. The increasing size of the developmental range with age thus seems to extend well beyond the years of childhood into at least the years of early adulthood.

The reflective-judgment results thus illustrate the generality of the developmental range across domains and ages. People show one developmental level—one competence—when they act in a spontaneous context and a much higher developmental level—a different competence—when they act in a socially supportive context. The difference is remarkably robust. Not only does it occur across many domains, but practice and simple instruction do not eliminate it.

## DYNAMICS OF COMPETENCE IN A NEURAL NETWORK IN CONTEXT

The robustness and generality of the developmental range suggest that it is a basic characteristic of human cognition, a property of the way the human nervous system operates in context. To begin to understand the neural foundations for developmental range, we looked to modern neural network theory, especially models of parallel, distributed networks that involve a collaboration between top-down processes in the network itself and bottom-up processes from input to the network. Adaptive resonance theory (ART) has these properties and has been used with success to model many cognitive processes (Bullock, Carpenter, & Grossberg, 1991; Grossberg, 1980). ART networks have the capacity to learn and to function in many ways like intelligent organisms. As parallel distributed networks, they use a set of input to make generalizations about the form of that input, often producing surprises not built into the original network. Building on these properties, they achieve great power through specifying particular, diverse network architectures like those of human neural systems.

### Developmental Range in Neural Networks

Within adaptive resonance theory, neural networks have exactly the dynamic properties we anticipated: They generate not merely one competence but a range of competences affected powerfully by input from the context in which the network is functioning. Especially relevant to this developmental range is the role of contextual input in stimulating complex neural activity that is sustainable through short-term memory processes.

The networks contain short-term memory components that can be activated without being directly encoded into long-term memory. Indeed, complex neural systems exhibiting short-term memory, long-term memory, and differentiation of the two would seem inevitably to produce a property like developmental range. When the short-term memory components are activated by context, they allow the consequences of the transient contextual input to persist without any input from long-term memory components. For a significant interval after the contextual input, the network exhibits this competence, but the ability is fragile because it depends on the induced short-term memory components, which are not subject to long-term memory encoding at the current level of network maturity. Therefore, after intervening activities push the system into some other state, the network cannot autonomously re-enter the state originally induced by the context. The competence associated with having entered the contextually induced state is real, but the state itself cannot be regenerated by the network alone without appropriate contextual input.

In general, when bottom-up input (like that coming from context) and top-down input (like that coming from individual goals or plans) show an appropriate match, they produce resonance in the circuit. When the match is absent because of the absence of one or the other input, the network can still function, but it functions differently, in a less complex way. Thus a single network can show one organization when it is functioning without matching inputs and a more complex organization when it is functioning with both contextual input and matching top-down input, such as that from short-term memory.

The structure of this network is illustrated in a highly schematic way in Fig. 4.4. The output process involving network sites $R_1$ and $R_2$ produces a simple activity state at an early stage of development when it is activated by signals along pathways $S_1$ and $S_2$. As development proceeds, this process is reorganized by hierarchical inputs from sites $C_1$ and $C_2$ to sites $R_1$ and $R_2$ along pathways $S_3$ and $S_4$. When sites $C_1$ and $C_2$ are activated even briefly, they can maintain their active state by virtue of the excitatory feedback loop (shown with the + sign to indicate its excitatory nature). That is, when contextual inputs $I_1$ and $I_2$ activate $C_1$ and $C_2$, the pattern can be maintained in reverberatory short-term memory and continue to enable reorganized processing through sites $R_1$ and $R_2$—optimal level behavior.

**FIGURE 4.4    A neural network that shows the phenomena of developmental range**

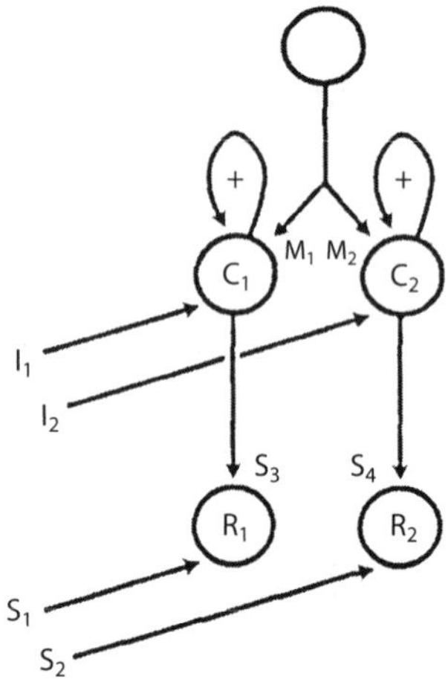

*Key:* Circles mark neural network sites, and arrows mark activation pathways. C and R designate hierarchically organized sites, with C providing input to R. The + sign indicates excitatory feedback loops, which sustain short-term memory for a site. S designates pathways of activation from one neural site to another. I marks input from the context. M designates memory pathways. The diagram shows only the part of the network central to the text. The open circle at the top and activation pathways $S_1$ and $S_2$ show links to other parts of the network.

However, when the system is reset by, for example, a change in context, the loop will be interrupted, and the reorganized processing will cease. Now all that the system can sustain is the simpler activity produced by signals $S_1$ and $S_2$—functional level behavior. To overcome this functional-level limit, the system must be able to generate the more complex activity through sites $C_1$ and $C_2$ on its own without contextual inputs $I_1$ and $I_2$. This development occurs when the long-term memory pathways $M_1$ and $M_2$ to sites $C_1$ and $C_2$ become functional. As further development and learning bring these long-term memory pathways into operation, a child can permanently encode the pattern induced at $C_1$ and $C_2$ in long-term memory. As a result, the child becomes able to endogenously regenerate the induced state at a later time in the absence of immediate contextual support. Now, what was previously optimal level becomes functional level: Behavior that previously depended on contextual support can now be produced spontaneously.

The partial independence of short- and long-term memory processes is only one part of the general complexity and diversity of animal nervous systems. A central nervous system (CNS) is made of many components in composite structure, including diverse neural circuits and diverse inputs to those circuits. The components are not only parallel and distributed but often distinct in structure. Advanced brains are built up from many separate local circuits that operate in partial independence of other local circuits. Although all regions of the CNS are ultimately linked, partial independence is assured by variability in linkage strengths, occurrence of both cooperative (mutually excitatory) and competitive (mutually inhibitory) interactions, radical differences among networks in sensitivities to inputs of various types, and highly diverse inputs from the environment and the body. In addition, partial independence is also assured by developmental delays in effective interaction between many component networks (Fischer & Rose, 1993; Thatcher, 1994), as in the delay in development of the M components in Fig. 4.4. Given all the complexity and independence of components, it is inevitable that among the system's multiple activity states, some will be dependent on specific contexts. In addition, some of these context-dependent states will eventually develop so that a child can generate them autonomously.

### Advantages of Multiple Levels of Competence

In time, children typically develop the capacity to evoke the complex activity at sites $C_1$ and $C_2$ on their own through long-term memory sites $M_1$ and $M_2$. That is, after some key experiences, a child becomes capable of autonomously generating the developmentally advanced performance earlier exhibited only transiently—a capacity that Bullock, Carpenter, and Grossberg (1991) called autonomous supercession of (endogenous) control. This capacity has major advantages, of course, but there also seem to be good reasons that its development is delayed.

The advantages of autonomous control are clear. It is advantageous to be able to re-enter a state that generates an adaptive behavior without strong dependence on exogenous input such as social contextual support. Instead of a lengthy process of search for the supportive context to produce the behavior, the organism can directly generate the desirable behavior. Such re-entry to desirable states is a theme in both Piagetian theory, with its emphasis on circular reactions and the regeneration of sensorimotor states (Piaget, 1936/1952; see also Kaufmann, 1980), and conditioning theory, with its emphasis on the regeneration of positively reinforcing states (Skinner, 1969). In fact, there are many different kinds of autonomous supercession of control within and across species (Bullock, 1981; Bullock et al., 1991; Fischer & Bullock, 1984). Because of the emphasis on autonomous control, neural network theories of perceptual and motor skill learning have focused on showing how more endogenously activated input pathways to component networks can gracefully supercede more exogenously activated input pathways, as illustrated with the supercession of control by long-term memory in Fig. 4.4. (Note that in neural network models the supercession effect is graded rather than all-or-none.)

Despite all these obvious advantages, children do not develop autonomous control quickly in all domains. Instead, they develop it slowly and hierarchically, with vast arenas of behavior requiring social contextual support for years before children gain autonomous control over them. Of course, it is these delays that produce the developmental range, the difference between optimal and functional levels. This aspect of developmental range has not been a major subject of research in neural network theory or in other parts of cognitive science.

The key questions are: What does an organism have to gain by delaying the time that a level of supercession of control matures, and how is the delay achieved? Of these two aspects of the problem, how the delay could be achieved is easier to answer. The full functioning of neural connections can be readily delayed by many processes, including slow myelination of pathways. For example, if learned supercession of control depends, as in Fig. 4.4, on the correlated activation of sites $C_1$ and $C_2$ with long-term memory pathways $M_1$ and $M_2$, which project to $C_1$ and $C_2$ from remote brain regions, then supercession can be prevented by delayed myelination of pathways $M_1$ and $M_2$ prior to that time. Without myelin, signals will be transmitted slowly and with great attenuation along $M_1$ and $M_2$. The result will be negligible long-term memory encoding of $C_1$ and $C_2$ activations, even if the cells that give rise to pathways $M_1$ and $M_2$ show functional connections within the local circuit to $C_1$ and $C_2$. In fact, myelination is a slow developmental process in human beings (Yakovlev & Lecours, 1967), and there are many other processes as well that delay the full functioning of neural connections (Thatcher, 1994).

Questions about the adaptive value of such delays have seldom been asked by developmentalists. They seem to assume that developmental delays are explained in terms of intrinsic maturational factors, such as the inherent dependence of upper levels of a hierarchy on prior development of lower levels. We have argued since the early 1980s that timing of developmental transitions arises from a set of dynamically interacting factors, not merely from intrinsic maturation (Fischer, 1980; Fischer & Bullock, 1981).

The advantages of delaying autonomous supercession of control, we hypothesize, center on the relation between levels of organization in a hierarchy. When a higher level assumes control, there is truncation of the search process at the lower level—that is, reduction in the scope of search for adaptive combinations for generalization at the lower level. Consequently, delaying supercession of control by level n + 1 prolongs the search for new adaptive combinations at level n.

Delaying the control of level n + 1 not only allows time to find adaptive combinations at level n, but it reduces the risk of finding inadequate combinations there. The form that activity takes in a neural network depends very much on the input it experiences—its sampling base. With insufficient experience at level n, poor generalizations can be formed there. Delays in supercession of control to a higher level will avoid powerful generalizations drawn from insufficient sampling.

A self-organizing hierarchy can produce compact representations together with great generative power, but this potential requires that its generalizations be well suited to its task environments. The effectiveness of its generalizations are directly related to the thoroughness of its sampling of task environments. Indeed, Elman (1992) showed this limitation in a parallel, distributed network that learned to speak based on experience. For the network to learn adequate generalizations about lower levels of speech production, it required extensive experience at a lower level before moving to a higher level. When the network was not required to function at a lower level first, it missed important generalizations. There is a selective benefit to prolonging lower level sampling well beyond the minimum that is strictly necessary for construction of skills to begin at the next level.

Even while there is a disadvantage to truncating lower level sampling too early, there is also an advantage to being able to activate higher level generalizations that have been successful. The developmental-range phenomenon provides a way of having both advantages at the same time by separating the two levels. A child can sustain higher level generalizations when the context induces them, but the child can simultaneously delay higher level control in order to have extensive opportunity for learning important generalizations at the lower level. This kind of process has been outlined not only for development but also for multiple memory systems in primates (Levine & Prueitt, 1989; Mishkin, Malamut, & Bachevalier, 1984) and for alternative substrates for learning in neural networks (Grossberg, 1978).

The coexistence of lower level and higher level functioning in the developmental range essentially separates sampling and generalization processes. The collapsing of these separated processes would pose serious problems for a developing organism dependent on learning. Some neural network theories, such as back propagation models (McClelland & Rumelhart, 1986), have architectures that virtually collapse sampling and generalization, and as a result the networks must learn very slowly in order to prevent premature, poor quality generalizations (Bullock & Grossberg, 1990; Grossberg, 1987; see also Prince & Pinker, 1988).

The separation of competences evident in the phenomena of developmental range thus make sense in terms of how neural networks function and in terms of the demands of adaptation to a complex environment.

## SUMMARY AND CONCLUSIONS: THE DYNAMICS OF COMPETENCE

Across domains and ages, context contributes directly to competence. That is, skill level is a characteristic not only of a person but also of a context. People do not have competences independent of context.

The phenomenon of developmental range shows one way that this person-environment collaboration works. Immediate context contributes directly to skill, affecting the developmental level of a child's behavior. By evoking specific skill components, context induces a particular skill. This effect is powerful, with performance varying from moment to moment up and down a developmental scale as a function of degree of contextual support for high-level functioning. When the support changes, the child's level changes.

Traditional conceptions of competence and performance fail because they treat competence as a fixed characteristic of the child, analogous to a bottle with a fixed capacity. Performance factors are seen as somehow interfering with this capacity. The concept of skill overcomes these limitations by providing a dynamic framework for analyzing variations in behavior with context.

Our research shows that children do indeed have stable levels of competences when domain and degree of support are held constant across assessment contexts. In optimal contexts—with high support, familiar tasks, and motivation to perform—children show a true upper limit on performance, called their optimal level. In spontaneous contexts—with minimal support—children show a much lower upper limit, their functional level. The optimal level develops in a stagelike way, while the functional level develops slowly and gradually.

Neural networks based in adaptive resonance theory show the same separation of levels of functioning. When contextual support induces an optimal-level organization, short-term feedback can sustain that level until the circuit is disrupted. Without contextual support, the network functions at a simpler, functional level. This property of separation of levels allows children to function at a high level when the context demands it while at the same time keeping lower levels of functioning open to new learning from experience. In this kind of system, there is no single fixed competence like that of a glass but a dynamic range of competences reflecting the complexity of human behavior and experience.

## ACKNOWLEDGMENTS

The work in this chapter was supported by grants from the MacArthur Network on Early Childhood, the Spencer Foundation, and Harvard University. We would like to express appreciation to Gail Goodman, Helen Hand, Karen Kitchener, Michael Mascolo, Malcolm Watson, and Robert Wozniak for their contributions to the ideas and research reported here.

## REFERENCES

Beilin H. (1971). "Developmental stages and developmental processes." In D. R. Green, M. P. Ford, & G. B. Flamer (Eds.), *Measurement and Piaget*. New York: McGraw-Hill.

Bidell T. R., & Fischer K. W. (1991). "Beyond the stage debate: Action, structure, and variability in Piagetian theory and research." In R. Sternberg & C. Berg (Eds.), *Intellectual development* (pp. 100–140). New York: Cambridge University Press.

Bronfenbrenner U. (1979). *The ecology of human development: Experiments by nature and design*. Cambridge, MA: Harvard University Press.

Broughton J. M. (1981). "Piaget's structural developmental psychology, III. Function and the problem of knowledge." *Human Development*, 24, 257–285.

Bruner J. S. (1982). "The organization of action and the nature of adult-infant transaction." In M. Cranach & R. Harre (Eds.), *The analysis of action* (pp. 280–296). New York: Cambridge University Press.

Bullock D. (1981). "On the current and potential scope of generative theories of cognitive development." In K. W. Fischer (Ed.), *Cognitive development. New Directions for Child Development* (Vol. 12, pp. 93–109). San Francisco: Jossey-Bass.

Bullock D., Carpenter G. A., & Grossberg S. (1991). "Self-organizing neural network architectures for adaptive pattern recognition and robotics." In P. Antognetti & V. Milutinovic (Eds.), *Neural networks: Concepts, applications, and implementations* (Vol. 1, pp. 33–53). Englewood Cliffs, NJ: Prentice-Hall.

Bullock D., & Grossberg S. (1990). "Motor skill development and neural networks for position code invariance under speed and compliance rescaling." In H. Bloch & B. I. Bertenthal (Eds.), *Sensory-motor organizations and development in infancy and early childhood* (pp. 1–22). Dordrecht: Kluwer Academic.

Chomsky N. (1965). *Aspects of the theory of syntax*. Cambridge: MIT Press.

Cole M., & Scribner S. (1974). *Culture and thought: A psychological introduction*. New York: Wiley.

Elman J. (1992). "Incremental learning, or the importance of starting small." In *Proceedings of the Thirteenth Annual Conference of the Cognitive Science Society.* Hillsdale, NJ: Lawrence Erlbaum Associates.

Elmendorf D. (1992). *Development of distortions in children's understanding of intentions behind physically harmful acts.* Unpublished doctoral dissertation, University of Denver. *Dissertation Abstracts International.*

Fischer K. W. (1980). "A theory of cognitive development: The control and construction of hierarchies of skills." *Psychological Review,* 87, 477–531.

Fischer K. W., & Bidell T. R. (1991). "Constraining nativist inferences about cognitive capacities." In S. Carey & R. Gelman (Eds.), *The epigenesis of mind: Essays on biology and knowledge* (pp. 199–235). Hillsdale, NJ: Lawrence Erlbaum Associates.

Fischer K. W., & Bullock D. (1981). "Patterns of data: Sequence, synchrony, and constraint in cognitive development." In K. W. Fischer (Ed.), *Cognitive development. New Directions for Child Development* (Vol. 12, pp. 69–78). San Francisco: Jossey-Bass.

Fischer K. W., & Bullock D. (1984). "Cognitive development in school-age children: Conclusions and new directions." In W. A. Collins (Ed.), *The years from six to twelve: Cognitive development during middle childhood* (pp. 70–146). Washington, DC: National Academy Press.

Fischer K. W., & Elmendorf D. (1986). "Becoming a different person: Transformations in personality and social behavior." In M. Perlmutter (Ed.), *Minnesota Symposium on Child Psychology, Vol. 18: Cognitive perspectives on children's social and behavioral development* (pp. 137–178). Hillsdale, NJ: Lawrence Erlbaum Associates.

Fischer K. W., & Farrar M. J. (1987). "Generalizations about generalization: How a theory of skill development explains both generality and specificity." *International Journal of Psychology,* 22, 643–677.

Fischer K. W., Hand H. H., Watson M. W., Van Parys M., & Tucker, J. (1984). "Putting the child into socialization: The development of social categories in preschool children." In L. Katz (Ed.), *Current topics in early childhood education* (Vol. 5, pp. 27–72). Norwood, NJ: Ablex.

Fischer K. W., & Hogan, A. (1989). "The big picture for infant development: Levels and variations." In J. Lockman & N. Hazen (Eds.), *Action in social context: Perspectives on early development* (pp. 275–305). New York: Plenum.

Fischer K. W., & Pipp S. L. (1984). "Processes of cognitive development: Optimal level and skill acquisition." In R. J. Sternberg (Ed.), *Mechanisms of cognitive development* (pp. 45–80). New York: Freeman.

Fischer K. W., & Roberts R. J., Jr. (1991). "The development of classification skills in the preschool years: Developmental level and errors." Cambridge, MA: Cognitive Development Laboratory Report, Harvard University.

Fischer K. W., & Rose S. P. (1993). "Development of coordination of components in brain and behavior: A framework for theory and research." In G. Dawson & K. W. Fischer (Eds.), *Human behavior and the developing brain.* New York: Guilford Press.

Fischer K. W., Shaver P., & Carnochan (1990). "How emotions develop and how they organize development." *Cognition and Emotion,* 4, 81–127.

Flavell J. H., & Wohlwill J. F. (1969). "Formal and functional aspects of cognitive development." In D. Elkind & J. H. Flavell (Eds.), *Studies in cognitive development*. London: Oxford University Press.

Gibson J. J. (1979). *The new ecological approach to visual perception*. Boston: HoughtonMifflin.

Grossberg S. (1978). "A theory of human memory: Self-organization and performance of sensory-motor codes, maps, and plans." In R. Rosen & F. Snell (Eds.), *Progress in theoretical biology* (Vol. 5, pp. 233–374). New York: Academic Press.

Grossberg S. (1980). "How does a brain build a cognitive code?" *Psychological Review*, 87, 1–51.

Grossberg S. (1987). "Competitive learning: From interactive activation to adaptive resonance." *Cognitive Science*, 11, 23–63.

Hand H. H. (1982). "The development of concepts of social interaction: Children's understanding of nice and mean." *Dissertation Abstracts International*, 42(11), 4578B. (University Microfilms No. DA8209747)

Kaufmann G. (1980). *Imagery, language, and cognition*. Oslo: Universitetsforlaget.

Kitchener K. S., & Fischer K. W. (1990). "A skill approach to the development of reflective thinking." In D. Kuhn (Ed.), *Developmental perspectives on teaching and learning thinking skills. Contributions to human development* (Vol. 21, No. 4, pp. 48–62). Basel, Switzerland: S. Karger.

Kitchener K. S., & King P. M. (1981). "Reflective judgement: Concepts of justification and their relation to age and education." *Journal of Applied Developmental Psychology*, 2, 89–116.

Kitchener K. S., Lynch C., Fischer K. W., & Wood P. (1993). "Developmental range of reflective judgement." *Developmental Psychology*.

Klahr D., & Wallace J. G. (1976). *Cognitive development: An information-processing view*. Hillsdale, NJ: Lawrence Erlbaum Associates.

Lamborn S. D., & Fischer K. W. (1988). "Optimal and functional levels in cognitive development: The individual's developmental range." *Newsletter of the International Society for the Study of Behavioral Development*, 2(14), 1–4.

Levine D. S., & Prueitt P. S. (1989). "Modeling some effects of frontal lobe damage: Novelty and perseveration." *Neural Networks*, 2, 103–116.

Magnusson D. (1988). *Individual development from an interactional perspective: A longitudinal study*. Hillsdale, NJ: Lawrence Erlbaum Associates.

McClelland J. L., & Rumelhart D. E. (Eds.). (1986). *Parallel distributed processing*. Cambridge, MA: MIT Press.

Mishkin M., Malamut B., Bachevalier J. (1984). "Memories and habits: Two neural systems." In G. Lynch, J. McGaugh, & N. Weinberger (Eds.), *Neurobiology of learning and memory* (pp. 65–77). New York: Guilford.

Neisser U. (1976). *Cognition and reality*. New York: Freeman.

Overton W. F., & Newman J. L. (1982). "Cognitive development: A competence-activation/utilization approach." In T. M. Field, A. Huston, H. C. Quay, L. Troll, & G. E. Finley (Eds.), *Review of human development*. New York: Wiley.

Pascual-Leone J. (1970). "A mathematical model for the transition rule in Piaget's developmental stages." *Acta Psychologica*, 32, 301–345.

Piaget J. (1952). *The origins of intelligence in children* (M. Cook, Trans.). New York: International Universities Press. (Original work published 1936)

Piaget J. (1971). "The theory of stages in cognitive development." In D. R. Green, M. P. Ford, & G. B. Flamer (Eds.), *Measurement and Piaget*. New York: McGraw-Hill.

Piaget J. (1987). *Possibility and necessity* (2 vols., H. Feider, Trans.). Minneapolis, MN: University of Minnesota Press. (Original work published 1981 and 1983).

Prince A., & Pinker S. (1988). "Rules and connections in human language." *Trends in Neuroscience*, 11, 195–202.

Rogoff B., & Lave J. (Eds.). (1984). *Everyday cognition: Its development in social context*. Cambridge, MA: Harvard University Press.

Rose S. P. (1990). *Levels and variations in measures of perspective-taking*. Unpublished doctoral dissertation, University of Denver, Denver, CO.

Rotenberg, E. J. (1988). *The effects of development, self-instruction, and environmental structure on understanding social interactions*. Unpublished doctoral dissertation, University of Denver, Denver, CO.

Skinner B. F. (1969). *Contingencies of reinforcement: A theoretical analysis*. New York: Appleton-Century-Crofts.

Thatcher R. W. (1991). "Maturation of the human frontal lobes: Physiological evidence for staging." *Developmental Neuropsychology*, 7, 397–419.

Thatcher R. W. (1994). "Cyclic cortical reorganization: Origins of human cognitive development." In G. Dawson & K. W. Fischer (Eds.), *Human behavior and the developing brain*. New York: Guilford.

Vygotsky L. (1978). *Mind in society: The development of higher psychological processes* (M. Cole, V. John-Steiner, S. Scribner, & Ellen Souberman, Trans.). Cambridge, MA: Harvard University Press.

Watson M. W., & Fischer K. W. (1980). "Development of social roles in elicited and spontaneous behavior during the preschool years." *Developmental Psychology*, 16, 484–494.

Woo N. S. (1990). *The development of person categorization in Korean preschool children: Understanding and use of age and sex categories*. Unpublished doctoral dissertation, Harvard University, Cambridge, MA.

Wood D. J. (1980). "Teaching the young child: Some relationships between social interaction, language, and thought." In D. R. Olson (Ed.), *The social foundations of language and thought*. New York: Norton.

Yakovlev P. I., & Lecours A. R. (1967). "The myelogenetic cycles of regional maturation of the brain." In A. Minkowsky (Ed.), *Regional development of the brain in early life* (pp. 3–70). Oxford: Blackwell.

*Originally published as K. W. Fischer, D. Bullock, E. J. Rotenberg, & P. Raya. (1993). The dynamics of competence: How context contributes directly to skill. In R. Wozniak & K. W. Fischer (Eds.),* Development in context: Acting and thinking in specific environments *(pp. 93–117). Hillsdale, NJ: Erlbaum. Reprinted with permission of Elsevier Ltd. via Copyright Clearance Center.*

# CHAPTER FIVE

# LEARNING FROM OUTLIERS

The Universal Design for Learning framework makes several strong assumptions about learning variability, including the assumption of "innovation from the margins"—the notion that the study of extreme instances of variability (so-called *outliers*) yields meaningful insights about the nature of learning that are applicable (and valuable) for all students. This view stands in stark contrast to classic models of learning, which focus on average performance and ignore outliers.

In recent years the value of learning from outliers has become increasingly recognized and accepted in certain areas of education, such as curriculum development, instructional design, and educational technologies. In contrast, educational assessment has not made the same kind of progress in dealing with variability in general and outliers in particular. A continued focus on typical or average performance prevents the assessment field from developing more accurate and effective measures of student learning. Focusing on variability, by focusing on outliers, as is a core approach in developing the UDL framework, will be critical if we are to leverage the power of digital technologies to create assessments that are cost-effective and accurate for a broader range of students.

In their comprehensive discussion of the role of knowledge representations (KRs) in assessment, "On the Roles of External Knowledge Representations in Assessment Design," Robert Mislevy and his co-authors focus on designing assessment models that are "more explicit, more valid, and more efficient." KRs, or means of depicting "entities and relationships in some domain, in a way that can be shared," come from cognitive psychology; the authors argue that they are relevant to assessment in several ways, including, primarily, making explicit that the assessment itself is a KR and that design KRs can support instruction and assessment. This article broadly frames the purpose and design of assessments and provides an insightful perspective on assessments as a single representation of a learner's understanding or skills that will necessarily be limited and shaped by the decisions made in the KRs of the domain being assessed and in the choices made by the assessment designers.

Using as an example the framework of evidence-centered assessment design, Mislevy and his coauthors describe the many layers of decisions and representations of knowledge that contribute to creation and delivery of assessments. This complexity makes clear the need in assessments for awareness of goals and assumptions and attention to principled design, opening a perspective and an opportunity where UDL can contribute.

It is from this vantage point that we approached Michael Russell to discuss his understanding of the roles of KR and assessment and their relevance to UDL. The conversation focused not on KRs in particular but on key concepts and frames of thinking in assessment design, based on observation of outliers and considerations of variability. These concepts could represent aspects of the design KRs that Mislevy and colleagues seek—perhaps a UDL-based one.

A renowned researcher in the field of computer-based assessment, Russell explores the ways technology and assessment can improve teaching and learning. Because of his innovative work in the field, we asked Russell to guide us in considering the relationship between variability, outliers, and educational assessments. In talking with him we discovered that his ideas in the area of assessment were informed by early (and largely serendipitous) work with outliers.

More than a decade ago Russell was approached to work with a consortium of states seeking to understand how to better use technology to support students with and without disabilities. In the course of this work, he found himself considering variability that was made evident by these outliers, whether in terms of biology, cognition, language, past experience, or behavior (among others). This early work was formative in that it opened his thinking to the challenge of measuring performance among students who differ in ways that are unrelated to the construct being measured. From our conversation with Russell, three key ideas emerged as particularly instructive.

### Who Is the Burden On?

Russell emphasizes the need to be clear about the underlying assumption of testing in education. He tells us that "scholars in the field of testing often assume students are meant to be trying to demonstrate their knowledge and skills, as opposed to the scholars trying to measure what a student knows." This distinction, he argues, is critical to understanding ways to create precise assessments. In the first condition—where assessment creators assume that the student is trying to demonstrate knowledge, and particularly when the goal is to compare students— it would be appropriate to use standardized conditions in order to ensure fairness. In contrast, if the assumption is that the tester is responsible for trying to measure something about the student, then, as Russell points out, "to get a purer measure, you wouldn't want to have a standardized condition."

To make the point, Russell uses the example of a doctor trying to measure the temperature of various patients. She will have different thermometers to use, depending on whose temperature she is measuring—"you are not going to ask an infant to hold a traditional thermometer under their tongue for two minutes. You are going to use a different instrument that's going to work better for that person, but you might not use that same instrument for an adult." In education, Russell argues, we are using the same instrument regardless of the individual.

### Outliers, Barriers, and a Pure(r) Measure

The second (related) point has to do with the issue of a "pure measure"—that is, the aim of assessment is to create instruments that measure only those things that are relevant to the construct that you are trying to assess. Russell speaks about the value of studying outliers in terms of understanding the obstacles that get in the way of obtaining a purer measure and how these obstacles are different for different students. He says that once you gain a clearer understanding of some of the obstacles that vary by student—by studying students in the margin—it allows you to consider "how we can vary the way in which we are measuring students to overcome those obstacles"—and in this way get closer to a purer measure for all students.

### Inference

The final point emerging from the conversation with Russell has to do with the inferences we make about students based on our assessment measures. He argues that education "hasn't been particularly good about being specific about inferences" and gives the example of state assessment programs. While just about everyone agrees the point is to make inferences about student learning, there is rarely consideration of questions such as "Under what context?" or "For what purposes?" He argues that these questions are not asked often enough, although they are essential to understanding how to develop purer assessments and how to draw appropriate inferences from these measures.

For example, Russell says, imagine a consortium that wants to make inferences about student readiness for college. "Does that mean they are making inferences about students' development along a path or a set of paths that they believe to be important for college? Or are they talking about students being able to demonstrate knowledge and skill today in contexts . . . that are likely to be similar to those they'll experience in college?" The answer to this question is critical, since with the first inference—measuring students' progress toward knowledge and skills believed to be important for college—we get a purer measure if we allow variations in how we are assessing the students. In contrast, with the second inference—where we see it as inferences about how well students are going to perform in specific contexts, we might want to limit some of those same variations, if the variations aren't expected to exist in those contexts.

## FOR FURTHER READING

Dolan, R. P., Hall, T. E., Banerjee, M., Chun, E., & Strangman, N. (2005). Applying principles of universal design to test delivery: The effect of computer-based read aloud on test performance of high school students with learning disabilities. *Journal of Technology, Learning, and Assessment, 3*(7), 1–33. Retrieved from http://ejournals.bc.edu/ojs/index.php/jtla/article/view/1660/.

Hattie, J., & Timperley, H. (2007). The power of feedback. *Review of Educational Research, 77*(1), 81–112.

Russell, M., Higgins, J., & Hoffman, T. (2009). Meeting the needs of all students: A universal design approach to computer-based testing. *Innovate, 5*(4). Retrieved from http://www.innovateonline.info/pdf/vol5_issue4/Meeting_the_Needs_of_All_Students-__A_Universal_Design_Approach_to_Computer-Based_Testing.pdf.

Willett, J. B. (1997). Measurement of change. In J. P. Keeves (Ed.), *Educational research, methodology and measurement: An international handbook* (2nd ed., pp. 671–678). Oxford: Pergamon Press.

# On the Roles of External Knowledge Representations in Assessment Design

ROBERT J. MISLEVY, JOHN T. BEHRENS, RANDY E. BENNETT,
SARAH F. DEMARK, DENNIS C. FREZZO, ROY LEVY, DANIEL H. ROBINSON,
DAISY WISE RUTSTEIN, VALERIE J. SHUTE, KEN STANLEY,
AND FIELDING I. WINTERS

*Authors' Abstract:* People use external knowledge representations (KRs) to create, identify, depict, transform, store, share, and archive information. Learning to work with KRs is central to becoming proficient in virtually every discipline. As such, KRs play central roles in curriculum, instruction, and assessment. We describe five key roles of KRs in assessment: An assessment is itself a KR, which makes explicit the knowledge that is valued, ways it is used, and standards of good work. The analysis of any domain in which learning is to be assessed must include the identification and analysis of the KRs in that domain. Assessment tasks can be structured around the knowledge, relationships, and uses of domain KRs. "Design KRs" can be created to organize knowledge about a domain in forms that support the design of assessment. KRs in the discipline of assessment design can guide and structure domain analyses (re #2), task construction (re #3), and the creation and use of design KRs (re #4). The third and fourth roles are developed in greater detail, through an "evidence-centered" design perspective that reflects the fifth role. Recurring implications of technology that leverage the impact of KRs in assessment are highlighted, including task design supports and automated task construction and scoring. Ideas are illustrated with "generate examples" tasks and simulation tasks for computer network design and troubleshooting.

## INTRODUCTION

Knowledge representation is a central theme in cognitive psychology. Internal knowledge representation refers to the way that information about the world is represented in our brains, and as such lies at the center of learning, interacting, and problem-solving of all kinds. This paper concerns external forms of knowledge representation. An external knowledge representation (abbreviated KR below), or inscription (Lehrer & Schauble, 2002), is a physical or conceptual structure that depicts entities and relationships in some domain, in a way that can be shared among different individuals or the same individual at different points in time. KRs are human inventions that overcome obstacles to human information processing with respect to working memory limitations, faulty long-term memory over time and in volume, coordinating actions across individuals, and providing common ways of thinking about some phenomenon of shared interest. Examples of KRs include maps, lists, graphs, wiring diagrams, bus schedules, musical notation, mathematical formulas, object models for business systems, and the 7-layer OSI model for computer networks.

This paper considers the roles of KRs in educational assessment, with an eye toward making the activities of assessment design more explicit, more valid, and more efficient. A red thread highlighting the implications of technology runs through the discussion. Technological developments make KRs possible that are more interactive, support automated transformations, and enable collaboration in ways that are transforming the practice of assessment—"assessment engineering," to use Luecht's (2002, 2007) term. We aim to bring to the surface the interplay among psychology (through the lens of KRs), technology, and assessment theory upon which this transformation is grounded.

The following section provides a brief review of important features of KRs. Five roles of KRs in assessment are then outlined. We note how KRs connect expertise with learning and assessment in a domain, and hence shape both instructional and assessment design. We then further develop and illustrate two of these roles, namely the design of assessment tasks around domain KRs and the creation of special KRs that help the assessment designer accomplish this. We place this discussion in the context of evidence-centered assessment design (ECD; Mislevy, Steinberg, & Almond, 2003; Mislevy & Haertel, 2006) to take advantage of KRs emerging from that work. The ideas are illustrated with examples from three assessment projects.

A relatively simple example based on Butterfield et al. (1985) concerning inductive reasoning tasks is interleaved through the discussion. Two more-complex examples are discussed in greater detail later in the paper. They concern a "generating examples" task type developed at Educational Testing Service (Bennett et al., 1999; Bennett, Morley, & Quardt, 2000; Katz, Lipps, & Trafton, 2002) and Cisco Systems' computer network simulation (CNS) assessments of design and troubleshooting (Behrens et al.,2004, Frezzo & Stanley, 2005, Williamson et al., 2004).

## KNOWLEDGE REPRESENTATIONS IN ASSESSMENT

KRs play a central role in human cognition, as a means of identifying, expressing, communicating, and utilizing information in social spheres. Generally speaking, KRs are a vehicle for discourse, used either by a single individual (mediated cognition) or among individuals (distributed cognition), at one point in time or across multiple time points. They concern entities, relationships, and processes in some domain, and their organizational form is used to create, gather, store, transform, and use information more easily than would be accomplished without them. Markman's (1999, pp. 5–8) definition of a KR has four components:

- A represented world: The domain that the representations are about. The represented world might be the world outside the cognitive system or some other set of representations inside the system. That is, one set of representations can be about another set of representations.
- A representing world: The domain that contains the representations. (The terms "represented world" and "representing world" come from a classic paper by Palmer, 1978.)
- Representing rules: The representing world is related to the represented world through a set of rules that map elements of the represented world to elements of the representing world.
- A process that uses the representation: It makes no sense to talk about representations in the absence of processes. The combination of the first three components (a represented world, a representing world, and a set of representing rules) creates merely the potential for representation. Only when there is also a process that uses the representation does the system actually represent, and the capabilities of a system are defined only when there is both a representation and a process. Increasingly, as

we will see in the case of assessment, these processes can be carried out digitally as well as perceptually, cognitively, or mechanically, as has been the case historically.

Some KRs, such as mathematical notation and computer languages, gain their power through symbol manipulation. After information has been encoded in the required form, operations can be carried out on the symbols to transform or combine the information in ways that would be difficult or impossible for a human to do unaided. A quotation from Whitehead (1911) is a propos:

> By relieving the brain of all unnecessary work, a good notation sets it free to concentrate on more advanced problems, and, in effect, increases the mental power of the race. . . . Civilisation [sic] advances by extending the number of important operations which we can perform without thinking about them (pp. 59, 61).

Other KRs, such as graphs and maps, encode information in ways that capitalize on humans' strengths in recognizing patterns and interpreting spatial relationships (see, for example, Lewandowsky & Behrens, 1999, on statistical graphs and maps):

> The greatest possibilities of visual display lie in vividness and inescapability of the intended message. A visual display can stop your mental flow in its tracks, and make you think. A visual display can force you to notice what you never expected to see. One should see the intended at once; one should not even have to wait for it to appear (Tukey, 1990, p. 367).

Many KRs use both symbolic and perceptual representation in varying mixtures (e.g., Tufte, 1990). A table exploits spatial arrangement to communicate the relevance of the organizing concepts of rows and columns for the subject of each cell (Mosenthal & Kirsch, 1989). Technology extends the power of KRs in several respects. Interactivity, as in working through a wizard to complete a tax form, and collaboration over a distance, as in online meeting workspaces that share computer applications, are two familiar examples. Digital KRs are particularly amenable to automated symbol manipulation, in ways and at speeds that far outstrip unaided human cognition. A central problem in human-computer interaction is developing and tuning the KRs through which people interact with computers to exploit these capabilities.

### Properties of Knowledge Representations

Several properties of KRs are relevant to their roles in assessment. One of the most important is that a KR does not attempt to include everything in the represented world, only certain entities and relationships. It highlights those entities and relationships, and facilitates thinking about them, talking about them, and working with them. This is the ontology of the KR. Unrepresented aspects of the represented world are considered irrelevant. The velocity of a falling body is represented by v0 + g t, whether the body is a cannonball or a feather, whether it is falling in Austin or Tokyo. The breadth of applicability of KRs can be a strength. It is also a potential weakness in application when what is omitted from the mapping is important in the real-world situation, as when the velocity of a falling feather is lower because of air resistance. While carrying out reasoning within the representing world is important in learning to use KRs, it is just as important to learn when to apply them gainfully and how to recognize a potentially hazardous misfit (a central topic in statistics, for example; e.g., Belsley, Kuh, & Welch, 1980, on diagnostics in regression analysis).

In addition to focusing on only certain aspects of situations in the represented world, KRs are optimized for certain uses regarding those aspects. A domain of any complexity typically has many KRs, each tuned to different relationships and purposes. For example, matrix algebra, path diagrams, and computer code input are all used to represent factor analysis and structural equation models (SEMs) in psychometrics (Figure 5.1 shows two different representations of the same factor analysis model). The matrix equations admit to symbol-manipulation procedures for taking derivatives, which support algorithms for finding the values of the variables that fit the data best—finding maxima of multivariable likelihood functions is not something people do well in their heads. But graphical representations have advantages at the model-building stage, because the qualitative relationships among variables are immediately apparent and rapidly specified. Computer programs such as EQS (Bentler, 2006) allow the user to specify a model by working with a graphical interface, then generate code automatically to estimate the parameters with algorithms derived under the algebraic representation.

Note the essential role of technology in this process: The user working with a graphical interface is using an interactive computer-based representation that facilitates spatial thinking about relationships among variables; the computer representation is a digital encoding of the sequence of drags, drops, clicks, and typed characters; the computer program transforms this digital representation of user actions into another digital representation that would correspond in turn to an algebraic expression, upon which to carry out mathematical operations. The outcomes of these operations are re-expressed as human-friendly KRs such as graphs and tables of results, including human-accessible traces of processing such as changes in the log likelihood function at each cycle of an iterative process on computer friendly KRs. We will see later in the CNS example how similar algorithmic conversions from one knowledge form to another provide advantages in computer-based assessment systems for domain analysis, task authoring, task presentation, interaction with the examinee, and automated scoring.

This attunement of KRs to different processes and purposes explains the presence of multiple KRs in a given domain (Ainsworth, 1999). Multiple KRs also occur when the complexities of real-world situations lend themselves to modeling at different levels or from different perspectives. In transmission genetics, for example, there are KRs for expressing relationships at the levels of species, individuals, cells, and molecules. Although each KR highlights entities and relationships at a certain level of analysis, relationships and constraints can cross levels and representational forms as well. The similarities of elements' chemical properties in a column of Mendeleev's periodic table correspond to similarities in electron shell diagrams. Translating information from one form to another is often a target of learning in content domains, as the process of solving a problem can take the form of a sequence of transformations within and between models, mediated by operations carried out with KRs.

One can speak of KRs at various levels of generality. For example, the elements and representational capabilities of Cartesian graphs and their attendant elements can be addressed at a general level, to display kinds of relationships that can be used to represent among variables in any domain. Certain knowledge associated with graphs can thus be learned and used (and assessed) across domains. Scatter plots in statistics and acceleration graphs in physics are both special cases of Cartesian graphs that can be studied in their own right, as patterns in graphs correspond to more specialized representations such as acceleration formulas, which are in turn grounded in the generative principles of that particular domain. KRs have value because people can do things with them. Well-chosen KRs incorporate subtle and hard-won insights into a form that can be applied mechanically. Fifty years ago, an economist could win a Nobel prize for generating and solving from first principles the kinds of systems of linear equations

**FIGURE 5.1**   **Matrix algebra and path diagram representations of a factor analysis model**

$$
\begin{pmatrix} y_1 \\ y_2 \\ y_3 \end{pmatrix} = \begin{pmatrix} \lambda_1 \\ \lambda_2 \\ \lambda_3 \end{pmatrix} \eta + \begin{pmatrix} \varepsilon_1 \\ \varepsilon_2 \\ \varepsilon_3 \end{pmatrix}
$$

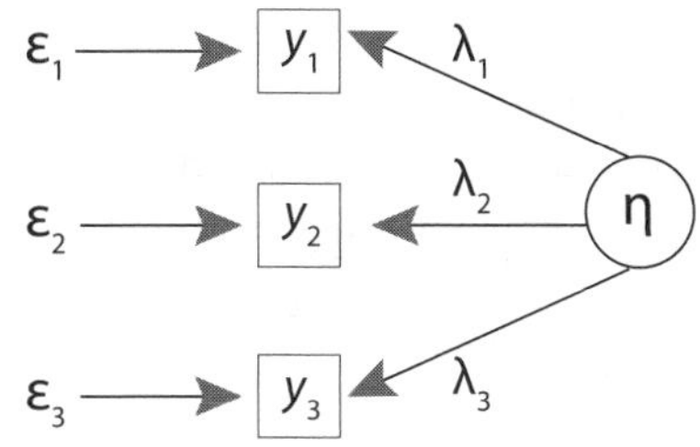

that EQS users can apply today without knowing either calculus or matrix algebra. It is an advantage of a KR that a user can exploit deep principles without knowing them explicitly. To enjoy these benefits, however, the user must become attuned to the ways the KR offers to create, display, or transform information—its affordances, to use Gibson's (1966) term. The problem of designing KRs to best communicate information and affordances receives both practical and academic attention in fields such as graphics (e.g., Pinker, 1990) and human-computer interfaces (e.g., Card, Moran, & Newell, 1983). This research is prompted in part by the fact that KRs that can be expressed in symbolic form support multiple views and automated transformations. For example, CNS works back and forth between perceptual KRs for presenting and capturing information from examinees and symbolic KRs for evaluating their work and transforming information from one form to another.

How do KRs facilitate work? By focusing on recurrent patterns at a level above the particulars of any problem, KRs facilitate analogies across problems and domains. They make it easier to acquire and structure information. They coordinate work in projects that are so large or complex that no one can know all the details of all their facets. In such cases, KRs such as Gantt charts and object models help people understand their roles and connect their work with that of others. They provide a common language for people to express information and work with it in ways that tacitly incorporate experience from other times and other people. The form of a

KR can indicate when information is missing. For example, representing text information in a matrix graphic organizer rather than text makes missing information more salient (Figure 5.2). KRs such as blueprints, agendas, schedules, to-do lists are significant in planning, because they indicate what information is needed, how it is to be acted upon, and what a solution will look like. Collins and Fergusen (1993) emphasize that people can create new knowledge by using KRs by referring to them as "epistemic forms," and the ways that people use them as "epistemic games."

### Roles of Knowledge Representations in Assessment

Looking at educational assessment through the lens of KRs reveals their presence throughout the enterprise, at different stages, at different levels, and with different purposes. The following sections discuss five key roles that KRs play in assessment:

1. An assessment is in itself a KR, which makes explicit the knowledge that is valued, ways it is used, and standards of good work.
2. The analysis of any domain in which learning is to be assessed must include the identification and analysis of the KRs in that domain (that is, the "domain KRs").
3. Assessment tasks can be structured around the knowledge, relationships, and uses of domain KRs.
4. "Design KRs" can be created to organize knowledge about a domain (including its domain KRs) in forms that support the design of instruction and assessment.
5. KRs from the disciplines of instructional design and assessment design can guide and structure the domain analyses noted in (2), the task construction noted in (3), and the creation and use of design KRs noted in (4).

### Assessments Are Themselves Knowledge Representations

The analogy of assessment to measurement is vital to its conduct, but it is not sufficient. A student taking an assessment is engaged in a form of socially construed discourse (Gitomer & Steinberg, 1999), no less than a teenager playing a video game or a taxpayer completing an IRS 1040 form. This observation holds implications for assessment designers and students alike. Designers must always be aware that an assessment constitutes the most direct statement of the knowledge and skills that are valued, in effect if not in intention. The process of constructing an assessment, done thoughtfully, elicits an understanding of the knowledge that is targeted, the actions of

**FIGURE 5.2    What information is presented about moths but not butterflies? The missing element is easier to see from the matrix organizer than in the text**

**Moths and Butterflies** *(text)*

A moth has two sets of wings. It folds the wings down over its body when it rests. The moth has feathery antennae and spins a fuzzy cocoon. The moth goes through four stages of development.

A butterfly also goes through four stages of development and has two sets of wings. Its antennae, however, are long and thin with knobs at the ends. When a butterfly rests, its wings are straight up like outstretched hands.

**Moths and Butterflies** *(matrix organizer)*

|             | Moths           | Butterflies             |
|-------------|-----------------|-------------------------|
| Wings       | Two sets        | Two sets                |
| Rest        | Wings over body | Wings outstretched      |
| Antennae    | Feathery        | Long, thin, with knobs  |
| Cocoon      | Fuzzy           | —                       |
| Development | Four stages     | Four stages             |

students that provide evidence about it, and the circumstances under which that knowledge should be brought to bear (Wiggins, 1998). An assessment is a KR that communicates the targets of learning and the standards of performances to all stakeholders, and its construction serves educative purposes before the first examinee ever sees it.

In order to perform well in an assessment, students must not only have become facile with the targeted knowledge and skills, but they must also be able to work with them in the forms and under the conditions that characterize the assessment situation. That is, the students must be attuned to the affordances of the assessment as a form of KR. The more complex an assessment is, in terms of the embedded KRs students will interact with and the standards by which KRs that students produce will be evaluated, the more important it is to ensure that this attunement has taken place before the assessment begins. For students attempting to solve an interactive chemistry investigation with an unfamiliar computer interface, the interface can present more difficulties than the chemistry. Similarly, students cannot "explain" a solution to a mathematics problem until they understand the nature, the forms, and the expectations of exposition that are required to produce a "satisfactory explanation."

*Identifying the Knowledge Representations of a Domain*

Becoming an expert in a domain is a process of learning about the nature of knowledge in the domain, including terms, principles, patterns, and exemplars, and the nature of interaction among those who participate in that domain (Ericsson, 1996). The kinds of knowledge highlighted under both an acquisition metaphor and a participation metaphor (Sfrad, 1998) are required. KRs play central roles in both. KRs embody the important ideas and relationships in a domain, organize them so that they are the vehicle for doing work in the domain, define the language by which people acquire and communicate information in that domain, and coordinate the interactions of people as they work toward common ends. It is not much of an understatement to say that learning in a domain is learning to use the KRs of the domain—the domain KRs, as we call them here.

No analysis of a learning domain can be complete without an investigation of the KRs that are used in the domain and the situations in which they are used. Learning materials such as textbooks and exemplars are a natural place to begin, but the selection of KRs used in instruction can be biased toward "academic" KRs. Additional KRs used in practical work, perhaps informal or embedded in tools, are also part of the targeted domain, and learning how and when to use them is part of the targeted learning.

*Structuring Tasks Around Domain Knowledge Representations*

Assessment is reasoning about what students know, can do, or have accomplished more broadly, from evidence in the form of a relative handful of particular things they say, do, or make in particular situations. The situations in which the student is to act are defined in no small part through KRs. The various KRs that constitute an assessment task provide information about a situation to the student, suggest the nature of the problem, suggest the terms in which the problem is to be approached, offer clues as to the nature of a solution and the criteria of evaluation, and provide affordances for getting started. This is as true of open-ended performances or portfolios as it is of objective tests consisting of multiple-choice items.

Furthermore, what the student says, does, or makes in response—the work products—are typically structured in terms of the KRs of the domain as well. Scalise and Gifford (2006) describe how, in technology-supported environments, having examinees complete or construct representations not only increases fidelity to the domain, but facilitates construct-driven automated scoring. Indeed, it is increasingly common, especially in simulation-based tasks like the CNS tasks, that complex interactive KRs constitute the environment in which the examinee thinks and acts.

Research on expertise reveals increasing expertise in the use of domain KRs as proficiency increases, in ways that hold implications for designing tasks and evaluating performances. As a first example, Kindfield's (1999) study of experts' and novices' use of diagrams to reason through genetics problems revealed an interesting reversal: Novices' drawings were often more complete and better proportioned than experts', but what distinguished experts' diagrams was that only the salient features tended to be shown, and the relationships important to the problem at hand were rendered with whatever accuracy was needed to solve the problem. That is, the experts' diagrams were more efficacious than those of the novices. As a second example, Cameron et al. (2000) found increasing proficiency in dental hygienists at increasing levels of experience with respect to their use of KRs such as radiographs, hard and soft tissue charts, and probing depth charts. Early stages of learning were marked by the ability to identify and interpret key features on a given single representation. Expert hygienists were distinguished from recently licensed hygienists by a superior ability to integrate information across multiple representations of different types, effectively constructing a model of a patient about whom all the representations were different, yet coherent, views of the same person.

A central idea for assessment design, and a central topic of the CNS example, is that a systematic analysis of the KRs in a domain—what they are, their features, and how people use them—is a foundation for principled generation of assessment tasks. An understanding of the entities and relationships of each KR and the relationships among them is developed in conjunction with an understanding of the kinds of reasoning or actions that one wants students to carry out using the KRs. The outcomes of this analysis lay the groundwork for schemas of tasks that focus on valued work in the domain in explicit ways, and exist at some level of generality above particular tasks. The level of generality of the KRs and the resulting schemas depends on the intended use, with the usual understanding that broad applicability of general forms trades off against the power of specific forms. These task construction schemas can themselves be expressed in terms of KRs. Hively, Patterson, and Page's (1968) item shells and Haladyna and Shindoll's (1989) item forms represented initial research along these lines, while more recent technology-based task construction frameworks include those of Bejar et al. (2003), Gierl, Zhou, and Alves (2008), and Mislevy et al. (2003).

At this point, we introduce an example from Butterfield et al. (1985) concerning theory-based generation of letter series tasks, a measure of inductive reasoning (Thurstone & Thurstone, 1941). Here are two examples based on the Primary Mental Abilities test battery (Thurstone &Thurstone, 1962):

> Fill in the next letters in the series:
>
> C D C D C D __ __ __
>
> A T B A T A A T B A T __ __ __

This KR is an example of an item type—a particular kind of KR used in assessment to present information to an examinee and set expectations for a response. This particular KR consists of a series of symbols, read from left to right, arranged according to a pattern, or rule, that both explains the appearance of the symbols that are depicted and sets expectations for the symbols that would come next. The student's task is to determine the rule and make predictions. The blanks are affordances—the natural place to write the symbols that extend the pattern if you understand what the KR is about, but mysteries if you do not. Although these items require no specialized content knowledge other than the alphabet, they reflect the kind of reasoning required in more-complex inductive problems that do require more substantive knowledge, such as scientific inquiry. Because this is the representational form that the student works with, it is the domain KR in our first assessment example.

*Representations for Designing Assessments in Given Domains*
Advantages can be gained when the characteristics of the KRs can themselves be represented in higher-level KRs that are devised to serve the purposes of assessment design. We may call these "design KRs." Design KRs are related to domain KRs, but they are built for the purpose of generating domain KRs to be used in tasks. They describe salient features of task situations, in ways that both imply domain representations and indicate the kinds of reasoning and knowledge that the student will need to call upon. We shall see that the same representations can provide information to KRs used in other stages of assessment design and delivery, such as task selection and psychometric modeling (Bejar, 2002; Embretson, 1998).

Butterfield et al. (1985) created a design KR for the domain of letter series tasks described in the previous section. Letter series tasks had been used at least as early as Thurstone's research in 1941, in both practical applications and psychometric research. Task generation was idiosyncratic, however, and systematic examinations of both the structure of tasks and how people solve them were lacking (Butterfield). Simon and Kotovsky (1963) devised a symbol system to describe such tasks after they have been written, and their analysis is Butterfield's starting point for a KR that supports automated task generation in this domain. An abbreviated version and a few examples of the design KR for letter series rules convey the key ideas: Letter series tasks are composed of one or more strings of letters. Within a string, special relationships hold for moving from one letter to the next, such as identity (I), next letter (N), and back a letter (B). A rule is expressed by the relationships of letters within a string, and the strings' relationships to one another. The rule underlying the series CDCDCD is denoted by I1 I2, instantiated with C and D as the initial values of the first and second strings. The same rule instantiated with R and T as the initial values yields RTRTRT. The series MABMBCMCD is expressed as I1 I2 N2, with initial values M and A.

This design KR for expressing rules is obviously distinct from letter series tasks themselves, but they are related in ways that serve the purposes of the assessment designer. A rule expressed in the design KR grammar and initial string values suffices to produce a letter series task. Operations can be defined on rules expressed in the grammar of the KR to address issues of form, such as when two rules produce identical series. Other operations on rules address psychological issues such as memory load, as a function of calculable properties such as "Counts = # moving strings * (period – # adjacent identity relations)." Related operations can be used to address psychometric issues such as task difficulty (as in Embretson, 1998). The design KR for letter series tasks, therefore, has pragmatic connections to the task authoring, psychological argument, and measurement modeling layers of the assessment enterprise.

An early example of generative design KRs is Hively, Patterson, & Page's (1968) idea of "item forms" for generating whole number arithmetic items, two of which appear as Figure 5.3. Another example appears in Bormuth's (1970) work on generating "wh" questions from text. The KR is a syntactic representation of one or more propositions, which is amenable to symbolic transformations that yield questions that can be used to assess basic comprehension. Both of these examples provided KRs that enabled an assessment designer to map the structures and content of domain KRs (arithmetic items and English text) into more-abstract KRs that support transformations into tasks. The "generating examples" and CNS examples in later sections illustrate more recent work, in which the capability of computers to carry out symbol manipulation is exploited more fully in the automated construction of tasks through technology-based design KRs. At the time Bormuth (1970) introduced the "generating questions" approach mentioned above, for example, tasks were generated algorithmically but needed to be constructed by hand; few applications were carried out (Roid & Finn, 1977, describes one such application). With current natural-language processing capabilities, it would be a simple matter to construct "wh" questions from English text automatically.

### Knowledge Representations in the Discipline of Assessment Design

As long as assessment has been practiced, KRs have been developed to aid designers. Familiar examples include the aforementioned item types and item forms, test specifications (Davidson & Lynch, 2001, for a recent in-depth discussion), and content-by-process matrices often based on Bloom's (1956) taxonomy of educational objectives. These KRs are used to help designers generate items and assemble test forms. KRs used in the analysis of test data are also familiar, from the symbolic representations used in psychometric models to innovative displays used to summarize patterns in performance for students and their teachers. Schemas for rubrics to evaluate open-ended task performances are also widely used, allowing an assessor (such as a classroom teacher) to adapt a tested evaluation procedure to locally customized tasks; a number of tools are available in interactive formats on the Internet. Wiggins (1998) offers designers of performance assessment a number of templates and flowcharts, all with an eye toward connecting what is assessed with the goals of instruction.

Designing assessments of any complexity involves considerations at many levels: substantively grounded evidentiary arguments, design of operational elements such as tasks and scoring models, implementing the design in terms of specific tasks, and all the operational activities involved in actually carrying out the assessment. No single KR can encompass all this work; multiple, coordinated representations are required. Developing frameworks for assessment design, complete with a conceptual rationale and multiple supporting KRs, has been a focus of research in the assessment community in recent years (e.g., Almond, Steinberg & Mislevy, 2002; Embretson, 1998; Luecht, 2002, 2007; Wilson, 2005). The next section discusses one such approach in greater detail.

**FIGURE 5.3**   Two "item forms" from Hively, Patterson, and Page (1968)

| Descriptive Title | Sample Item | General Form | Generation Rules |
|---|---|---|---|
| Basic fact; Minuend > 10 | 13 <br> –6 | A <br> – B | 1. A=1a ; B=b <br> 2. (a<b) ε U <br> 3. {H, V} |
| Borrow across zero | 403 <br> –138 | A <br> – B | 1. # digits = {3,4} <br> 2. A=a1a2...; B=b1b2... <br> 3. (a1>b1), (a3<b3), (a4≥b4), ε U0 <br> 4. b2 ε U0 <br> 5. a2 = 0 <br> 6. P{{1,2,3},{4}} |

Capital letters represent numerals, lower case represent digits.

x ε { — } means chose x with replacement from the set.

U = {1,2,...,9}; U0={0,1,..., 9)

## A CLOSER LOOK AT KRS AND ASSESSMENT DESIGN

Evidence-centered assessment design (ECD) is a process of assessment design that involves gathering, organizing, and transforming information in a variety of representational forms, within the framework of a clearly articulated assessment argument. Under the ECD framework, KRs are integral at every step in the process of developing and using an assessment. This section starts with a brief overview of ECD and then, through this perspective, discusses and provides examples of KRs in assessment design.

### A Brief Overview of Evidence-Centered Assessment Design

Central ideas in ECD are the assessment argument, layers of the assessment, and the role of KRs in designing and implementing assessments. Messick (1994, p. 16) concisely lays out the key aspects of an assessment argument by asking "what complex of knowledge, skills, or other attributes should be assessed? Next, what behaviors or performances should reveal those constructs, and what tasks or situations should elicit those behaviors?" All of the many terms, concepts, representations, and structures in ECD are aimed at constructing a coherent assessment argument and building machinery to implement it.

Adapting a "layers" metaphor from architecture and software engineering, ECD organizes the design process in terms of the following layers: domain analysis, domain modeling, conceptual assessment framework, assessment implementation, and assessment delivery (Mislevy & Riconscente, 2006). The fundamental work in assessment design can be viewed as creating, transforming, and using information in the form of KRs within and between these layers. Table 5.1 summarizes these layers in terms of their roles, key entities (for example, concepts and building-blocks), and the KRs that assist in achieving each layer's purpose.

The layering suggests a sequential design process, but cycles of iteration and refinement across layers are the norm.

The first layer in the process of designing an assessment, domain analysis, lays the foundation for later layers by defining the knowledge, skills, and abilities (KSAs) that assessment users want to make inferences about, the student behaviors they can base their inferences on, and the situations that will elicit those behaviors. A critical part of domain analysis includes identification of KRs important to the domain, because expertise in a domain necessarily includes knowledge of and understanding of how and when to use the KRs in that domain.

At the next layer, domain modeling, KRs within the domain of assessment design come into play in the form of assessment argument diagrams (Bachman, 2003, Mislevy, 2003, 2006; see Figure 5.4 for the basic structure, adapted from Toulmin, 1958), content-by-process matrices, and the design patterns that will be discussed in more depth in the next section. Using these KRs, domain modeling structures the outcomes of domain analysis in a form that reflects the structure of an assessment argument, in order to ground the more technical student, evidence, and task models that are required in the subsequent Conceptual Assessment Framework (CAF) layer.

The *conceptual assessment framework* (CAF) concerns the technical specifications for the materials and processes that embody assessments. The central models in the CAF are the student model, the evidence model, and the task model (Figure 5.5). In addition, the assembly model governs how tasks are assembled into tests, a presentation model indicates the requirements for interaction with a student (for example, simulator requirements), and the delivery model specifies requirements for the operational setting. An assessment argument laid out in narrative form at the domain-modeling layer is here expressed in terms of specifications for tasks, measurement models, scoring methods, and delivery requirements. Details about

**TABLE 5.1   Layers of evidence-centered design**

| Layer | Role | Key Entities | Examples of Knowledge Representations |
|---|---|---|---|
| Domain Analysis | Gather substantive information about the domain of interest that has direct implications for assessment: how knowledge is constructed, acquired, used, and communicated. | Domain concepts, terminology, tools, knowledge representations, analyses, situations of use, patterns of interaction. | Content standards, concept maps (e.g., Atlas of Science Literacy, AAAS, 2001). Representational forms and symbol systems of domain of interest, e.g., maps, algebraic notation, computer interfaces. |
| Domain Modeling | Express assessment argument in narrative form based on information from domain analysis. | Knowledge, skills, and abilities; characteristic and variable task features; potential work products and observations. | Assessment argument diagrams, design patterns, content-by-process matrices. |
| Conceptual Assessment Framework | Express assessment argument in structures and specifications for tasks and tests, evaluation procedures, measurement models. | Student, evidence, and task models; student model, observable, and task model variables; rubrics; measurement models; test assembly specifications. | Test specifications; algebraic & graphical KRs of measurement models; task template; item generation models; generic rubrics; automated scoring code. |
| Assessment | Implement assessment, including presentation-ready tasks, scoring guides, or automated evaluation procedures, and calibrated measurement models. | Task materials (including all materials, tools, affordances); pilot test data for honing evaluation procedures and fitting measurement models. | Coded algorithms to render tasks, interact with examinees, evaluate work products; tasks as displayed; IMS/QTI representation of materials; ASCII files of parameters. |
| Assessment Delivery | Coordinate interactions of students and tasks: task- and test-level scoring; reporting. | Tasks as presented; work products as created; scores as evaluated. | Renderings of materials; numerical and graphical score summaries; IMS/QTI results files. |

**FIGURE 5.4   An assessment argument diagram**

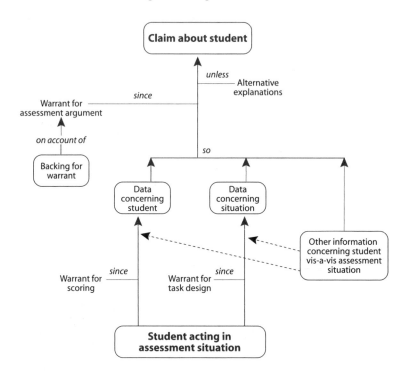

task features, measurement-model parameters, stimulus material specifications, and the like are expressed in terms of KRs and data structures that we
will say more about later in this section, which guide their implementation
and ensure their coordination.

With information from the models in the CAF, delivery of an assessment
from an ECD perspective is defined by a four-process architecture (Figure
5.6). Starting in the upper left corner of Figure 5.6, the activity selection
process selects a task (tasks include items, sets of items, or other activities)
and directs the presentation process for display to the examinee. When the
examinee has finished interacting with the item, the results (a work product)
are sent to response processing. Information from the task model defined in
the CAF provides the basis for the presentation process and work product
specifications. From information outlined in the evaluation model of the
CAF, the response process identifies essential observations about the results
and passes them to the summary scoring process, which updates the scoring

**FIGURE 5.5   The central models of Conceptual Assessment Framework (CAF)**

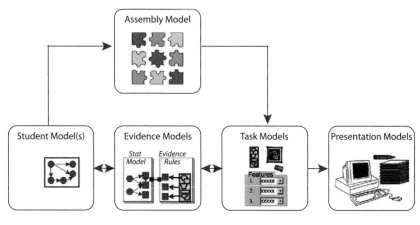

**Delivery Model**

record about the examinee. The scoring record describes knowledge about the student-model variables articulated in the student model of the CAF. All four processes add information to the results database. The activity selection process again makes a decision about what to do next, based on the current scoring record of the participant or other criteria.

The preceding brief outline is not sufficient to explain the roles and interplay of the processes, or the way that this structure supports the design of technology-based assessment tasks and delivery systems; the reader is referred to Almond, Sternberg, & Mislevy (2002). What is important for this presentation is that every message that passes from one process to another is expressed in terms of some KR. It has been produced by the sender, be it a human or computer, and provided in a form that the receiver, again a human or a computer, can use to carry out some other function essential to the operation of the assessment. The following sections provide examples.

*Domain Reasoning, Knowledge Representations, and Task Design*

The ECD process affirms the idea that analysis of the KRs central to a given domain is integral to generating assessment tasks in that domain. Essential to this idea is the connection between a given domain KR itself, reasoning in the domain, and the way people use it in practice. This is critical because the knowledge needed to use a domain KR in a particular circumstance is

FIGURE 5.6  The four principles processes in the assessment cycle

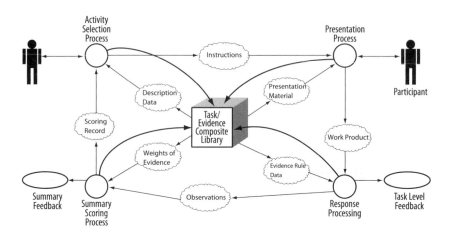

often what we want to draw inferences about. Identifying and articulating the relationship between using specific KRs in particular situations and the type of knowledge elicited is an important link in the assessment design process. Identification of these relationships during the domain analysis process sets up the construction of arguments in domain modeling, which in turn sets up the creation of schemas for designing tasks.

Butterfield et al.'s (1985) letter series example provides an example of the interplay between KRs and knowledge. In this example, the KR, a pattern of letters, provides a way for both task designers and examinees to reason about the underlying pattern. In essence, this KR allows for assessment of the inductive reasoning ability of the test-taker; the KR structure itself becomes a tool for assessing this knowledge.

Checklists and behavioral inventories are examples of KRs that have long been used to ground licensure and certification tests. As epistemic forms, they provide structure to the job analyst's task of identifying the nature and frequency of tasks professionals carry out, from which assessment tasks will be devised.

More recent work in cognitive task analysis addresses the nature, organization, and use of knowledge that tasks employ (Schraagen, Chipman & Shalin, 2000). This allows for distinctions between different types of knowledge and skills that one may want to evoke from an examinee, including declarative, procedural, or strategic knowledge, which may all be associated with one particular domain KR. The information is collected during the domain analysis phase of the assessment design. For example, Shute, Torreano, and Willis's (2000) automated knowledge elicitation tool DNA (Decompose, Network, Assess) provides structured, user-friendly web forms to elicit domain experts' input on declarative, procedural, and conceptual-knowledge requirements of common tasks in the domain. The DNA tool is an interactive design KR, capitalizing on technology and the wizard metaphor to elicit and structure domain information from subject matter experts, and to store it in digital forms that can be transformed to support domain modeling, the next step in the design process.

In addition to the argument schema shown in Figure 5.4, another KR that has been developed for work in the domain modeling layer is the design pattern (Mislevy et al., 2003). Design patterns encapsulate knowledge about ways to address assessment challenges that recur across domains or within particular domains, organized in categories that connect to elements of an assessment argument on the one hand, and point ahead toward the more technical elements of the CAF. For example, Table 5.2 shows selected portions of a design pattern for problem-solving in finite systems, a valued skill in both everyday life (why won't this door close?) and in technical domains such as aircraft repair, computer programming, and the troubleshooting of computer networks addressed by the CNS tasks.

A design pattern for this particular skill can be utilized across domains because it capitalizes on similar patterns of problem-solving reasoning in each. Within any given domain, multiple design patterns can be used to target the knowledge, skills and abilities of interest—such as building a teamwork task around troubleshooting, working-in-groups, and self-monitoring design patterns.

The design pattern structure can be used to address the type of proficiencies that people employ when using domain KRs. For example, in model-based reasoning an initial model, usually expressed in the form of a KR, is created and iteratively revised as it is tested in real-world situations (Stewart & Hafner, 1994). The Architectural Registry Examination (ARE; Bejar & Braun, 1999) utilizes this type of reasoning with a computer-aided design (CAD) system that has examinees produce a domain KR in the form of a site plan. At each step in this iterative process, examinees react to and modify their design based on their previous designs and remaining constraints for the design (Katz, 1994). The steps examinees take in this process (all, it may

**TABLE 5.2   Portions of a design pattern for problem-solving in finite systems**

| | |
|---|---|
| *Summary* | Students are presented a problem of determining the state of a system, and methods for gathering information about its state. No available diagnostic procedure is definitive; each rules in some possibilities and rules out others. |
| *Rationale* | Integrated knowledge structures, characteristic of effective problem solvers, are displayed in the ability to represent a problem, select and execute goal-directed strategies, monitor and adjust performance, and offer complete, coherent explanations. |
| | In particular, problem-solving to determine the state of a finite system with a set of tests requires an understanding of the procedures that can be applied to rule sets of states in or out, being able to interpret the results of the tests, synthesizing their information to determine what states are still possible after a series of tests, and being able to choose a next test that will effectively narrow the search space. |
| *Focal knowledge, skills, and abilities* | • Ability to apply knowledge of system and component functioning to solve a problem.<br>• Ability to generate and elaborate explanations of task-relevant concepts.<br>• Ability to build a mental model or representation of a problem to guide solution.<br>• Ability to devise and manage problem-solving procedure. |
| *Additional knowledge, skills, and abilities* | • Domain knowledge.<br>• Capability to carry out tests.<br>• Ability to coordinated problem-solving with others (if required). |
| *Characteristic task features* | • Statement of problem provides system, initial conditions, and set of test procedures.<br>• System with imperfectly known state (e.g., fault, unknown components).<br>• There is a finite (though possibly large) space of possibilities of the system state.<br>• Each test procedure rules some aspects of system state in and others out. |
| *Variable task features* | • Level and nature of content knowledge required to solve problem.<br>• Degree of domain familiarity required.<br>• What is the fault(s)?<br>• Fault simple, compound, intermittent?<br>• Complexity of system to troubleshoot.<br>• Degree of scaffolding or prompting.<br>• Individual work, work with a partner, or as a member of a group?<br>• Number of diagnostic procedures to choose from.<br>• Redundant diagnostic procedures?<br>• Overlapping diagnostic procedures? |

| | |
|---|---|
| *Potential observable variables* | • Correctness of solution.<br>• Quality of evidence to support conclusions.<br>• Quality of explanation of task-specific concepts.<br>• Adequacy of problem representation or problem-solving plan.<br>• Appropriateness of solution strategies.<br>• Frequency and flexibility of self-monitoring.<br>• Efficiency of solution.<br>• Accuracy of deductions at each step. |
| *Potential work products* | • Written or verbal description/identification of where the problem is or what the solution is to the problem.<br>• Illustration of problem solution and/or written justification for "Here is how I know."<br>• Verbal or written description of anticipated problem-solving approach.<br>• Verbal or written explanation of task-specific concepts.<br>• Log or observation of student actions.<br>• Observation data/log-file/think-aloud protocols during solution.<br>• Indication of possibilities are ruled in or out by a given test procedure.<br>• Indication of which possibilities are ruled in or out by all test procedures given thus far, at any point during the solution. |

be noted, within the technology-based simulation environment that is itself an interactive KR) become a critical aspect of assessing their level of expertise in architectural design.

Thus, the design pattern KR serves first as an epistemic form to synthesize experience and analysis of classes of valued work in ways that will support assessment design. It is then a source of information for the task author creating such specific tasks or task models for a specific context. It provides grounding for the validity of tasks created in this manner by making explicit the link between the features, requirements, and evaluation procedures of a task and the knowledge and skills that are valued in the domain (Bennett & Bejar, 1998).

While the sample design pattern illustrated in Table 5.2 is a static form, affordances provided by technology have been employed to facilitate their construction by geographically dispersed design teams and their interactive use by task authors. That is, the usefulness and efficiency of design patterns as a KR has been leveraged by embedding them in digital form, and taking advantage of technological affordances to help people build them and use them. The form in which design patterns are created is an object model that can be built by a dispersed team in real time over the Internet using a collaborative virtual work space (Hamel & Shank, 2005).

A "writer-friendly" online version of the design pattern structure presents item writers with a concise summary version of the pattern but allows them to follow links for additional discussion and examples of the various attribute entries, and to highlight entries from different attribute categories that are related to one another with regard to task design choices (Mislevy & Liu, 2009).

### Knowledge Representations for Creating, Presenting, and Scoring Tasks

After the evidentiary argument has been defined at the domain analysis and domain modeling layers, the next layers focus attention on structuring and generating actual tasks. These are the CAF layer, in which student, evidence, and task models are articulated, and the Implementation layer, which includes task generation. This section notes roles that KRs play in these processes.

*Task Creation*    In domain analysis, the designer identifies situations in which practitioners in a domain use the KSAs of interest, and on this basis in domain modeling the designer frames, in the KR of design patterns, paradigmatic situations to elicit those KSAs (recall Table 5.1). In the CAF, more detailed task models are created. A task model is a design KR that structures the authoring of the actual tasks that will be presented to the student. Itdescribes the environment in which students will act to provide the data necessary to make inferences about KSAs, including the domain KRs that will be used to provide information to the examinees and to serve as work spaces and tools for them, and in which they will express the products and processes of their work. The values of the task model variables identified in a task model provide specifications such as the form of the work product, the materials necessary, and other features of the setting, all of which are grounded in the original assessment argument and play a variety of roles in task construction, presentation, scoring, and interpretation of results (Mislevy et al., 2002).

Figure 5.7 shows a schematic diagram of the relationship between the task model variables (on the right-hand side) and the assessment implementation and delivery process. The task model variables, which in this example include the language in which the task will be presented, inform the task design as well as the evidence portion of the process. As described in Mislevy et al. (2002), these attributes in the task model KR provide information for KRs used in task authoring, task selection, automated scoring, psychometric modeling, and score reporting.

**FIGURE 5.7   Schematic showing the roles of task model variables**

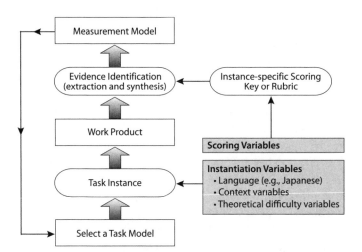

A task model, then, is a design KR that includes details about how the information the tasks elicit is related to other components of the assessment. The task model also explicates what particular features are necessary to include and which are variable, or optional. This general idea has been embodied in a variety of particular forms. For illustration we use here the task template (Riconscente, Mislevy, & Hamel, 2005) developed in the Principled Assessment Design for Inquiry (PADI) project to describe task models more specifically. Task authors can use the template as a blueprint to create actual tasks that are grounded in the original assessment argument, without needing to reconstruct this reasoning. As an example, Figure 5.8 shows an example of a PADI task template for BioKIDS, a project that helps students learn science inquiry (Gotwals & Songer, 2006). As can be seen in this example, the template lays out the student and measurement models in conjunction with the task model. Further, the template articulates particular materials, activities, and tools associated with the task template. In this way, the task template is connected to the chain of reasoning that occurs at the domain analysis and domain modeling layers.

Another advantage of task models as design KRs, beyond ensured instantiation of the assessment argument at the task level, is their potential for guiding the reusability and adaptability of tasks to different forms or assessments. Hively et al.'s "item forms" provide an early example of this type of design KR. Item forms and item models provide item-level templates that can be adapted to a number of different assessments through changes in task features. Such templates allow the assessment designer the flexibility of adapting particular item types or tasks without losing the connection to the original assessment argument. This provides both efficiency and validity in task creation. Continuing with the example from the Butterfield et al. (1985) letter-series task, one can imagine using an "item form" approach whereby particular features of the letter-series task change (for example, letters, pattern) to create distinct items assessing the same reasoning.

When a task model is in digital form and the slots are appropriately filled, the resulting form can serve as input to subsequent processes to create tasks in the forms in which they are needed in implementation and presentation (as in Bejar et al., 2003, Gierl et al., 2008, Hamel, Mislevy, & Winters, 2008, and Hamel & Schank, 2006). Two examples of programs that can facilitate task authoring using the idea of item templates are Mathematics Test Creation Assistant (TCA, Singley & Bennett, 2002) and the Free-Response Authoring, Delivery, and Scoring System (FRADSS, Katz, 1995). Both of these tools allow for creation of multiple items from particular item models or item objects that are at a more general level of abstraction. Like PADI task templates, item forms and models support efficiency in their potential for reusability, as well as validity in their connection to the assessment argument laid out in the domain analysis phase.

KRs play an important role in the decisions that are made about the environment around the task. For example, choice of the format (for example, paper and pencil or computer-based; multiple-choice or diagram with essay) and the materials (for example, physical manipulatives) will all be shaped by the KRs that are critical to the domain, as identified in the domain analysis phase and carried through to the task template. This aspect of task authoring is discussed in further depth in the next section on task presentation.

*Task Presentation*  KRs are important for task presentation in several ways. First, the tasks themselves can be considered KRs. They are designed, based on the assessment argument, to be KRs that examinees must respond or react to in some manner, producing a work product that will be subsequently evaluated. Most often, a task employs important domain KRs to achieve this. Mathematics tasks use diagrams and mathematical notation, social studies tasks use maps and graphs, and music tests use musical notation. The CNS utilizes symbols of network systems to assess examinees' understanding of network troubleshooting. Thus, the presentation of the tasks in this environment necessarily includes KR symbols, formats, and manipulations that the test-taker must be able to understand and use.

An example of a task as the examinee experiences it (in contrast to the task object KR, in the IMS/QTI xml form that the presentation process uses to render this view) is depicted in Figure 5.9. This screen shot is of a task from the Full Option Science System (FOSS) project, in which science phenomena are simulated in a computer environment. For this particular example, examinees are asked to interact with the symbols on the screen to simulate electrical circuits. A number of domain KRs are present in this example, such as the battery and switch. As a technology-based KR itself, the simulation environment affords interaction to the examinees so that the real-world implications of their actions with the simulated components can be visualized. In this way, the KRs have been tuned both to cognition in the domain and to the elements of an assessment argument.

Decisions regarding what stimulus materials, resources, and levels of scaffolding will be provided to examinees are all described in the task model. These decisions are often affected by the type of work product that is derived for a particular task. With the FOSS example, the work products produced for this item are similar in form to many others from the tasks created with the same template.

Just as specifications for particular tasks are articulated in the task model, the presentation model provides specifications for rendering the task in a particular environment. For example, a presentation model for a computer-based assessment will be different from one for a paper-based test, even though the two might have identical task and evidence models. This flexibility is yet another example of the way in which the ECD approach enables adaptability and reusability of tasks.

Finally, design KRs also play a role in facilitating presentation of tasks across the various aspects of assessment delivery. For example, the IMS Question and Test Interoperability (QTI) specification is an assessment KR that allows for interchange of information between authoring tools, item banks, test construction systems, and assessment delivery systems. In this way, the QTI aids in creating and presenting tasks more efficiently, by providing a shared language for KRs that are used and produced in computer-based assessment (Almond, Steinberg, & Mislevy, 2002).

*Task Scoring*   Articulating the student model requires specifying the student-model variables. Each student-model variable corresponds to some

FIGURE 5.8 A BioKIDS template in PADI design system

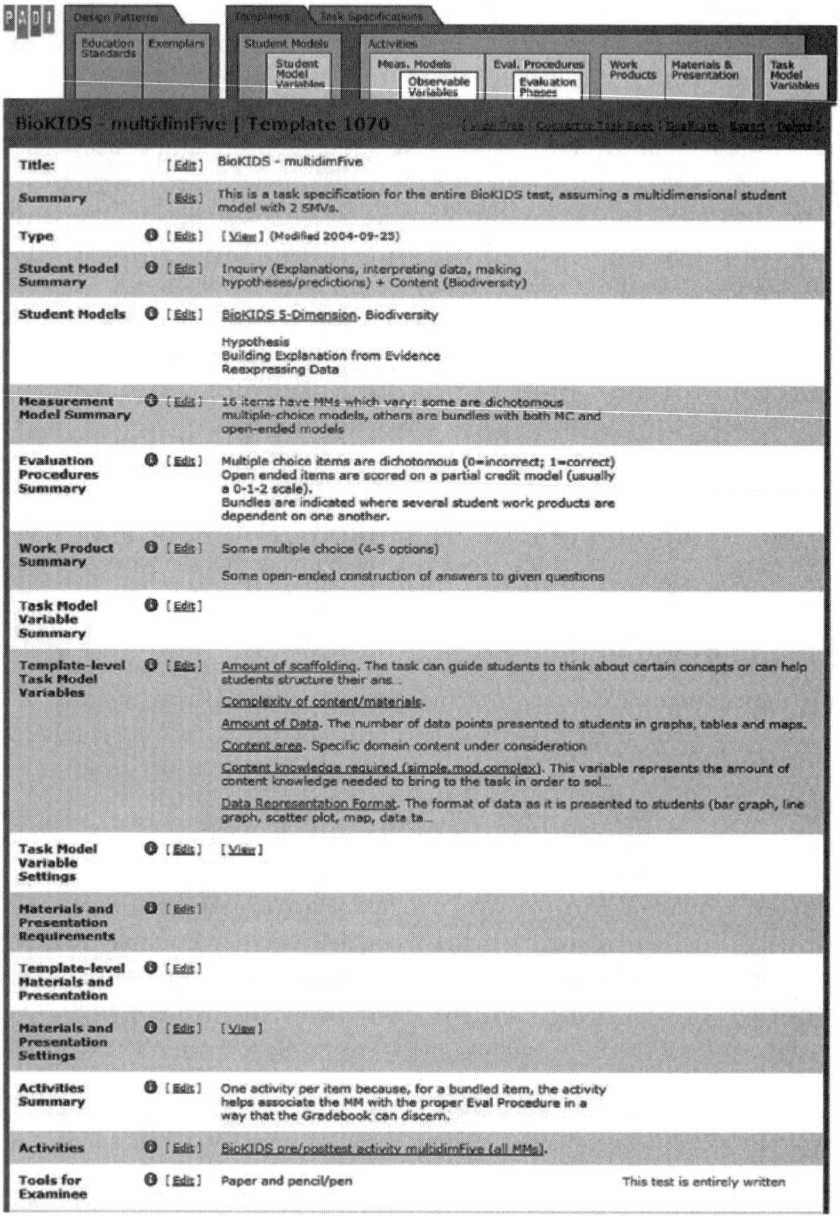

aspect of knowledge, skill, ability, or proficiency, presumed to drive probabilities of observable responses. They will be the variables in a latent variable model such as an IRT, latent class, cognitive diagnosis, or Bayes net model. Psychometric models such as these use probability-based methods to ground inferences about students. From the perspective of ECD, the student model and the measurement submodel of the evidence model are KRs that support probability-based reasoning about examinees based on evaluations of their performances. Structured around recurring evidentiary themes, measurement model fragments can be fit together flexibly for different problems and different kinds of data (Conati, Gertner, & VanLehn, 2002; Mislevy, 2006; Rupp, 2002). Being able to automatically assemble probability models in light of purposes and evolving conditions, as in simulation-based assessment, is an example of what engineers call "knowledge-based model construction" (Breese, Goldman, & Wellman, 1994). Its implementation depends on developing KRs that encode key features of situations to guide the assembly of the measurement model and student model KRs.

The *evaluative submodel* of the evidence model involves identifying and evaluating features of the examinee work product, in terms of values for the observable variables that are used by the measurement submodel to update the values of student model variables. We have discussed how what examinees say, do, or make to provide evidence in assessments is often expressed in terms of domain KRs, which examinees create, complete, transform, or interrelate—this leveraging of domain KRs being central to proficiency in the domain of interest. Students produce these response KRs in their interactions with the presentation process. They constitute the message passed to the evidence evaluation process.

What is important here from the perspective of representation is that the form of the work product, as a KR, can be tuned to identifying and evaluating the features that convey evidence about the examinee's proficiencies. The work product KR must capture traces of the cognitive processes that produced it, no matter whether the evaluation is carried out by humans or automatically (Messick, 1994). Taking advantage of developments in technology to evaluate performances requires attention not just to the form of the work product KR and the procedures to be carried out, but also to virtually every link in the chain of reasoning that comprises the assessment argument (Bennett & Bejar, 1998). To this end, the Williamson et al. (2006)–edited volume Automated Scoring of Complex Tasks in Computer-Based Testing contains chapters describing various methodologies for

**FIGURE 5.9** Prompt from FOSS/ASK simulation

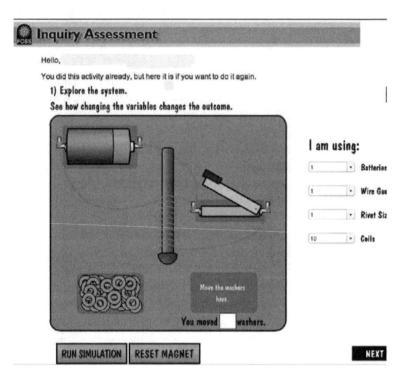

automated scoring of KRs from performance assessments from the perspective of ECD. In a later section, we discuss automated scoring procedures used in CNS tasks, which adapt ideas from both the rule-based algorithms for scoring the log of patient management problems in the National Board of Medical Examiners' Primum assessment (Margolis & Clauser, 2006) and the natural language processing techniques used in automated scoring of essays (Deane, 2006).

The KR of multiple-choice response format revolutionized testing first when it was introduced in the early decades of the twentieth century, because it virtually eliminated judgment in evaluation, and then again in the middle of the twentieth century when machine-based scoring of multiple-choice items made standardized testing economical at vastly larger scales. Current work focuses on the use of more ecologically valid KRs as work products; that is, examinees' performance in directly constructing, completing, or transforming domain KRs. To accomplish this objective economically requires KRs that in one view the examinee can interact with, but that in another view support both customizable automated evaluation procedures and flexible reuse across assessment domains and purposes. The key to successful automated scoring is the articulation of the cognitive psychology underlying the use of the domain KRs, which determines how assessment design and implementation KRs are structured and processed to provide the necessary evidence in the assessment argument.

## "GENERATING EXAMPLES" TASKS

This section looks more closely at an innovative task family for use in large-scale testing, through the lens of KRs. Bennett, Steffen, Singley, Morley, and Jacquemin (1997) developed the mathematical expression (ME) response type that allows presentation of any item for which the answer is a rational symbolic expression. It was created primarily to present mathematical modeling problems such as the following:

> A normal line to a curve at a point is a line perpendicular to the tangent line at the point. The equation of the normal line to the curve $y = 2x2$ at the point (1,2) is given by _____.

Such questions typically describe a situation in one representational form (verbal), which the examinee must then translate to a symbolic form more suitable for mathematical procedures. Translating between alternative representations is key to success in any technical field. In most applied fields—mathematics, engineering, architecture, and computer programming are good examples—a key activity is to translate the verbally stated requirements of a client to the representational forms of the field, because it is those representational forms that can be more effectively and efficiently operated on to satisfy client requirements (Larkin & Simon, 1987). This notion of translating verbal into more graphic or pictorial KRs is also consistent with research demonstrating the advantages of having students construct graphic organizers or concept maps from text (e.g., Lambiotte, Dansereau, Cross, & Reynolds, 1989; Robinson, 1998).

In addition to using the ability to translate between KRs as the object of measurement, how this response type uses KRs in scoring is of interest. One of the attractions of ME items is that they have no single correct answer. Rather, there can be many—perhaps an infinite number—of correct answers because there are numerous ways to express the same mathematical relationship. For ME, examinee responses always share the same basic KR, a mathematical expression. However, correct responses will almost certainly vary in their surface features. Thus, the scoring challenge is one of mathematical paraphrase. For example, in field trials, the following were among the correct responses examinees produced for the preceding problem:

$$-1/4x + 9/4(-1 *x + 9)/4 - 1/4 * x + (9/4)$$
$$1/4 * (9-x) - x/4 + 9/4(-x + 9)/4$$
$$-.25x + 2.25(9-x)/42 - 1/4 * (x - 1)$$

To score answers automatically, each response is compared against a *key expression*, where that key expression can be any paraphrase of a correct answer. The comparison is done by substituting values in the examinee's expression, evaluating it, substituting the same values in the key expression, evaluating it, and subtracting one expression from the other. If the result is repeatedly zero (that is, across many different substitutions), the examinee response is considered to be correct. ME scoring works, then, by manipulating KRs. It does nothing more than compare the contents of the examinee's KR to a representation expressed in the same symbol system, which might differ in its surface configuration but, if the response is right, not in semantics. Although examiners have evaluated answers for value rather than expression for centuries, the capability of manipulating algebraic expressions digitally enables designers to employ open-ended responses as work products in this representational form in large-scale tests.

Bennett et al. (1999) also developed the "generating examples" (GE) response type in which problems present constraints but do not present enough information to determine the answer uniquely, and ask examinees to pose one or more instances that meet those constraints. GE questions thus relax the problem structure, although unlike Simon's (1978) "ill-structured" problems, GE items give enough information to determine whether a posed solution is a member of the universe of correct responses. And, unlike ME, this universe is not composed of only paraphrases but also includes quantitatively different responses. The following is a sample item:

> If n and m are positive integers and 11n – 7m = 1, what are
> two different possible sets of values for n and m?

The GE item class overlaps with the ME class. That is, we can pose GE items for which the work product is a constructed algebraic expression. That expression can take many quantitatively different forms and each of those forms can, in turn, have many paraphrases. Neither the paraphrases nor the quantitatively different forms may be completely specifiable in advance.

The GE response type can also accommodate other representational forms including numbers, letter patterns, graphs, or geometric figures (see Bennett, Morley, Quardt, & Rock, 2000). From the perspective of KRs, GE can be used to pose a problem in one representational form (for example, verbal) and collect a response in another (for example, symbolic, numeric, figural). But in contrast to ME, GE scores responses using a KR that differs from the examinee's production. This KR is an executable key—computer code that tests each examinee response against the constraints expressed in the item stem. Thus, the executable key is nothing more than an alternative KR of the problem statement, optimized for use by a computer.

For the sample item, the executable key would essentially check each response to see if it:

- Contained two pairs of values,
- Had a second pair different from the first,
- Had each member of each pair be a positive integer,
- Returned for the first pair a true result when its values are substituted for n and m in the equation, $11n - 7m = 1$, and
- Returned for the second pair a true result when its values are substituted for n and m in the equation, $11n - 7m = 1$.

For this question, then, multiple KRs are in play. The examinee works with verbal and symbolic representations in translating the problem, and then with symbolic and numerical ones in formulating a response. The scoring works with the numerical response and its own logical representation to process that response.

## CISCO NETWORK SIMULATOR (CNS) PERFORMANCE ASSESSMENTS

The Cisco Networking Academy Program (CNAP; http://cisco.netacad.net) is a public-private partnership that teaches apprentice-level design, installation, and troubleshooting of computer networks in more than 50,000 locations ("academies") throughout the globe. Since its inception, CNAP has employed hands-on, instructor-administered performance (skills) examinations. When well administered, these exams constitute a "gold standard" for assessing proficiency in the program. With more than 10,000 instructors and little local control, however, their reliability and validity can vary substantially from one site to another. The web-based CNS provides all academies with high-quality simulation-based performance assessment to complement local hands-on exams (Frezzo & Stanley, 2005). The CNS tasks discussed in the following sections grew out of research of the NetPass project (Behrens et al., 2004, Williamson et al., 2004), which produced the initial versions of the presentation process and automated scoring procedures. This section considers the roles of KRs in the development and use of CNS tasks. The interpenetrating roles of technology, cognition, and assessment design theory are clear throughout the discussion.

### The CNS Assessment as a Knowledge Representation

The CNS assessment is itself a KR, which coordinates information about the curriculum and instruction that occurs in the Cisco Networking Academy Program, expert-novice studies on design and troubleshooting (Williamson et al., 2004), and research on assessment design in order to provide evidence about student proficiency at the end of the program. Figure 5.10 shows the web page that the students taking the CNS exam see as they work. This page contains a title, instructions for submitting the assessment, a timer, and tabs that link to key domain KRs that will be discussed further in the following section. The affordances that appear on the web page were designed to mirror other tools that students have used, including real networking devices.

The "assessment as knowledge representation" of CNS is of paramount importance in CNAP. The widely varying quality of skills assessments across thousands of academies meant that instructional goals and performance expectations were not being clearly communicated to instructors and students. CNS was seen as a cost-effective way to use technology to provide this information widely, and to provide students with opportunities to work through the cognitive aspects of design, configurations, and troubleshooting with CNS learning tasks as well as summative exams.

### Domain Analysis of KRs in Networking

Subject matter experts analyzed CNAP curriculum materials to survey the KRs used in instructional materials and in real-world problems at the targeted level of skills. They found usage of both general-purpose KRs, such as tables and graphs, populated with networking information and KRs that were particular to the domain.

One example of a critical domain KR in the domain of computer networking, and thus for CNS, is the logical topology representation. The logical topology is an abstracted map of the networking device nodes and

**FIGURE 5.10    The CNS examinee interface**

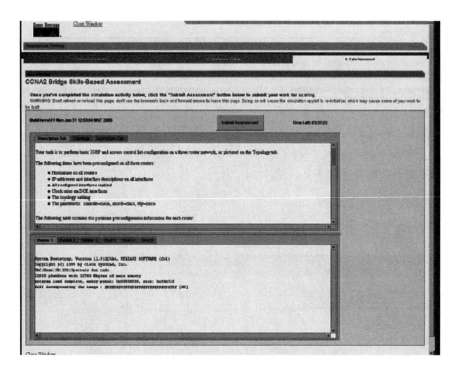

the interconnections between those nodes (Frezzo & Stanley, 2005). Figure 5.11 shows an example of a logical topology, with icons representing PCs and icons representing routers. Two other domain KRs are shown at the bottom of this figure: the command-line interface (CLI), which allows students to interact with the virtual routers, and Cisco's Internetwork Operating System (IOS), which is the control and programming language for networking the switches and routers in the logical topology KR. Both are inherently interactive and technology-based as people use them in actual practice, and as examinees need to use them in CNS tasks. As an aspect of knowledge about the domain, students are expected to be able to understand each type of KR and how the representations interact to describe a given network—that is, what each representation tells one about the network and what it does not, where the representations share information in different forms and must therefore be consistent, and how each representation supports different aspects of reasoning about the network when troubleshooting.

**FIGURE 5.11** Two key domain KRs, the logical topology (top) and the Cisco IOS command-line interface (CLI) (bottom)

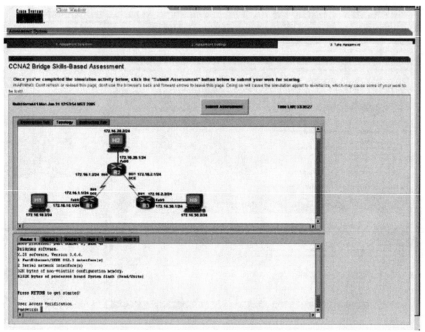

### Structuring Tasks Around Domain KRs

KRs play a central role in assessment in determining the context in which students will provide evidence of their knowledge, skills, and abilities, which includes knowledge and proficiencies with domain KRs. CNS network configuration tasks illustrate the interactions between a student and the delivery system in the presentation, creation, and transformation of KRs.

The initial presentation of the problem to the student takes the form of domain KRs, in the form of verbal descriptions using networking terminology and concepts (Figure 5.10), a logical topology diagram (upper window in Figure 5.11), and a CLI for configuring the devices in the network (lower window in Figure 5.11). The student uses the CLI to configure the network devices by means of the Cisco IOS control language, which is a symbol-system KR through which humans and network devices communicate with other devices. We note the fidelity of the CNS configuration tasks to real-world device configuration: The CNS environment uses the same

Cisco IOS language and the same CLI interface as when configuring real devices remotely from a terminal, and the simulator provides the same messages back as real devices would. This correspondence, made possible by the simulation environment, supports the construct-representation line of argumentation for the validity of these tasks (Embretson, 1983).

As the student proceeds, two new KRs are created and others are transformed. The KRs that are transformed are the representations of the devices inside the simulator. These are symbol system KRs as well, representing the state of each hypothetical network device in a digital form that the simulation program can use to compute device responses to communicate back to the student or to modify the behavior of other devices. These are not KRs of the learning domain, but rather of the simulation domain used in the presentation and evidence identification processes in the assessment delivery system. They are optimized to support the processes of the delivery system for presentation and scoring, and are not visible to the student.

The KRs that are created are called the running configuration and the log file. The running configuration file for a router is the result of using the CLI to issue commands to change the active configuration of the router and its traffic control behavior. Figure 5.12 shows an example. Running configuration files are of great importance in the networking domain, and serve as the key work product in CNS configuration tasks. As a work product, a running configuration file indicates the final status of the network when a student completes the problem. The log file additionally captures all the commands that a student issues during the course of the work and the responses from the network.

Running configuration files and log files are domain KRs, produced by examinees as they interact with a (simulated) network system using the Cisco IOS symbol-system that they are learning for just this purpose. As work products, they are assessment KRs that can be operated on by the evidence identification process of the CNS delivery system to identify and evaluate evidence about student proficiency. The interplay between humans—students and instructors—and the CNS system continues in the automated scoring and reported processes discussed in a later section of this paper.

### Using Design KRs to Support Task Creation

Another way in which KRs played a crucial role in the development of the CNS is through the design KRs called design patterns, noted earlier. In the case of CNS, design patterns were used to create multiple forms to

**FIGURE 5.12** Router running configuration file serves as a student work product

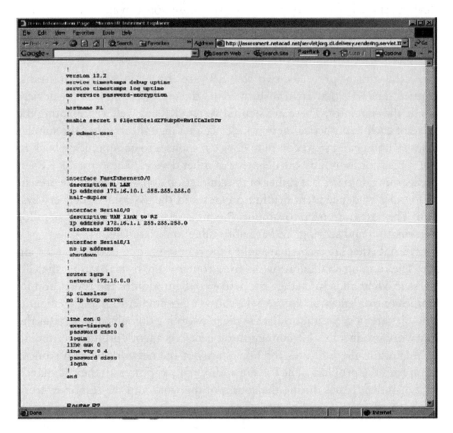

ensure exam security. Design patterns that are of interest to the CNS are those related to network design, implementation, and troubleshooting tasks (Wise, 2005). More-focused design patterns were developed from the Problem-Solving in a Finite System design pattern presented earlier, which incorporated the specialized domain knowledge and context of troubleshooting computer networks.

Task shells are another KR used in CNS. CNS task shells are built around the specification of stimulus domain KRs, key aspects of their contents in terms of task model variables, and targeted KRs in terms of work products. Figure 5.13 is an example of the part of a task shell that test developers use to create instances from a family of simple network design tasks.

**FIGURE 5.13**    Shell for CNS design task problem statement (boldface phrases are variables)

1. *Setting sentence:* A(n) **setting** is [create something that is a typical activity for this setting].

2. *Building size sentence:* The **setting** is **buildingLength** long.

3. *Network type sentence:* The **setting** has been asked to install a(n) **EthernetStandard** network for this [the typical activity for this setting created above].

4. *Subgroup 1 specification:* The **subgroup1** connections require a bandwidth of **bandwidthforASubgroup1**.

5. *Subgroup 2 specification:* The **subgroup2** connections require a bandwidth of **bandwidthforASubgroup2**.

6. *Subgroup 3 specification:* The **subgroup3** connections require a bandwidth of **bandwidthforASubgroup3**.

7. *"Force closets" sentence?:* No networking equipment can be stored in **Subgroup123** area.

8. *Location of POP sentence:* The link to the Internet is located **locationOfExternalConnection(POP).**

### Using KRs to Create Tasks and Manage Assessment Systems

CNS has revolutionized assessment in the Cisco Networking Academy Program, and in turn teaching and learning, by making high-fidelity simulations of the cognitive aspects of the domain available at low cost throughout the program over the Internet. Obviously, the KRs transmitted over the Internet to and from the examinee, in terms of stimulus conditions, interactions with the simulated network, and work products, must be represented in digital form, and transformations from one form to another are necessary to communicate between people and computer processes, and between one process and another.

Many domain KRs and design KRs, some of which are mentioned in the previous sections, are used in the design, implementation, and delivery of CNS tasks. In this section we point to two particular ways that KRs are used in computer-supported task design and computer-based delivery—namely, task authoring and automated scoring. These leverage points concern the way that assessment designs can use technology to more efficiently create the domain KRs examinees interact with, and capture and evaluate the KRs they produce.

As noted earlier, task shells like those used in CNS are not a new idea. They are a KR that has been used for decades to synthesize knowledge in learning domains and knowledge about assessment, to improve efficiency and validity. What is new is the expression of task shells in computer-based forms that facilitate the work of test developers by allowing them to work with interfaces that create task specification KRs and automated or semiautomated procedures that operate on these forms to generate the KRs used in assessment delivery. Figure 5.14, for example, shows a screen from a CNS task authoring tool in which a test developer selects stimulus and work product KRs for troubleshooting tasks. Having specified that a topology diagram will be present in a task, the test developer then specifies and configures a network that meets the conditions indicated in the task model variables, using an interface similar to the one that a student uses in a design task. The output of this interaction is another KR, an XML file whose format can be used by the presentation process to display the topology diagram, and by the simulator to create the network and govern its behavior.

CNS uses automated scoring procedures in the evidence identification process. They consist of computer programs that scan for salient features of the KRs produced by students' interactions with the presentation process, namely configuration files, log files, and network topology XML files. The scoring rules for the running configuration in configuration tasks, for example, produce values for graded response observable variables for accuracy of the routing protocol, whether access control lists (ACLs) are assigned to appropriate devices, and the correctness of the ACL rules. Log files contain more information—for example, about strategy use and efficiency—but these would present greater scoring challenges because they can vary considerably from one student to another. The NetPass prototype used logical rules to identify the presence or absence of key features of the interaction, systematicity of steps, and number and seriousness of errors (Williamson et al., 2004). Clauser et al. (1997) describe this style of automated scoring for interactive problem solving in simulated patient management problems at the National Board of Medical Examiners.

Viewing the interaction between an engineer and a network as a conversation carried out in the Cisco IOS language, DeMark and Behrens (2004) took a statistical language processing approach to analyzing the log files, with promising results in classifying learners along a novice-to-expert curriculum.

The resulting observable variables are a KR that is sent the reporting process to produce the student score report. A computer program thus trans-

**FIGURE 5.14    Screen from CNS task authoring interface**

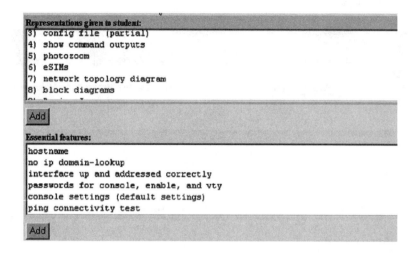

forms information in the form of machine-readable KRs containing values of observables into a KR that summarizes results on this task for human students and instructors. The reporting process creates an accompanying KR called an item-information page (Figure 5.15), which details by item how the student responded and the scoring rubric that was applied.

KRs play roles in managing and coordinating the various aspects of building an assessment. For CNS, aspects of the curriculum, instruction, and assessment are intertwined around the domain and design KRs. Many actors, including learners, instructors, subject-matter experts, programmers, psychometricians, and automated delivery processes use the KRs that are embodied in the assessment to interact and communicate with one another. Several benefits have accrued from explicating and exploiting the roles of KRs in assessment design (DeMark, West, & Behrens, 2005). These include improving alignment among curriculum, assessment, and instruction; providing efficiency and scalability in task and test construction; and grounding the defensibility of tasks in high-stakes tests.

In more recent work, assessment designers have extended these ideas to more local customization for instructors for learning exercises and formative assessment. A dynamic software environment called Packet Tracer allows instructors to create tasks and students to use and manipulate the multiple KRs it contains (Frezzo, 2009; Frezzo, Behrens, & Mislevy, 2009). Figure 5.16 shows an example with multiple interactive KRs, including the logical

**FIGURE 5.15** Item information page including student model variables, feedback, and work product

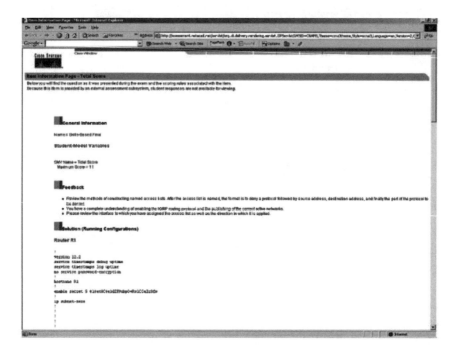

topology and command-line interface. The central development team used design patterns for network design, configuration, and troubleshooting to create sample tasks and a help system to assist instructors in using Packet Tracer effectively.

## CONCLUSION

These are exciting times in assessment, with rapid developments in fields that are fundamental to the conception, design, and use of educational tests. These include statistics, measurement models, technology, cognitive psychology, and learning domains. The challenge is how to put new insights to work to improve assessment. Knowledge representation plays a central role in this endeavor. Two primary ways in which external KRs play a role in assessment can be described as domain KRs and design KRs.

Domain KRs are representations that are used to express ideas and to carry out work in domains. They concern the "what" of assessment.

FIGURE 5.16    Packet Tracer's multiple interactive KRs, Including logical topology, Cisco IOS CLI, OSI model view, router state table, and animated "Packet Movie" mode

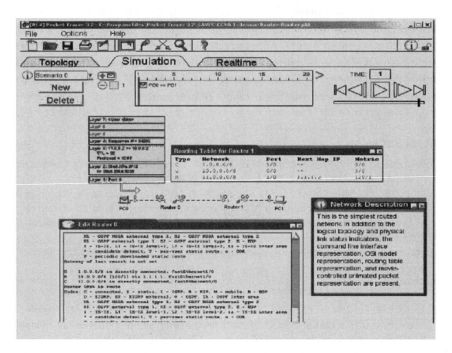

Insights from the cognitive, situative, and sociocultural perspectives in psychology help us to understand the roles of KRs in the development of competence and of expertise. They are critical for understanding the domain; hence they are pivotal points in learning and in assessment. Learning to think in their terms is a target of learning; they are used in assessment to help define the environments that students work in and to serve as vehicles for carrying out the work, and as they are produced, they constitute work products for evaluation. Continual advances in technology mean that KRs are increasingly interactive and amenable to digital representations. It is through the psychology of using KRs and the theory of assessment design that we will understand how to present information, afford interaction, and capture work products in these forms.

Making assessment design more efficient requires greater understanding of the assessment enterprise. Recent work on "assessment engineering" (e.g., Luecht, 2002; Mislevy et al., 2003) aims not only to make the underlying principles explicit, but also to embed the underlying principles in design

KRs that help assessment professionals structure, and at times automate, their work (Mislevy & Haertel, 2006). Assessment design KRs thus concern the "how" of assessment. They facilitate communication between different levels of the assessment design and provide capacity for reusing assessment ideas and task components. Advances in technology equally provide opportunities to design and deliver assessments more effectively. It is through improved frameworks of assessment design that we will understand how to create design KRs to capitalize on these opportunities.

## REFERENCES

Ainsworth, S. E. (1999). A functional taxonomy of multiple representations. *Computers and Education, 33*, 131–152.

Almond, R. G., Steinberg, L. S., & Mislevy, R. J. (2002). Enhancing the design and delivery of assessment systems: A four-process architecture. *Journal of Technology, Learning, and Assessment, 1*(5). http://www.bc.edu/research/intasc/jtla/journal/v1n5.shtml.

American Association for the Advancement of Science. (2001). Atlas of science literacy. Washington, D.C.

Bachman, L. F. (2003). Building and supporting a case for test use. *Language Assessment Quarterly, 2*, 1–34.

Behrens, J. T., Mislevy, R. J., Bauer, M., Williamson, D. M., & Levy, R. (2004). Introduction to evidence centered design and lessons learned from its application in a global e-learning program. *International Journal of Testing, 4*, 295–301.

Bejar, I. I. (2002). Generative testing: From conception to implementation. In S. H. Irvine & P. C. Kyllonen (Eds.), *Item generation for test development* (pp. 199–217). Hillsdale, NJ: Lawrence Erlbaum Associates.

Bejar, I. I., & Braun, H. I. (1999). *Architectural simulations: From research to implementation.* Final Report to the National Council of Architectural Registration Boards. (ETS RM-99-02). Princeton, NJ: Educational Testing Service.

Bejar, I. I., Lawless, R. R., Morley, M. E., Wagner, M. E., Bennett, R. E., & Revuelta, J. (2003). A feasibility study of on-the-fly item generation in adaptive testing. *Journal of Technology, Learning, and Assessment, 2*(3). Available from http://www.jtla.org.

Belsley, D. A., Kuh, E., & Welch, R. E. (1980). *Regression diagnostics: Identifying influential data and source of collinearity.* New York: John Wiley.

Bennett, R. E., & Bejar, I. I. (1998). Validity and automated scoring: It's not only the scoring. *Educational Measurement: Issues and Practice, 17*(4), 9–17.

Bennett, R. E., Morley, M., & Quardt, D. (2000). Three response types for broadening the conception of mathematical problem solving in computerized tests. *Applied Psychological Measurement, 24*, 294–309.

Bennett, R. E., Morley, M., Quardt, D., Singley, M. K., Katz, I. R., & Nhouyvanisvong, A. (1999). Generating examples: A new response type for measuring quantitative reasoning. *Journal of Educational Measurement, 36*, 233–252.

Bentler, P. M. (2006). *EQS 6 structural equation modeling software*. Encino, CA: Multivariate Software, Inc.

Bloom, B. S. (Ed.) (1956). *Taxonomy of educational objectives: The classification of educational goals. Handbook I, cognitive domain*. New York: Longman.

Bormuth, J. R. (1970). *On the theory of achievement test items*. Chicago: University of Chicago Press.

Breese, J. S., Goldman, R. P., & Wellman, M. P. (1994). Introduction to the special section on knowledge-based construction of probabilistic and decision models. *IEEE Transactions on Systems, Man, and Cybernetics, 24*, 1577–1579.

Butterfield, E. C., Nielsen, D., Tangen, K. L., & Richardson, M. B. (1985). Theoretically based psychometric measures of inductive reasoning. In S. E. Embretson (Ed.), *Test design: Developments in psychology and psychometrics* (pp. 77–148). New York: Academic Press.

Cameron, C. A., Beemsterboer, P. L., Johnson, L. A., Mislevy, R. J., Steinberg, L. S., & Breyer, F. J. (2000). A cognitive task analysis for dental hygiene. *Journal of Dental Education, 64*, 333–351.

Card, S. K., Moran, T. P., & Newell, A. (1983). *The psychology of human computer interaction*. Hillsdale, NJ: Lawrence Erlbaum Associates.

Clauser, B. E., Ross, L. P., Clyman, S. G., Rose, K. M., Margolis, M. J., Nungester, R. J., Piemme, T. E., Chang, L., El-Bayoumi, G., Malakoff, G. L., & Pincetl, P. S. (1997). Development of a scoring algorithm to replace expert rating for scoring a complex performance-based assessment. *Applied Measurement in Education, 10*, 345–358.

Collins, A., & Ferguson, W. (1993). Epistemic forms and epistemic games: Structures and strategies to guide inquiry. *Educational Psychologist, 28*, 25–42.

Conati, C., Gertner, A., & VanLehn, K. (2002). Using Bayesian networks to manage uncertainly in student modeling. *User Modeling & User-Adapted Interaction, 12*, 371–417.

Davidson, F., & Lynch, B. K. (2001). *Testcraft: A teacher's guide to writing and using language test specifications*. New Haven: Yale University Press.

Deane, P. (2006). Strategies for evidence identification through linguistic assessment of textual responses. In D. M. Williamson, R. J. Mislevy, and I. I. Bejar (Eds.), *Automated Scoring of Complex Tasks in Computer Based Testing* (pp. 313–371). Mahwah, NJ: Lawrence Erlbaum Associates.

DeMark, S. F., & Behrens, J. T. (2004). Using statistical natural language processing for understanding complex responses to free-response tasks. *International Journal of Testing, 4*, 371–390.

DeMark, S. F., West, P. A., & Behrens, J. T. (2005). Explorations in domain analysis and task model specification sensitive to underlying knowledge representations. Presented at the annual meeting of the American Education Research Association, April 15, 2005, San Francisco, CA.

Embretson, S. (1983). Construct validity: Construct representation versus nomothetic span. *Psychological Bulletin, 93*, 179–197.

Embretson, S. E. (1998). A cognitive design system approach to generating valid tests: Application to abstract reasoning. *Psychological Methods, 3*, 380–396.

Ericsson, K. A. (1996). *The Road to Excellence: The Acquisition of Expert Performance in the Arts and Sciences, Sports, and Games*. Mahwah, NJ: Lawrence Erlbaum Associates.

Frezzo, D. C. (2009). Using activity theory to understand the role of a simulation-based learning environment in a computer networking course. Unpublished doctoral dissertation, University of Hawai'i, Manoa.

Frezzo, D. C., Behrens, J. T., & Mislevy, R. J. (2009). Design patterns for learning and assessment: Facilitating the introduction of a complex simulation-based learning environment into a community of instructors. *The Journal of Science Education and Technology*. http://www.springerlink.com/content/566p6g4307405346/fulltext.pdf.

Frezzo, D. C., & Stanley, K. (2005). Knowledge representations driving the design of computerized performance assessments in a complex simulated environment. Presented at the symposium Knowledge Representation in Assessment, at the Annual Meeting of the American Educational Research Association, April 15, 2005, Montreal, Canada.

Gibson, J. J. (1966). *The senses considered as perceptual systems*. Boston: Houghton Mifflin.

Gierl, M. J., Zhou, J., & Alves, C. (2008). Developing a taxonomy of item model types to promote assessment engineering. *Journal of Technology, Learning, and Assessment, 7*(2). Available from http://www.jtla.org.

Gitomer, D. H., & Steinberg, L. S. (1999). Representational issues in assessment design. In I. E. Sigel (Ed.), *Development of mental representation* (pp. 351–370). Hillsdale, NJ: Lawrence Erlbaum Associates.

Gotwals, A., & Songer, N. (2006). Cognitive Predictions: BioKIDS Implementation of the PADI Assessment System (PADI Technical Report 10). Menlo Park, CA: SRI International.

Haladyna, T. M. & Shindoll, R. R. (1989). Shells: A method for writing effective multiple-choice test items. *Evaluation and the Health Professions, 12*, 97–104.

Hamel, L., Mislevy, R. J., & Winters, F. (2008). Design rationale for an assessment task authoring system: a wizard for creating "mystery inquiry" assessment tasks (PADI Technical Report 19). Menlo Park, CA: SRI International.

Hamel, L., & Schank, P. (2005). Participatory, example-based data modeling in PADI (PADI Technical Report 4). Menlo Park, CA: SRI International.

Hamel, L., & Schank, P. (2006). A Wizard for PADI assessment design (PADI Technical Report 11). Menlo Park, CA: SRI International.

Hively, W., Patterson, H. L., & Page, S. H. (1968). A "universe-defined" system of arithmetic achievement tests. *Journal of Educational Measurement, 5*, 275–290.

Katz, I. R. (1994). Coping with the complexity of design: Avoiding conflicts and prioritizing constraints. In A. Ram, N. Nersessian, & M. Recker (Eds.), *Proceedings of the Sixteenth Annual Meeting of the Cognitive Science Society* (pp. 485–489). Mahwah, NJ: Lawrence Erlbaum Associates.

Katz, I. R. (1995). FRADS: A system for facilitating rapid prototyping by end users. In Y. Anzai & K. Ogawa (Eds.), *Proceedings of the Sixth Annual International Conference on Human-Computer Interaction*. Amsterdam: Elsevier Science Publishers.

Katz, I. R., Lipps, A. W., & Trafton, J. G. (2002). Factors affecting difficulty in the generating examples item type. ETS Research Report RR-02-07. Princeton, NJ: Educational Testing Service.

Kindfield, A. C. H. (1999). Generating and using diagrams to learn and reason about biological processes. *Journal of the Structure and Learning and Intelligent Systems, 14*, 81–124.

Lambiotte, J. G., Dansereau, D. F., Cross, D. R., & Reynolds, S. B. (1989). Multirelational semantic maps. *Educational Psychology Review, 1*, 331–367.

Larkin, J. H., & Simon, H. A. (1987). Why a diagram is (sometimes) worth ten thousand words. *Cognitive Science, 11*, 65–99.

Lehrer, R., & Schauble, L. (2002). Symbolic communication in mathematics and science: Co-constituting inscription and thought. In E. D. Amsel & J. Byrnes (Eds.), *Language, literacy, and cognitive development: The development and consequences of symbolic communication.* (pp. 167–192). Mahwah, NJ: Lawrence Erlbaum Associates.

Lewandowsky, S., & Behrens, J. T. (1999). Statistical graphs and maps. In F. T. Durso, R. S. Nickerson, R. W. Schvaneveldt, S. T. Dumais, D.S. Lindsay, & M. T. H. Chi (Eds.). *Handbook of Applied Cognition* (pp. 513–549). Chichester, UK: Wiley.

Luecht, R. M. (2002). From design to delivery: Engineering the mass production of complex performance assessments. Paper presented at the Annual Meeting of the National Council on Measurement in Education, New Orleans, LA.

Luecht, R. M. (April, 2007). Assessment engineering in language testing: From data models and templates to psychometrics. Invited paper presented at the annual meeting of the National Council on Measurement in Education, Chicago, IL.

Margolis, M. J., & Clauser, B. E. (2006). A regression-based procedure for automated scoring of a complex medical performance assessment. In D. M. Williamson, R. J. Mislevy, and I. I. Bejar (Eds.), *Automated Scoring of Complex Tasks in Computer Based Testing* (pp. 132–167). Mahwah, NJ: Lawrence Erlbaum Associates.

Markman, A. B. (1999). *Knowledge representation.* Mahwah, NJ: Lawrence Erlbaum Associates.

Messick, S. (1994). The interplay of evidence and consequences in the validation of performance assessments. *Educational Researcher, 23*(2), 13–23.

Mislevy, R. J. (2003). Substance and structure in assessment arguments. *Law, Probability, and Risk, 2*, 237–258.

Mislevy, R. J. (2006). Cognitive psychology and educational assessment. In R. L. Brennan (Ed.), *Educational measurement* (4th ed.) (pp. 257–305). Westport, CT: American Council on Education/Praeger Publishers.

Mislevy, R. J., & Haertel, G. (2006). Implications for evidence-centered design for educational assessment. *Educational Measurement: Issues and Practice, 25*, 6–20.

Mislevy, R. J., Hamel, L., Fried, R. G., Gaffney, T., Haertel, G., Hafter, A., Murphy, R., Quellmalz, E., Rosenquist, A., Schank, P., Draney, K., Kennedy, C., Long, K., Wilson, M., Chudowsky, N., Morrison, A., Pena, P., Songer, N., & Wenk, A. (2003). Design patterns for assessing science inquiry (PADI Technical Report 1). Menlo Park, CA: SRI International.

Mislevy, R. J., & Liu, M. (2009). Design patterns in the project "Leveraging evidence-centered design within scenario-based statewide science assessment." Presented at the Annual Meeting of the American Educational Research Association, San Diego, CA, April 13, 2009.

Mislevy, R. J., & Riconscente, M. M. (2006). Evidence-centered assessment design: Layers, structures, and terminology. In S. Downing & T. Haladyna (Eds.), *Handbook of Test Development* (pp. 61–90). Mahwah, NJ: Lawrence Erlbaum Associates.

Mislevy, R. J., Steinberg, L. S., & Almond, R. G. (2002). On the roles of task model variables in assessment design. In S. Irvine & P. Kyllonen (Eds.), *Item generation for test development* (pp. 97–128). Mahwah, NJ: Lawrence Erlbaum Associates.

Mislevy, R. J., Steinberg, L. S., & Almond, R. G. (2003). On the structure of educational assessments. *Measurement: Interdisciplinary Research and Perspectives, 1*, 3–67.

Mosenthal, P., & Kirsch, I. (1989). Understanding documents: Intersecting lists. *Journal of Reading, 33*, 210–213.

Palmer, S. E. (1978). Fundamental aspects of cognitive representation. In E. Rosch & B. B. Lloyd (Eds.), *Cognition and categorization* (pp. 259–303). Hillsdale, NJ: Lawrence Erlbaum Associates.

Pinker, S. (1990). A theory of graph comprehension. In R. Freedle (Ed.), *Artificial intelligence and the future of testing* (pp. 73–126). Hillsdale, NJ: Lawrence Erlbaum Associates.

Riconscente, M. M., Mislevy, R. J., & Hamel, L. (2005). An introduction to PADI task templates. (PADI Technical Report 3). Menlo Park, CA: SRI International.

Robinson, D. H. (1998). Graphic organizers as aids to text learning. *Reading Research and Instruction, 37*, 85–105.

Roid, G., & Finn, P. (1977). Algorithms for developing test questions from sentences in instructional materials. Interim Report, January–September. San Diego, CA: Navy Personnel Research and Development Center.

Rupp, A. A. (2002). Feature selection for choosing and assembling measurement models: a building-block-based organization. *International Journal of Testing, 2*, 311–360.

Scalise, K., & Gifford, B. (2006). Computer-based assessment in E-Learning: A framework for constructing "Intermediate Constraint" questions and tasks for technology platforms. *Journal of Technology, Learning, and Assessment, 4*(6) [online journal]. http://escholarship.bc.edu/jtla/vol4/6.

Schraagen, J. M., Chipman, S. F., & Shalin, V. J. (2000). *Cognitive task analysis*. Mahwah, NJ: Lawrence Erlbaum Associates.

Sfard, A. (1998). On two metaphors for learning and the dangers of choosing just one. *Educational Researcher 27*, 4–13.

Shute, V. J., Torreano, L. A., & Willis, R. E. (2000). DNA: Toward an automated knowledge elicitation and organization tool. In S. Lajoie (Ed.), *Computers as cognitive tools: No more walls, II*. Mahwah, NJ: Lawrence Erlbaum Associates.

Simon, H. A. (1978). Information-processing theory of human problem solving. In W. K. Estes (Ed.), *Handbook of learning and cognitive processes* (Vol. 5), Human information processing (pp. 271–295). Hillsdale, N.J.: Lawrence Erlbaum Associates.

Simon, H. A., & Kotovsky, K. (1963). Human acquisition of concepts for sequential patterns. *Psychological Review, 70*, 534–546.

Singley, M. K., & Bennett, R. E. (2002). Item generation and beyond: Applications of schema theory to mathematics assessment. In S. Irvine & P. Kyllonen (Eds.), *Item generation for test development* (pp. 361–384). Hillsdale, NJ: Lawrence Erlbaum Associates.

Stewart, J., & Hafner, R. (1994). Research on problem solving: Genetics. In D. Gabel (Ed.), *Handbook of research on science teaching and learning* (pp 284–300). New York: Macmillan.

Thurstone, L. L., & Thurstone, T. G. (1941). Factorial studies of intelligence. Psychometric Monographs, No. 2.

Thurstone, L. L., & Thurstone, T. G. (1962). *Primary mental abilities* (Rev. ed.). Chicago: Science Research Associates.

Toulmin, S. E. (1958). *The uses of argument.* Cambridge: Cambridge University Press.

Tufte, E. (1990). *Envisioning information.* Cheshire, CT: Graphics Press.

Tukey, J. W. (1990). Data-based graphics: Visual display in the decades to come. Statistical *Science, 5,* 327–339.

Whitehead, A. N. (1911). *An Introduction to mathematics.* New York: Holt.

Wiggins, G. P. (1998). *Educative assessment: Designing assessments to inform and improve student performance.* San Francisco: Jossey-Bass.

Williamson, D. M., Bauer, M., Steinberg, L. S., Mislevy, R. J., & Behrens, J. T. (2004). Design rationale for a complex performance assessment. *International Journal of Testing, 4,* 303–332.

Williamson, D. M., Mislevy, R. J., & Bejar, I. I. (Eds.). (2006). *Automated scoring of complex tasks in computer based testing.* Mahwah, NJ: Lawrence Erlbaum Associates.

Wilson, M. R. (2005). *Constructing measures: An item response modeling approach.* Mahwah, NJ: Lawrence Erlbaum Associates.

Wise, D. (2005). Design patterns for assessing troubleshooting in computer networks. Presented at the annual meeting of the American Education Research Association, April 15, 2005, San Francisco, CA.

*Originally published as R. J. Mislevy, J. T. Behrens, R. E. Bennett, S. F. Demark, D. C. Frezzo, R. Levy, D. H. Robinson, D. W. Rutstein, V. J. Shute, K. Stanley, & F. I. Winters. (2010). On the roles of external knowledge representations in assessment design.* Journal of Technology, Learning, and Assessment, 8(2). *Retrieved from http://www.jtla.org. Reprinted with permission of JTLA and Robert J. Mislevy.*

# CHAPTER SIX

# MODELING VARIABILITY

Human variability is not only a normal and valuable part of learning and development, it is in fact the essence of adaptive behavior. This assumption, although contrary to classic models of learning, is an essential premise of Universal Design for Learning and is entirely consistent with emerging research from the modern learning sciences. In particular, variability and its importance is anchored in dynamic systems theory, which has generated new insights into the many pathways of human development from infancy forward that depend on varied and interacting, individual and environmental factors. Indeed, perhaps the most consistent finding to come from this work is that no matter what aspect of learning is studied, no matter how precise the instruments used, and no matter the level of analysis, variability is the rule not the exception.

The shift toward dynamic systems—and the corresponding change in how variability is viewed in the context of learning—is an important conceptual advancement that has undoubtedly had a major influence on the way that scientists think about student learning. However, we argue that simply shifting the conceptual framework will not be enough to produce meaningful results in education. In fact, we think there is a danger in applying systems concepts to learning, in the tendency to adopt a concept (e.g., "variability-as-information" or "contextualized learning") in general without being specific about how exactly it functions. From a UDL perspective, full realization of a dynamic approach to learning—one that is capable of sustaining not only the interdisciplinary study of learning but also the challenges of research and practice translation—depends on pinning down dynamic concepts and building models that go beyond conjecture to make these concepts testable and falsifiable (and therefore scientific).

Fortunately, in recent years significant gains have been made in the methods and models available for analyzing variability in learning and development, and we believe these same models can (and should) anchor the kind of complex research that is needed to sustain meaningful interdisciplinary and translational science at the nexus of research and practice. For this reason, we invited Paul van Geert to guide us in understanding the changing landscape of dynamic systems modeling and what this means for learning science and educational practice. Van Geert has done pioneering work in the field of dynamic systems theory, particularly as it is applied to developmental phenomena but also to the study of learning and behavior.

In "Focus on Variability: New Tools to Study Intra-Individual Variability in Developmental Data," Paul van Geert and his colleague Marijn van Dijk provide both context and justification for the need to move beyond treating variability in learning performances as error and instead understanding such changes within the individual, or across individuals, as important information that needs to be measured and modeled. They suggest that the premise that variability in data reflects measurement error is implicitly assumed by many social scientists and by the statistical approaches they use.

Together, the authors investigate methods designed to capture intra-individual variability in individual time-serial data of repeated observations by applying them to data of early language development. They then go on to offer three alternative models for responding to the "vicious circle of neglect" of variability as important information and underscore the importance of treating variability as a "phenomenon of interest."

Van Geert has done pioneering work in building dynamic systems models and theories in the field of language and cognitive development, education, social development, and the general theory of developmental mechanisms. His models are based on theories from ecology and action theory and describe dynamics on the short- and long-term time scales. In addition to model building, he has also explored the study of intra-individual variability as an indicator of underlying developmental processes and the use of statistical simulation techniques in the description of individual-based time-serial data sets. He is one of the relatively few scholars who has successfully integrated the concepts and the powerful nonlinear mathematical models required to truly realize the transformative potential of dynamic systems. From our conversation with van Geert, three core ideas relevant to the UDL framework emerged.

### The Importance of Intra-Individual Variability

Van Geert emphasizes the need for researchers to focus not only on variability that exists among individuals (i.e., *inter*-individual variability) but also on variability within the same individual that manifests over time and across different contexts (i.e., *intra*-individual variability)—"both are essential to dynamic systems, and both are important explanatory factors for development." At the same time, he stresses the need to recognize that while the two kinds of variability can often go together, they are not the same and need to be studied on their own terms. He also stresses the need for a greater focus on differences within the individual, suggesting that intra-individual variability is the natural starting point for dynamic systems modeling.

In addition, van Geert emphasizes the need for research not only about intra-individual variability but also on "the extent to which intra-individual variability can be manipulated for educational reasons." Illustrating this point is a project he is working on in the Netherlands focusing on issues of talent and excellence. The challenge, he says, is that "there is a lot of talent in the schools" that is not revealed by current learning and assessment practices; he is interested in discovering ways in which that hidden talent can be uncovered.

What piqued our curiosity is how he characterizes talent, arguing that "the starting point of any definition of excellence and talent is the variability in the individual." He says that if approaches to teaching reduce intra-individual variability, then a child's abilities will be necessarily constrained. In contrast, if a learning environment encourages high intra-individual variability, students will be more likely to explore areas where they are not talented as well as areas where they are—thus, they will show high intra-individual variability. Currently this would be viewed in a negative light, if measured by traditional metrics of success (such as standardized assessments); however, van Geert argues that it is the best way to shift a whole population toward greater excellence, building many more "planks" from which children can take the leap toward excellence. He maintains that this view is important even for those students who are already excellent by definition (the top 20 percent in the class), since "they have the same unexplored region of variability as everyone else."

### Groups Versus Individuals

Another key point that van Geert raised in our conversation is the need for everyone in education, from educators to policy makers, to keep in mind the difference between levels of analysis in particular, the difference between groups and individuals. There are fundamental differences, he points out, between information about group differences and information about individual differences (whether inter- or intra-individual). He uses the example of information about student performance at the group level—a "group sample–based thinking"—and how this information may in fact be important and informative for questions at the policy level. However, he argues that the error occurs if the group-based instruments are used to try to monitor individual processes, since the individual process is about inter- and intra-individual variability as well as adaptability. "That's an entirely different logic," he says.

This confusion between groups and individuals, which we would argue is pervasive in education, particularly in the context of high-stakes tests, ultimately serves to impede effective teaching. Van Geert points out that the teacher is trying to "manipulate, govern steer the individual dynamic in the context of a class and interactions" and that this work is at a level that is literally on a "different dimension" compared to the group level of the policy dimensions. He maintains that it is important for people working at all levels (policy and practice) to recognize that the forms of assessment being used at each level, and the underlying thinking behind them, are entirely different. "What people are doing now is they think a valid and reliable (group level) test is also valid and reliable on the level of the individual child." The important insight, he argues, is for policy makers to recognize they are monitoring group-based activity and teachers are monitoring the individual process.

### Playing with Nonlinear Models

During our conversation, van Geert spoke about the fact that most patterns of growth and change (including learning and development) showed nonlinear characteristics and that, historically, what scholars have done is force a set of linear models onto children's learning and development (even as learning continued to defy this type of statistical analysis). We strongly believe that young scholars need to become familiar with new nonlinear modeling techniques that are the backbone of dynamic systems theory, as they provide the best opportunity to model a student's learning in all its richness and complexity and without having to separate the individual from their context.

That said, we are aware that nonlinear models can be incredibly complex and, at times, difficult to understand. And so we asked van Geert—knowing what he knows now—where a young scholar should begin if they are interested in learning about nonlinear models. He suggests that the best starting point, in terms of its simplicity and applicability, is the logistic curve. In fact, to this day it is his favorite dynamic model "because it says something very, very, very fundamental about growth." To explain this, he asked us to imagine walking with him into a garden and measuring a single bean that was growing. The growth of that bean depends on (at a minimum) two things. First, it is a function of itself: "If you measure the growth of the bean you'll see that its daily growth is a function of how big it already is." Beyond that, growth will be determined by the availability of resources, which are almost always limited (meaning you cannot have infinite growth). He argues that the logistic model is critical to understand for dynamic systems because it combines both of these determinants of growth into a single equation and because it is applicable across an astonishingly broad array of phenomena. "It's one of the mathematical models that basically everybody should understand."

We agree.

## FOR FURTHER READING

Fischer, K. W., & Bidell, T. R. (1998). Dynamic development of psychological structures in action and thought. In R. M. Lerner (Ed.) & W. Damon (Series Ed.), *Handbook of child psychology* (5th ed., pp. 467–561). New York: Wiley.

Immordino-Yang, M. H. (2010). Toward a microdevelopmental, interdisciplinary approach to social emotion. *Emotion Review, 2*(3), 217–220.

Thelen, E., & Smith, L. B. (1994). *A dynamic systems approach to the development of cognition and action.* Cambridge, MA: MIT Press.

van Geert, P. (1998). A dynamic systems model of basic developmental mechanisms: Piaget, Vygotsky, and beyond. *Psychological Review, 105*(4), 634–677.

van Geert, P., & Steenbeek, H. (2005). Explaining after by before: Basic aspects of a dynamic systems approach to the study of development. *Developmental Review, 25*(3), 408–422.

# Focus on Variability

New Tools to Study Intra-Individual Variability
in Developmental Data

PAUL VAN GEERT AND MARIJN VAN DIJK

*Author's Abstract:* In accordance with dynamic systems theory, we assume that variability is an important developmental phenomenon. However, the standard methodological toolkit of the developmental psychologist offers few instruments for the study of variability. In this article we will present several new methods that are especially useful for visualizing and describing intra-individual variability in individual time-serial data of repeated observations. In order to illustrate these methods, we apply them to data of early language development. After reviewing the common techniques and measures, we present new methods that show variability in developmental time-series data: the moving min–max graph, and the progmax–regmin graph. In addition, we demonstrate a technique that is able to detect sudden increases of variability: the critical frequency method. Also, we propose a technique that is based on a central assumption of the measurement-error-hypothesis: namely the symmetric distribution of error. Finally, as traditional statistical techniques have little to offer in testing variability hypotheses, we examine the possibilities that are provided by random sampling techniques. Our aim with the present discussion of variability and the demonstration of some simple yet illustrative techniques is to help researchers focus on rich additional sources of information that will lead to more interesting hypotheses and more powerful testing procedures, adapted to the unique nature of developmental data.

## 1. INTRODUCTION

### 1.1. Overview

In the field of developmental psychology, intra-individual variability is often neglected as a meaningful phenomenon. In our perspective, which has been inspired by dynamic systems theory, variability is viewed as a potential driving force of development and a potential indicator of ongoing processes. It should therefore be treated as an important source of information.

In this introduction, we provide an overview of the theoretical issues and discuss the traditional vs. the more current approach to variability. We go on with a short overview of studies from the different domains of developmental psychology that have taken up on the study of variability. In spite of the potential importance of intra-individual variability, there are only few tools for presenting and studying variability in the context of developmental data sets. Our aim is to introduce and discuss a number of relatively simple techniques and approaches for specifying intra-individual developmental variability. In the major part of this article, we will introduce these techniques by applying them to a data set from language development.

### 1.2. Theoretical Issues: Traditional vs. Current Views on Variability

Developmental psychology has a long tradition of focusing on the regular, gradual aspects of change. Until today, the majority of developmental studies show smoothed developmental trajectories of the variable under investigation. Although it is seldom explicitly mentioned, the almost automatic retreat towards a smoothed trajectory testifies of a certain suspicion towards the meaningfulness of the actual data and a belief that the average captures the underlying true level better. In recent years, several authors have warned against the untimely use of statistical compression techniques and have strongly recommended a more descriptive, exploratory approach, with an emphasis on smart ways of graphically presenting the data (Loftus, 1996; Tukey, 1977). It is also striking that the majority of the developmental graphs found in the literature do not explicitly graph the ranges within which the data fluctuate.

Intra-individual variability can be defined as differences in the level of a developmental variable within individuals and between repeated measurements. In this article we will use the term "variability" to indicate these differences (in achievement or behavior) between measurement occasions. We also use the term "fluctuations" for the differences between consecutive points in a variable trajectory. The term "stability" is used to indicate the counterpart of (or the lack of) variability.

In recent years, an increasing number of researchers acknowledge the possible meaningfulness of intra-individual variability and show an increasing interest in these irregular aspects of change. The notion that people function at different levels of development at the same time and the belief that this variability can be an essential factor in promoting development, have become increasingly prominent in recent developmental literature. Examples from early development are the studies of De Weerth, van Geert, and Hoitink (1999) who focused on variability in infant emotional behavior, Bertenthal (1999) who studied variability in inter-limb coordination and postural control in infants, and Ruhland and van Geert (1998) who focused on variability in early language development. Variability also features in the microgenetic approach (e.g., Kuhn, 1995), which tries to increase the chances of observing developmental change by providing a subject frequent opportunities over a period of weeks or months to engage in the cognitive strategies under investigation. This increased density of the use of strategies may lead to change, allowing the researcher close observation of the process. This is shown, among others, in the work of Fischer, Bullock, Rotenberg, and Raya (1993), Fischer and Granott (1995), Goldin-Meadow, Alibali, and Church (1993), Granott (1993), Lautrey (1993), Lautrey, Bonthoux, and Pacteau (1996), Lautrey and Cibois (1994), and Siegler (1994, 1996, 1997).

One of the reasons variability is receiving increasing attention lies in the introduction of a new theoretical viewpoint, namely dynamic systems theory (e.g., Thelen & Smith, 1993; van Geert, 1994), and in particular, catastrophe theory (Thom, 1975; van der Maas & Molenaar, 1992). These theories share the importance they attribute to variability. Both take a radical departure from the measurement-error-hypothesis, which systematically considers variability (in the form of fluctuating developmental levels) as the result of measurement error. This error-hypothesis is closely related to true score theory (Cronbach, 1960; Lord & Novick, 1968; Nunnally, 1970) and is deeply rooted in psychology. The error-hypothesis is based on the assumption that every psychological measurement is subjected to random measurement error, which is expressed in the variability of repeatedly acquired scores. Since these random errors are, by definition, independent of the true value measured, they are symmetrically distributed around the true level. Thus, by averaging over these (supposedly random) fluctuations, the true underlying level can be approached. Again, dynamic systems theory radically rejects this automatic retreat to the error-hypothesis and claims that variability bears important information about the nature of the developmental process.

Thelen and Smith (1993) were among the first to apply the dynamic systems approach to developmental psychology. They build on the idea of development as a self-organizing system. Change is defined as the transition from one stable state to another. Highly attractive states are dynamically stable and exhibit fluctuations around the mean state that reflect the noisiness of their components. Thelen and Smith state that in self-organization, the system is attracted to one preferred configuration out of many possible states, but behavioral variability is an essential precursor (p. 56). Dynamic systems theory has specific predictions for the behavior close to a developmental transition. During a transition, variability is large and "the system is free to explore new and more adaptive associations and configurations" (p. 145). The dynamic approach turns variability within (and also between) individuals into an essential element in the developmental process. Variability is considered to be the harbinger of change. Variability is also the essential ground for exploration and selection. Thelen and Smith encourage researchers to investigate the variability in their data. They state: "If errors of design or execution are not at fault, think dynamical and use the variability as data. Does the variability change over time?" (Thelen & Smith, 1993, p. 342). Note that Thelen and Smith do not discard the existence of measurement error. Measurement error exists in the form of errors of design or execution.

Self-organization is also central in catastrophe theory (Thom, 1975), which can be considered as a specific branch of dynamic systems theory (van Geert, Savelsbergh, & van der Maas, 1997). According to catastrophe theory, self-organizational processes can be classified into a limited number of characteristic patterns of discontinuous change, depending on the number of fundamental variables that determine the change. As such, catastrophe theory offers concrete models and criteria for discontinuities in developmental processes. One of the types of discontinuous change that has been applied is the cusp model. Catastrophe theory provides eight so-called catastrophe flags to test the presence of a cusp model (Gilmore, 1981; see also van der Maas & Molenaar, 1992, for an application to cognitive development). One of these catastrophe flags is "anomalous variance," which indicates that variability is expected to be greater in the vicinity of a phase transition, in the same sense as indicated by Thelen and Smith. However, catastrophe theory takes this reasoning one step further by taking variability as one of the criteria that indicates a discontinuous transition.

### 1.3. Recent Findings in the Field of Infant Motor and Emotional Development

#### 1.3.1. Motor Development

Several research domains have taken up on the ideas of dynamic systems theory and catastrophe theory. Initially, the field of motor development was most forceful in this pursuit. It is important to note that these studies are of different kinds: some are one-dimensional and quantitative, while others are multi-dimensional and qualitative. This distinction (between one-dimensional quantitative and multi-dimensional qualitative) has it implications for the methodology. We will elaborate on this issue later on.

The motor development domain provided many empirical studies on variability. We will only name a few for illustrative purposes. For instance Thelen (1985) documented the process of transition in the supine kicks of infants followed longitudinally from 2 weeks to 10 months (see also Thelen & Smith, 1993). One of the motor behaviors studied was the coordination between kicks. During the first few months, kicks were predominately alternating. However, this period is followed by a period with great variability. This instability led to new forms of coordination between legs, for instance simultaneous kicking of both legs. It appears that the infants must free themselves from the stable patterns of the newborn period before they can assemble new behavioral modes. It is clear that Thelen places great importance on behavioral variability as a precursor of a new behavioral repertoire. Furthermore, Wimmers (1996) studied transitions in the development from reaching without grasping to reaching with grasping. This occurs in most infants between 16 and 24 weeks of age. He used Gilmore's catastrophe flags to detect a phase transition in the development of grasping. One of the findings was the detection of the flag "anomalous variance," which indicates that the changes in question were accompanied by loss of stability (Wimmers, Savelsbergh, Beek, & Hopkins, 1998a, 1998b).

Bertenthal (1999) discusses the meaning of variability in the development of crawling patterns in infants. He states "[ . . . ] this variability is not merely a correlate of change but instead a contributor to the change itself" (p. 105) (also see Bertenthal & Clifton, 1998; Newell & Corcos, 1993). Bertenthal goes on stating that variability offers flexibility, which drives development following "Darwinian" principles. Principles of variation and selection cause successful behaviors to be stored and repeated more frequently than the less successful. Bertenthal believes that studying the change of variation patterns offers important insights into how children change with age.

## 1.3.2. Emotional Development

The study of De Weerth et al. (1999) focused on variability in infant emotional behavior. After reviewing the literature on this subject, they concluded that there are indications that infants display variable behavior both within and between observations. This is for instance the case in the field of visual behavior (Canfield, Wilken, Schmerl, & Smith, 1995), sleeping and waking patterns (Dittrichova, Tautermannova, & Vondracek, 1992), visual recognition behavior (Wachs, Morrow, & Slabach, 1990), and infantile emotions and temperament (e.g., Crockerberg & Smith, 1982; St. James Roberts & Wolke, 1984). However, the idea that variability could be an intrinsic characteristic of a normal developing system has seldom been recognized, much less explored. De Weerth et al. (1999) found considerable intra-individual variability in four different types of emotional behaviors in infants (crying, fretting/fussing, body-contact, and smiling) that seemed to decline in the first year of life. Instead of attributing this variability to measurement error, they point at a possible adaptive strategy. They claim that variability in emotional behavior ensures the infant of continued maternal attention: "[ . . . ] mother and infant try out new ways of communicating with each other, and also change them over time.[ . . . ] [They] tune into each other and influence each other with their moods attitudes and developing skills, etc." (p. 11). As the infant grows older, he or she has access to more sophisticated means of communication, to insure himself or herself of maternal attention, and variability may decline.

### 1.4. Recent Findings in the Field of Language Development

In the domain of language development, the importance of variability has largely been neglected. However, there are solid indications that language development is characterized by large fluctuations. For instance, the classical study of Minifie, Darley, and Sherman (1963) found a lack of test–retest reliability in seven language measures, including the average utterance length. Furthermore, Chabon, Kent-Udolf, and Egolf (1982) found large temporal variability of MLU (Mean Length of Utterance as defined by Brown, 1973) in children from age 3;6 and older. Neither study elaborates on the meaning of this variability although the use of the term "reliability" in both studies suggests a tendency toward true score theory. The work of Ruhland and van Geert (1998), on the other hand, is inspired by dynamic systems theory and catastrophe theory. In their study, the language development of six children was followed from the first-word stage up to the differentiation stage. Focus of this study was the development of function words. The frequency with which function words occur in child language constitutes an important indicator of syntactic development, according to Ruhland and van Geert (1998). Although the shape of the developmental curves turned out to have great inter-individual differences, all children showed remarkable fluctuations. The peaks and wells immediately catch the eye. Inspired by dynamic systems theory and catastrophe theory, Ruhland and van Geert take variability as developmentally meaningful, by studying it in the context of the catastrophe flag "anomalous variance." Therefore, intra-session variability was investigated by dividing the observation sessions in two equal parts, and consequently comparing the first part with the second part. In two of the six subjects, these differences turned out to coincide with a sudden jump; the other four showed more moderate effects. In sum, the language development of all children showed considerable intra-individual variability. Recently, the study of Fenson et al. (2000) addresses variability (both between and within individuals) in the MacArthur Communicative Development Inventories (CDIs). The CDIs were criticized by Feldman et al. (2000) as having too little stability and insufficient ability to predict a possible language delay. Critique would limit the utility of this parent report instrument for the study of language development. Fenson, however, offers the possibility that the finding is real, and that individual differences in language ability are quite unstable in this age range. He states: "Language skills may simply not be sufficiently developed at age 1 to make accurate assessments" (p. 325) and "[ . . . ] the CDI is simply reflecting the non-linear character of development" (p. 326).

In summary, although the literature on language development has so far largely neglected the issue of variability, there are solid indications that variability is prominently present and may bear theoretical and empirical importance.

### 1.5. Purpose of the Article

Starting from the idea that variability is an undeservedly neglected and meaningful phenomenon, this article aims at presenting several new techniques for describing variability in developmental data. These techniques will be illustrated by applying them to data from the field of early language development. What these techniques have in common is that they focus on variability in individual trajectories. It is important to note we are convinced that this individual level is the starting point for analyzing patterns of variability. After the presentation of the techniques in an application to individual language trajectories, we will also indicate how they can be applied to cross-sectional data.

## 2. A CASE STUDY OF VARIABILITY [IN] CHILD LANGUAGE

### 2.1. Time-Serial Data of Language Development

Language development provides a good starting point for illustrating the techniques that will be introduced in the remainder of this paper. As we stated before, there are strong indications that language development is characterized by large instabilities. From a dynamic systems view, language development is especially relevant because of its dynamic interplay between the various linguistic elements and the non-linguistic domain. Moreover, the domain of language development shows several practical advantages for the study of variability. First of all, because the study of variability requires a relatively large collection of measurement points per individual, the measurement procedure itself must be as non-obtrusive as possible. The collection of spontaneous speech samples easily meets this demand. Secondly, language development provides quantitative data, which can be easily plotted and used for calculation. Thirdly, language is known to develop relatively quickly and shows a rapid increase in its complexity. Thus, meaningful data sets can be collected in relatively short periods of time (about 1–2 years, on average).

In this article, we will show the results of two developmental variables: MLU and spatial prepositions. The reason we present these two variables in particular is that they show very different developmental patterns, and thus illustrate different aspects of variability. While the data of MLU show a regular, continuous trend, the preposition data show a more irregular pathway.

### 2.2. Description of the Study

#### 2.2.1. Subjects

One subject (Heleen, a girl) was followed from age 1;6 to age 2;6. In the beginning of the study, Heleen was in the one-word stage. At the end of the observation period her language showed various characteristics of the differentiation stage (see for characteristics of the Dutch differentiation stage, Frijn & de Haan, 1994). Heleen was the first-born (and, during the observation period, only) child of middle class parents. The family lives in a suburban neighborhood in an average-size city in the North of The Netherlands. Heleen was raised in a monolingual Dutch environment. The family does not speak any apparent dialect. Heleen's general cognitive development was tested with the Bayley Developmental Scales 2/30 (Van der Meulen & Smrkovsky, 1983) a few months before her second birthday. She scored within the normal range (OI = 100).

### 2.2.2. The Measurements

The study is based upon videotaped observations of spontaneous speech in a naturalistic environment (the child's home). The child and parent were free to follow their normal daily routine. There were a few practical restrictions given to the parents' activities (such as not watching the television, and not having extensive phone conversations). In addition to the child, one of the parents and the observer were present during the observations. Observations took 60 min each. The camera was positioned in a corner of the living room, overviewing much of the living room space. There was a warming-up time of 5 min. In practice, the child hardly noticed the camera and did not behave differently with or without the camera. All child language and all child-directed adult language were transcribed according to Childes conventions (MacWhinney, 1991).

### 2.2.3. The Design

The measurement design was scheduled in such a way that variability could be optimally studied. The first level of variability is developmental variability, which in this case takes place over a timespan of a year or more. Questions that can be addressed at this level are for instance: what is the general shape of the development process, is it continuous or discontinuous, is it rapid or is it slow? Secondly, the measurement design was set up to also include short-term variability. At this level, we ask ourselves how capricious the developmental variables are within relatively small intervals. How large are the fluctuations in, for instance, a week? We will call this time scale day-to-day variability. At a still smaller time scale, we can study within-session variability, for instance by comparing the first half-hour of an observation with the second. For the record, we would like to point out once more that the present article is aimed at describing and illustrating a number of techniques for representing variability and does not intend to answer the previous questions.

It is important to incorporate all these time scales in our analyses, because it is highly likely that variability may be different on each time scale. For instance, a developmental variable may be slowly oscillating while gradually growing, while another variable may increase discontinuously with sharp day-to-day fluctuations. It is also conceivable that the kinds of differences in variability patterns, as described above, take place within the same variable, for different periods in time. A variable may initially show slow oscillations, but when approaching a developmental transition grow to be very unpredictable and capricious. Although these possibilities are speculative, the point is that we wanted the design to be able to display these kinds of differences.

In order to capture long-term change, the longitudinal study covered the period of a whole year. The general format of the design is based on the common 2-weekly measurement design from the Childes-database samples (e.g., the Groningen Dutch Corpus). This measurement frequency is considered adequate to study developmental changes. In order to study day-to-day variability, we alternated the 2-weekly observations with six intensive observation periods. Each intensive observation period consists of six measurements in two consecutive weeks (three measurements in each week). The intensive periods were equally divided over the total observation period of a year. In total, we collected 55 samples. There was only one missing value (August 5, a 2-weekly observation).

Each observation lasted about 60 min, which is relatively long. A commonly used observation length in language acquisition studies is the unit of 100 utterances. Brown (1973), for instance, suggested calculating Mean Length of Utterance on the first 100 utterances. The period of 60 min consists of at least 200 utterances each, which means that there is enough room to study intra-observation variability, the smallest unit of variability.

### 2.3. Variables Under Study

#### 2.3.1. Mean Length of Utterance

Mean Length of Utterance in words (MLU-w) was calculated by dividing the number of words in the total sample by the total number of utterances in the samples. Uninterpretable utterances, direct imitations, and yes/no-answers, songs and imitation games were excluded. MLU-w is not the same as Brown's original MLU in morphemes (MLU-m), but research has shown that the two measures are highly correlated in normally developing children (e.g., Arlman-Rupp, van Niekerk de Haan, & van de Sandt-Koenderman, 1976; Hickey, 1991; Thordardottir & Weismer, 1998). Because MLU-w is much simpler (both theoretically and in practice) MLU-w is considered the preferred measure of the two (Thordardottir & Weismer, 1998). In a pilot study, we also found a strong similarity between MLU-m and MLU-w, MLU-m being only a bit higher than MLU-w. Results in terms of variability did not differ significantly (van Dijk & van Geert, 1999).

### 2.3.2. Spatial Prepositions

All prepositions that belong to the set of spatial prepositions were selected, even if the context was not spatial. This was done with LEGro (Language-analysis Excel add-in Groningen, van Geert, 2000), an Excel-macro that can select utterances with different kinds of criteria. We selected utterances with spatial prepositions. These selections were used for quantitative and qualitative analysis. First, we counted the total frequency of prepositions that were uttered in a particular spatial context. This means that if the context showed that the child referred to an object in a spatial relationship to another object, that preposition was included. We also included contexts that referred to spatial actions that had just occurred, or that still had to happen. So for instance, if a child said "in chair" in the context of "I want to sit in my chair/mommy please put me in my chair?" the preposition was also included, the same for "ball under" in the context of "the ball is under the table." We counted all different spatial contexts. For instance if a child said "in chair" and "doll in bed," these were counted as two different spatial contexts. However, because we were interested in the child's ability to label spatial situations, we excluded repetitions. For instance, if a child repeatedly said "in chair, in chair," while the mother did not respond, this was counted as only one spatial preposition-in-context.

It might be argued that the variability we will eventually observe is based on the actual use of spatial prepositions and that this use is highly dependent on (linguistic and non-linguistic) context. Some contexts might be better suited to evoke spatial prepositions than others. Variability in the data therefore not only reflects the possible instability of the developing syntactical system, but also many situational factors. We agree that not all variability is a direct reflection of development, more precisely, of the processes of stabilization and destabilization that development might, among others, consist of. On the other hand, we must consider that there exists a mutual interaction between the developing infant and the spatial context. First of all, the behavioral repertoire of children of this age is filled with spatial activities. They climb on things, build with blocks, drive with cars around other objects, put dolls in beds and in chairs, etc. All these activities are in principle suited to evoke spatial prepositions and the child is an active agent in the selection and constitution of activities and topics. Thus, the variability is the result of this mutual relation between the developing child and the context. The child is not only dependent on and influenced by the linguistic and non-linguistic context, but also selects it and contributes to it. Therefore, we must not conceive of the development of prepositions as the development from one stable state (of no preposition use) to another stable state, namely that of having acquired prepositions and using them at a constant level of production. Instead, we must consider the fact that the end-state of development is not a "stable" category, but a category that is "dynamically stable" in the sense that the produced prepositions still show a considerably variable range dependent on situational factors. This range (of variability) of fully acquired preposition use should, however, be smaller than the range of preposition use in young children who are still acquiring this linguistic category. We have indications that this is indeed the case: children appear to be considerably more variable in their use of spatial prepositions than adults.[1] This indicates that at least part of the variability we wish to describe in this article is developmentally determined.

## 3. HOW CAN WE DESCRIBE VARIABILITY IN LONGITUDINAL DATA?

### 3.1. Focus on Variability in Developmental Data

The question of whether intra-individual variability exists is not a subject of discussion in developmental psychology. In fact, variability is a well-known "problem" for many researchers. It is no coincidence, therefore, that there exists a broad spectrum of techniques to eliminate fluctuations in longitudinal data. We have already referred to them under the term smoothing techniques. There are, however, far less common techniques that allow us to specify and visualize variability in time-serial data, with a limited number of measurements.

The reason smoothing techniques are so well developed and commonly accepted, is that variability is often considered to represent error. This opinion is so widely spread that it is not surprising that many developmental psychologists are only interested in revealing the "general developmental pathway," whatever that means. When analyzing a general trend, fluctuations are often considered to be inconvenient noise. In addition, developmental psychologists tend to use a rather limited set of idealized trend models (basically linear, quadratic and exponential growth models). By so doing, they reduce the information from the data even further. However, even if they acknowledge the possibility of meaningful variability, researchers will still be interested in describing a general developmental trend. They will still ask questions such as whether a developmental process is continuous or discontinuous, and whether there are developmental transitions. What techniques can be used to analyze both the general trend and take variability into account? In this article we will present several of these techniques that are essentially descriptive in nature and can be used with many kinds of individual time-serial developmental data.

### 3.2. Qualitative and Quantitative Variability

As we mentioned before, there is an important difference between (one-dimensional) quantitative and (multi-dimensional) qualitative variability. In the case of quantitative variability, each measurement consists of a level on a single dimension. This can be a frequency count, for instance the number of function words in an observation, but it can also be a number that expresses the level of some kind of psychometric variable, such as IQ. Variability in quantitative data shows itself in a fluctuating level of the variable at issue. This sort of data is typically obtained in the field of early infant emotions (for instance the percentage of crying time in De Weerth et al., 1999, see Fig. 6.1A), and language development (for instance the Mean Length of Utterance in Chabon et al., 1982). Fluctuating levels of this nature can easily be plotted in a line graph, such as Fig. 6.1A.

In the case of qualitative variability however, each measurement consists of a set of behaviors, which have a specific occurrence each. For example, a child uses one strategy A in 10% of all occasions, a second strategy B another 10%, while he or she predominantly uses strategy C (80% of all occasions; see also Siegler, 1996, 1997 for a similar model, applied to cognitive strategies). For instance the first measurement consists of the strategies A, B and C, the second of strategies A, D and E, and a third of B, E, F, and G. The most important difference is simply that this qualitative variability concerns additional dimensions. Not only are there differences in the level of the measured variables, but also completely new variables can be introduced. Variables can disappear, often to reappear later on. Note that this sort of variability is often studied in the field of motor development (for instance the different types of coordination between kicks in the development of supine kicking in Thelen, 1985 and the use of different muscle groups in the development of postural control, Hadders-Algra, Brogren, &

FIGURE 6.1    (A) Example of one-dimensional quantitative variability: Crying duration in percentage of observed time of one infant (infant S) (*Source:* De Weerth, 1998). (B) Example of multi-dimensional variability: Infant response patterns (labels a, b, c, d, e, and g given for present illustration) during Fw-translations of one infant (infant I) during postural response sitting tasks (*Source:* Hadders-Algra et al., 1996)

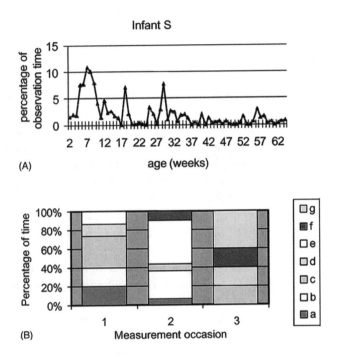

Forssberg, 1996, see Fig. 6.1B). These differences in measurements can easily be expressed in a stacked bar graph, such as Fig. 6.1B.

Most of the techniques we are going to present in the remainder of this article, are particularly suited for one-dimensional quantitative data. However, it is important to know that it is possible to transform qualitative data into a quantitative format. At this point in time, there is no measure that expresses all dimensions of qualitative variability into one single number. However, there are some options for further analysis. For instance, one can study each dimension separately, by taking the occurrence of the variable per measurement occasion. Additionally, the total number of behavior classes (for instance strategies) can be counted, or the total number of new classes.

### 3.3. Raw Data and Smoothing Techniques

#### 3.3.1. Mean Length of Utterance

As our first example, we will focus on the growth of Heleen's Mean Length of Utterance. The simplest, and commonly used, way to present the data on MLU, or any type of developmental data for that matter, is by putting the data in a simple XY-diagram, the X-axis showing the date of measurement, the Y-axis showing MLU (Fig. 6.2). Some measurements are closer together (intensive periods) than other measurements (2-weekly measurement rate).

The graph shows two striking facts. The first is the existence of a general trend, MLU growing from a little over 1 (one-word stage) to almost 3 (differentiation stage). Second, visual inspection clearly shows large fluctuations between measurement days. Especially the sixth intensive period seems to show dramatic differences within only a couple of days. Keeping Brown's initial MLU-stages in mind, Heleen seems to fit in three different MLU-stages within the timeframe of no more than 10 days. This can at least be called remarkable. It also confirms the results of another study on variability in early language development (van Dijk, De Goede, Ruhland, & van Geert, 2000), where both subjects' MLU levels fell into three distinct MLU-stages within a period of several weeks.

In Fig. 6.2 we also used a commonly known technique to show the developmental trend in the data: we plotted a trendline (using a polynomial of the second degree). As can be seen in the graph, this trendline completely smoothes (as it is supposed to do) all the fluctuations in the curve, which are especially large at the end of the curve. This already shows that using a smoothing technique will indeed lead to loss of information—information that may be valuable. Obviously in the case of MLU we are not dealing with something minor: the variability we eliminate by using a smoothing technique is indeed considerable.

Researchers who use these smoothing techniques, probably consider the variability as relatively uninteresting in itself, for instance because it is seen as a form of error fluctuation. The assumption behind this approach is that of an underlying, true level that can be approached by averaging over the fluctuations. The most common technique for doing this is by using moving averages. The fluctuating levels over a pre-specified time window, e.g., the period of 1 month, are used to specify the fluctuating level's central tendency. This central tendency is supposed to contain more reliable and meaningful information than each of the separate observations, respectively. Another technique consists of polynomial regression models. They make

FIGURE 6.2    Raw data of Heleen's MLU, including a linear trendline

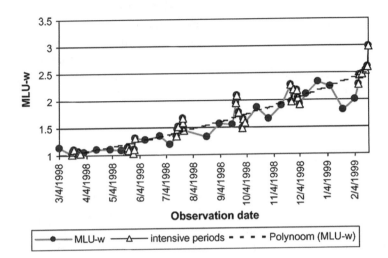

an estimation of a trendline based on a function of time. The trendline that shows the smallest average (squared) distance is considered the best representation of the developmental trend present. Thus, by averaging over, for instance, six observations in an intensive period, we try to estimate a central MLU level that we think characteristic of the period at issue. Regression models over time have yet another function, in addition to representing a supposed true central score. This other function is that they are very well suited for representing a direction, i.e., a motion vector. This can be seen as the simplest possible general trend of a range of score levels over time, in a way similar to a meteorologist's representation of the direction of the wind by a single arrow.

We noted earlier that developmental psychologists tend to confine themselves to an unnecessarily small set of smoothed trends. The statistical literature contains far more sophisticated smoothing models, which follow the actual rise and fall of the data as faithfully as one wishes. Examples are spline models, but also local polynomial regression models or loess smoothers that follow any non-linear trend in the data (Simonoff, 1996). The point is, however, that the smoothing model we opt for implicitly expresses our view on what we consider essential or important in the data and what information can be safely disregarded. The first kind of data to usually fall victim to our smoothing activities is the data about variability.

Heleen's fluctuations between an MLU of 1.6 and 3 can be summarized by presenting an average, say 2.3. The question is: to what extent do we reliably characterize Heleen's language development at the period at issue, by specifying that the average is 2.3? We do not claim that this average score does not bear any information in itself. We believe, however, that the particular range of scores can be highly informative of a child's level of language development. We will get back to this question further on, where we will show how the score range can be used to analyze the developmental data at issue.

### 3.3.2. Spatial Prepositions

Let us now turn to the data of Heleen's spatial prepositions. These data show a very different picture than the MLU data. The data points in Fig. 6.3, a simple XY-diagram, represent the total frequency of the prepositions per session, counted as the number of distinct spatial situations.

Based on the mere visual inspection of the data, it seems that the data can be cut into two clearly distinct periods. The first part of the data (up to observation number 38, November 12) shows a relatively stable, low frequency occurrence of prepositions. However, in the second part of the trajectory, we see a steep increase of prepositions. In this second part of the graph, large fluctuations immediately catch the eye. For instance note observation number 49 (February 4), where the frequency of prepositions is suddenly very low, and preceding and following measurement points show much higher numbers of prepositions.

When fitting a trendline to the data, using a second-degree polynomial of time, we obtain a continuous curve, with a moderate steepness. This also demonstrates the fact that the use of a standard smoothing technique indeed gives a completely different summary of the data than visual inspection of the actual data. While visual inspection points in the direction of two distinctive stages, the smoothing technique covers this fact up completely. Note that if we had used a less common smoother, namely a loess or weighted local regression smoother (Simonoff, 1996), the resulting smoothed curve would have displayed the stepwise increase in the data considerably more faithfully, thus supporting the suggestion of two distinct stages. The question of whether we indeed deal with two clearly distinctive parts of the developmental trajectory is in our opinion very important. Later on in this article, we will ask ourselves the question whether the two-stage pattern we see can also be justified by further statistical analysis.

**FIGURE 6.3    Raw data of Heleen's spatial prepositions, including a linear trendline**

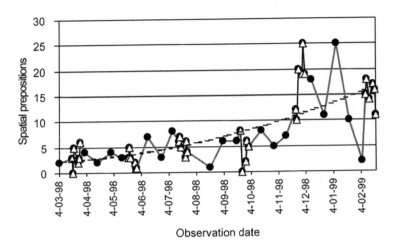

### 3.3.3. Variability as a Developing Range

As we showed in the preceding part, standard smoothing techniques eliminate much information from the actual data. The more current view that embraces variability asks for different techniques that visualize the essence of a developmental trajectory. In this view, the fact that Heleen's MLU shows fluctuations between three different MLU-stages is seen as highly informative of her present level of language acquisition. It is clear that she is capable of producing utterances that are of considerably higher relative complexity than the utterances she produced a few months earlier. However, although she is capable of doing so, it is not yet her habitual level of language production: there are days at which her level does not significantly exceed that of a few months earlier. In addition, during this period Heleen's MLU levels occupy almost any intermediary position between these two extremes. Although this observation seems trivial, it is not so in light of the fact that children sometimes oscillate between two different developmental states with no apparent states in between. For instance, in the study of van der Maas and Molenaar (1992) (where children were administered Piagetian conservation tasks) large variability in strategy use was found around the transition from the non-conserver stage to the conserver stage. At this point in time conservation and non-conservation strategies exist at the same time. Goldin-Meadow et al. (1993) found a similar situation in which two stages are simultaneously present in the system. They found that the shift from one (mathematical) strategy to a second, more advanced one, is characterized by the simultaneous presence of different strategies in different expressive modes (e.g., verbal and gestural). A final example of the simultaneity of distinct levels of problem solving is Siegler's model of overlapping waves in strategy use. Strategies at distinct levels of complexity are used in an alternating way. Learning and development amount to a change in the relative frequencies with which strategies are used, eventually resulting in the disappearance of less mature strategies (Rittle-Johnson & Siegler, 1999; Siegler, 1996, 1997).

In Heleen's MLU data, the phenomenon of interest is the broad range of Heleen's MLU levels, with the highest levels about twice as high as the lowest ones. One of the questions we could ask ourselves is whether or not this range is a developmental phenomenon in its own right. For instance, does the relative size of the range (let us say, the width in comparison to the central or average position) remain more or less stable across development? If this is so, the relative range itself is not specifically informative from a developmental viewpoint. However, if the range itself becomes either narrower or broader depending on various kinds of developmental phenomena or stages, the study of its properties becomes a worthwhile endeavor. We have seen that techniques for averaging or otherwise smoothing fluctuating data are readily available (moving averages, polynomials with time as a dependent variable, etc.). But what techniques do we have if we want to specify information that pertains to fluctuation and variability, as suggested by this new approach?

### 3.4. Showing Variability in a Graph

#### 3.4.1. Moving Minimums, Maximums and Averages

An elegant alternative technique, in which we can study the developmental trend, but that nevertheless also displays variability around a general trend is what we have called the moving min–max graph. This technique shows the data using the bandwidth of observed scores. Instead of displaying measurement points as simple dots, the moving min–max graph presents a score range for each measurement occasion. Instead of a single line graph, the data are presented in a bandwidth of scores. This method uses a moving window, a timeframe that moves up one position (measurement occasion) each time (the size of the window, e.g., five consecutive data points, 1 month, etc. is called its period). Each window partly overlaps the preceding windows, using all the same measurement occasions minus the first and plus the next. For instance, for every set of seven consecutive measurements we calculate the maximum and the minimum values. This is done by way of a predetermined moving window, such that we obtain the following series:

$$max(t1 \ldots t7), max(t2 \ldots t8), max(t3 \ldots t9), \text{etc.}$$
$$min(t1 \ldots t7), min(t2 \ldots t8), min(t3 \ldots t9), \text{etc.}$$

Technically these values are very easy to plot. Any commercially available spreadsheet program offers functions such as max and min that can easily be computed over moving data windows. Once the moving minimums and maximums are plotted, one can visually inspect whether they too show considerable fluctuations over time. The question one should ask is whether these fluctuations are developmentally meaningful or not. The fluctuations should again be contrasted with the eventual long-term changes in the minimums and maximums.

In addition to plotting maximums and minimums, one can also plot some form of central score. One possibility is to plot the median, the value that has a similar number of values above and below it. Another possibility, which combines these techniques with smoothing approaches, is to compute a moving average corresponding with the moving minimums and maximums data. Fig. 6.4A shows the moving minimums, maximums and averages of Heleen's MLUs, with a moving window of period 5.

The moving max–min method can be used to specify a value, for instance a child's test score, with respect to upper and lower boundaries of a time window chosen in advance. As a reasonable rule-of-thumb, one could take windows of a size of about one-tenth of the entire data set, but in principle no less than five data points. In the present study an irregular measurement design was used, with 2-weekly measurements alternated with intensive periods. This design results in windows that are very different from each other in terms of time. Five consecutive measurement points can cover a period of only 10 days (during the intensive measurement periods) but also 10 weeks (between the intensive periods). Therefore it is better not to use an absolute number of measurement points, but to choose a moving window on the basis of time. For instance, Fig. 6.4B uses a moving window of 18 days. Because of the differing number of days between measurement points (recall the irregular measurement design) the number of measurement points per window can vary.

Looking at Fig. 6.4B, it is possible to compare the width of the band with the general developmental trend. In the MLU case (Fig. 6.4) there is no obvious widening or narrowing in the range, but instead we see a general increase in bandwidth, with several mild oscillations. However, it is not clear that these oscillations are meaningful because they seem to coincide with the intensive periods. The fact that the intensive periods have more measurement points in the moving time window, might very well explain the mild fluctuations in the bandwidth. During the intensive periods, more observations are carried out and this increases the probability of hitting upon an "extreme" value, which is conserved across the length of the moving window.

It is obvious from the figure that MLU shows a general increase in its level in addition to a generally increasing bandwidth. When interpreting this observation, it is important to take notice of the increasing mean in the timeframe. It is a well-known fact that variability is related to the general mean. For instance, a data series with a mean of 100, is expected to have a larger range (for instance expressed in terms of standard deviation [SD]) than a data series with a mean of 10. Therefore it is to be expected that variability in the data increases solely on the basis of the increasing mean MLU.

Earlier, we stated that the range might be an important developmental phenomenon. When the range itself becomes narrower or broader depending on various kinds of developmental phenomena or stages, the range is indeed a developmental phenomenon in its own right. In the case of MLU we do not see any obvious widening or narrowing, we predominantly see a general widening with the growth of MLU. However we do not know enough about the relation between the increasing trend and the increasing bandwidth. Is variability accruing more quickly than the MLU trend, or is the slope of the MLU trend actually steeper than that of variability? If the latter were the case, variability would in fact decline if we were to correct for this growing mean. The graphs we showed so far, however, make one wonder how MLU behaves later on in development. Does the bandwidth decrease again at some point in time? If variability is indeed a developmental phenomenon, we do expect exactly that to happen. In the light of our remarks about the dynamically stable state of adult prepositions, it should be noted that we do not expect a disappearing bandwidth. Although we expect that adults show a significantly smaller bandwidth than developing children, their output is also variable to some degree.

**FIGURE 6.4   (A)** Application of the moving min–max methods to Heleen's MLU-w (5 positions). **(B)** Moving min–max graph of Heleen's MLU-w (timeframe 18 days, last window 15 days)

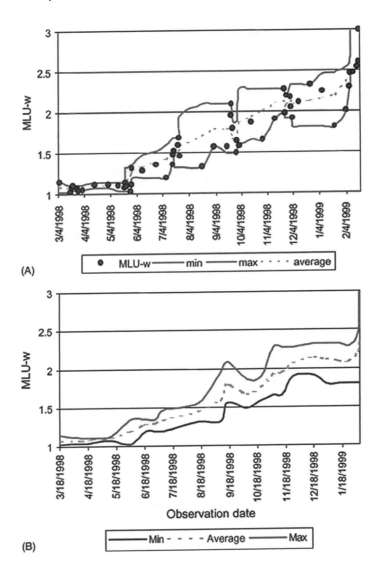

(A)

(B)

**FIGURE 6.5**  Moving min–max graph of Heleen's spatial prepositions (time window of 18 days, last window 15 days)

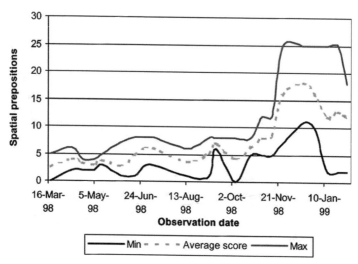

Fig. 6.5 shows the spatial preposition data in a moving min–max graph. Here, we see a completely different picture from what we saw with MLU. While MLU showed a general increasing bandwidth, with slow oscillations, prepositions show a moderate bandwidth in the beginning of the trajectory until observation 38. After this point, we first see a slight general increase, followed by a great widening of the range. This graph also suggests that something "different" occurs after observation number 38, which is probably a developmental transition in spatial prepositions.

### 3.4.2. Altitude Lines

The moving min–max graph provides a general overview of the moving range along the trajectory. As intended, this technique is highly sensitive to so-called extreme values. For a more in-depth study of the distribution of the values in the range, one might consider the following extension of the use of moving minimums and maximums. This method incorporates also intermediate positions in a so-called "altitude line graph." In that case, we do not only plot the minimum and maximum values in the moving window, but also the second highest, third highest value, etc. We then connect

**FIGURE 6.6    Application of the altitude lines method to Heleen's spatial prepositions (window of 5 positions)**

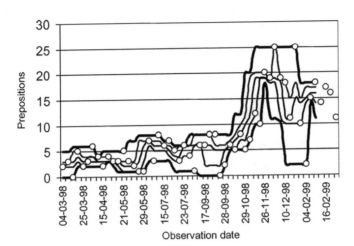

the corresponding data points by a line, comparable with altitude lines on a geographical relief map.

For instance, consider a piece of Heleen's data set of spatial prepositions (observations 22–27) with the values 7, 5, 3, 6, 4, 1. For the first window, the maximum value is 7, the second highest value is 6, the third highest value is 5, the fourth highest value is 4 and the fifth (or the minimum) is 3. For the second moving window, we get the values of, respectively 6, 5, 4, 3, 1. We can easily draw a graph linking all these (first, respectively second, third, etc.) positions with each other.

To give an illustration of these techniques we plotted Fig. 6.6 to show the altitude lines of the spatial preposition data of Heleen. The dots in this graph represent the actual data points, the outer lines are the moving minimums and maximums, and the intermediate lines are the intermediary positions.

In principle, these altitude lines can be interpreted in the same way as geographical lines representing the altitude and steepness of a physical relief. Our altitude lines, however, refer to the properties of the distribution of time-serial values. For instance, if they are concentrated either on the top or on the lower part of the range, they refer to a skewed distribution. Note that we can replace the actual data points by a polynomial approximation (e.g., in a linear regression model) or, more preferably, by a more flexible smoother such as a loess smoother. The polynomial or loess replacement results in a smoother and more easily interpretable representation of the longitudinal distribution of the data. Its disadvantage is that it conceals eventual sudden changes that may be indicative of discontinuities.

If the moving windows contain a sufficient number of data points, one may also plot the moving percentile scores, e.g., of the 90th, 10th and 50th percentiles. All these techniques serve to specify changes in the upper and lower boundaries of the scores and thus show the size of the range, in addition to the distribution of the actual data points over the range.

### 3.4.3. The Progmax–Regmin Method for Specifying a Range

Assuming that a developmental process in general amounts to an overall increase in some phenomenon or variable of interest, we should take high values or levels that occur in the beginning of the process as particularly informative, simply because they are less expected to occur at an earlier stage than later on. Thus, if a high level occurs at some early point in time, high levels that occur later but that are not as high as the early one should not replace it in our estimation of the variable's range or bandwidth. By the same token, low levels that occur at a later stage or point in time are particularly informative because they are less expected than higher values. They should not be concealed by low levels that occur at an earlier time and that are higher than the later one, if any such levels occur, of course. A simple way to implement this idea with longitudinal data points goes as follows. We specify a window with a period of 5, for instance, from the first data point on and compute the maximum value for that window. We then increase the window with one data point at a time, keeping its starting point (which is also the first point of our data series) constant and compute the maximum value of the extending window period. Similarly, we define a window, again with period 5, for instance, starting from the last point of our series and moving backwards. We compute the minimum value of that window and extend the window by one data point at the time, keeping the last point constant, which is also the last point of our data series. By doing so, we define the data series' progressive maximum and regressive minimum. The resulting line that circumscribes the collection of data points is closely related to the mathematical concept of an envelope or a so-called convex hull (see Fig. 6.7A and B). Note that this representation of the developmental range can again easily be achieved by means of any standard spreadsheet program.

FIGURE 6.7    (A, B) Application of the ordinary min–max method (window of 5 positions) (top) and the progmax–regmin method (bottom) to Heleen's spatial prepositions

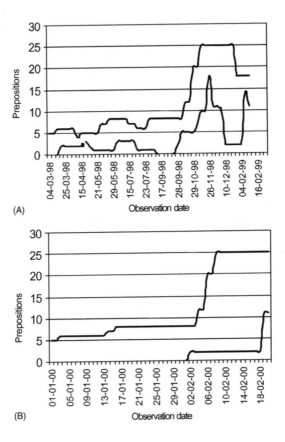

(A)

(B)

Fig. 6.7A and B shows that both max–min methods in fact convey different kinds of information about or present a different perspective on a longitudinal data series. The prog(ressive)reg(ressive) method shows the range specified across the whole time period (up to the time point of interest, e.g., at time $t_i$ it shows the range from the first point $t_0$ to that of time $t_i$, at time $t_j$ it shows the range from $t_0$ to $t_j$, and so forth), whereas the ordinary max–min method shows ranges defined over considerably smaller time windows. The difference between the methods allows us to look for changes in the range's bandwidth, for instance in the form of temporary regressions, that show themselves as gaps between the ranges specified by the progreg and the ordinary windows method, respectively.

Concluding, in the previous sections we showed several techniques that specify and depict the range in which the developmental scores occur. These techniques can be used to obtain a first impression of the general trend of the developmental curve and the way variability is related to this general trend. They also give us an indication of where we can look for meaningful changes in variability. Before proceeding to a discussion of standard measures of variability, we will first briefly discuss the application of the preceding techniques to cross-sectional data.

### 3.4.4. An Application to Cross-Sectional Data

The techniques introduced so far do not only apply to individual trajectories or time series, collected with a single child. Also cross-sectional data can be described in terms of variability and changing ranges. The major difference is that the variability does not apply to fluctuations within a child but to differences between children of similar and different ages. By way of example, we present data from an ongoing study on the development of children's Theory-of-Mind (Blijd-Hoogewys et al., 2003). Theory-of-Mind refers to the child's ability to understand thoughts, beliefs, emotions, desires and so forth of other people and the relations between these mental phenomena and people's behavior. Theory-of-Mind is measured by means of a test, the Theory-of-Mind Story Books, which contains six parallel versions (suited for longitudinal research) with each 77 dichotomous items. The present results are based on a cross-sectional study of 220 children equally divided over both sexes, ranging from 34 to 98 months. It is customary practice to present such data by first averaging the scores for age groups, the 3-year-olds, the 4-year-olds, and so forth, and then showing the increase of Theory-of-Mind understanding as the line through those averages. By so doing, interesting information about the relationship between inter-individual differences in children of approximately the same age and between children of different ages is lost. Instead, we argue for a representation of the data on the basis of the children's real ages. We can then apply the methods described earlier—the moving minmax, the progmax–regmin and the altitude lines—to the cross-sectional data set. These methods show the quantitative change in Theory-of-Mind understanding in the form of a variable range (see Fig. 6.8 for various possibilities).

**FIGURE 6.8**  (A–C) An application of the min–max, progmax–regmin, and altitude line methods to cross-sectional data on the development of Theory-of-Mind. (C) Specifies altitude lines for the 0, 25th, 50th, 75th, and 100th percentile

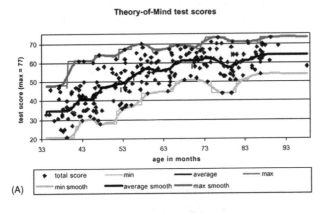

(A)

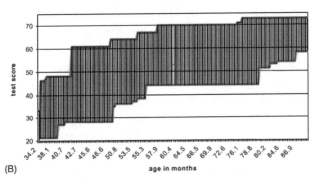

(B)

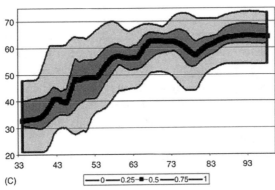

(C)

### 3.5. Standard Measures of Variability and Their Methodological Problems

In addition to showing variability in graphs, we would also like to express variability in some sort of standard measure, because it can be used for the comparison of variability in different samples. There are two common measures to describe variability in a sample: the SD and the coefficient of variation (CV). However, both have their own statistical problems when comparing variability in samples with different characteristics. The SD shows problems because of its sensitivity to the mean, and the CV shows problems with variables that have very low values. Data sets that begin with low values and show increasing means are called heteroscedastic (Kmenta, 1990). Heteroscedasticity, especially in the form of low initial values, increasing means and increasing variances, is likely to occur in developmental data.

Probably the best-known measure of variability is the SD. The SD is defined as the square root of the variance, which is in turn the average of the squared deviations from the mean. We can compute a SD for every meaningful data unit greater than one, and for every time unit. However, a problem arises if we want to compare SDs of different data sets. The reason for this is that the SD is very sensitive to the mean in a sample. We discussed this issue before when we showed the technique of moving minimums and maximums. The issue is that a higher mean is usually associated with a higher SD. Consequently, it is not possible to make a direct comparison between SDs of samples without taking the mean into account. In order to solve this issue, the CV is often used. The CV is defined as the standard deviation of a sample divided by its mean. We now have a measure that specifies the amount of SD in a standard unit of the mean, a measure that may indeed be helpful when comparing variability in different samples.

### 3.5.1. Mean Length of Utterance

One of the goals of our present study is to analyze variability in the developmental pathway. We ask ourselves if the amount of variability changes during the course of development. We want to investigate, for instance, if variability suddenly increases at some point in time. The study was also set up to analyze variability on different time scales. For the sake of illustration, we show here the results of the day-to-day measurements, and included only measurements from the intensive periods.

Table 6.1 shows the SDs, means and CVs of Heleen's MLU, for each of the six intensive periods. When we discussed the moving min–max graph, we

TABLE 6.1    General measures of variability in time scale two:
Day-to-day variability in MLU-w

|      | Period 1 | Period 2 | Period 3 | Period 4 | Period 5 | Period 6 |
|------|----------|----------|----------|----------|----------|----------|
| SD   | 0.03     | 0.10     | 0.12     | 0.23     | 0.14     | 0.24     |
| M    | 1.06     | 1.13     | 1.51     | 1.76     | 2.09     | 2.55     |
| CV   | 0.03     | 0.09     | 0.08     | 0.013    | 0.07     | 0.09     |

asked ourselves whether variability increases with time for MLU. Looking at the pattern of SDs, we would indeed be inclined to conclude this. However, as can be seen in the table, the means also increase with time for almost every consecutive period. Consequently, the CVs show a subtler picture. While, on average, lower values occur in the first part of the set (periods 1–3) and higher values occur in the second part (periods 4–6), there exists no obvious simple increasing trend comparable to that of SDs and means.

Given the small number of values (6) it seems hardly worthwhile trying to fit a regression line to see if the CVs show a statistically increasing trend. A simpler method is to check whether periods 1–3 are on average smaller than periods 4–6. This can be done with an exact permutation test, i.e., a test that computes all the different combinations of six elements into groups of three and compares the averages of those groups (Good, 1999). Since the number of groups that can be formed from six elements taken three by three is only 20, a p-value of 5% must correspond with the biggest difference out of the 20 possibilities. This difference occurs if the smallest values occur in periods 1, 2 and 3 and the larger values occur in periods 4, 5 and 6. It is easy to see that this is not the case (the second smallest CV, 0.07 occurs in period 5). Hence, the averages of periods 1, 2 and 3 and 4, 5 and 6 are not statistically significantly different at the 5% level. An exact permutation test reveals that the difference between the averages is the third smallest out of the 20 possibilities, which corresponds with a p-value of 15%. Further on in this article, we will get back to the possibilities random sampling techniques have to offer.

Concluding, in the case of MLU the SD as a general measure of variability would lead to an overestimation of the variability in the later part of the trajectory. Therefore, the SD is unsuitable for making comparisons between and within samples. So far, the CV seems to be the better candidate for such a goal.

### 3.5.2. Spatial Prepositions

Now we turn to the data of spatial prepositions. Here we asked ourselves the question whether the growth curve shows a shift in growth pattern from measurement point 38 (November 12) onwards. Visual inspection of the XY-graph, and the moving min–max graph certainly points in that direction. In the early part of the trajectory, there seem to be small fluctuations, while the later part shows dramatic peaks and wells. The demarcation point falls on November 12 and lies between the fourth and fifth intensive period. As a consequence, we expect the later two intensive periods to be more variable than the first four.

When looking at Table 6.2 such an effect turns out to be absent. Even stronger, the effect seems to be reversed. The highest CV values are to be seen in the first, second and fourth intensive period, while periods 5 and 6 show moderate values. The p-value of the difference between the averages of periods 1, 2 and 3 and 4, 5 and 6, respectively, calculated with an exact permutation test is .70. This means that the difference is far from significant. It might seem surprising that the CVs do not confirm the pattern we thought we recognized with visual inspection. Is it true that especially the early intensive periods are the most variable ones?

This hardly seems likely. In fact, the effect observed in the data is a good illustration of heteroscedasticity, a statistical problem that is very common if one deals with growth data. Heteroscedasticity is often associated with the presence of very low initial values. Such low values are unstable, because small absolute fluctuations are large in proportion to the values themselves. Consider for instance a variable where the values 1 and 2 succeed each other. These minimal fluctuations (there is no smaller measurement unit possible) lead to a very high CV, for the simple reason that this variable shows a fluctuation of a 100% (i.e., the proportion 1:1). The CV resulting for these data would be the same for a data set in which the values 100 and 200 succeed each other in a similar fashion, which would amount to an oscillation which magnitude is rather unlikely. The reason heteroscedasticity occurs is because in the study of language acquisition (and many other developmental domains), there is by definition an absolute point zero. Also, the unit of measurement reaches its lower limit, for instance with spatial prepositions the minimal unit is one. Smaller units are simply not possible.

Recapitulating, we have seen that the two common measures to describe variability (the standard deviation and the coefficient of variation) have their own statistical problems when comparing variability in samples. While the

TABLE 6.2    General measures of variability in time scale two:
Day-to-day variability in spatial prepositions

|     | Period 1 | Period 2 | Period 3 | Period 4 | Period 5 | Period 6 |
|-----|----------|----------|----------|----------|----------|----------|
| SD  | 2.14     | 1.52     | 1.47     | 3.25     | 5.54     | 2.48     |
| M   | 3.16     | 2.5      | 5.17     | 4.83     | 17.5     | 15.17    |
| CV  | 0.67     | 0.61     | 0.28     | 0.67     | 0.32     | 0.16     |

standard deviation shows problems because of its sensitivity to the mean, the coefficient of variation shows problems with variables with very low values because of heteroscedasticity. These problems are especially serious when analyzing development. In order to observe development, the data sets should combine these two characteristics: they ideally start out with very low values and further show considerable growth. Therefore, both the standard deviation and the coefficient of variation are not suitable as general measures of to analyze variability patterns in developmental trajectories.

### 3.6. The Critical Moment Method

There is another method to establish variability in data, or more precisely, to establish at what point in time variability significantly increases compared to a relatively stable period. This method is developed in the field of motor coordination (e.g., Verheul & Geuze, 1999) and can be applied to developmental research in general. The method is based on the following assumptions. First of all, a system is supposed to be relatively stable over some initial period of time. Second, this period must be followed by a period in which this system becomes "unstable," which results in large variability. The aim of this method is to establish if, and at what exact moment, the system loses its stability. We believe that the data of Heleen's early preposition use meet these assumptions in a satisfactory way. First of all, visual inspection of the developmental trajectory shows that there exists a period in which the system seems relatively stable. Secondly, at some point in time there is a period that shows larger fluctuations. This can very well be compared to a dynamic system that loses its stability. First, we ask ourselves if there is a point in time after which variability critically increases (comparable with the critical frequency which is used in the field of bimanual coordination, Kelso, Scholz, & Schöner, 1986; Verheul & Geuze, 1999). Secondly, we are interested in the pattern in which variability increases and eventually decreases again. Does the system gradually lose its stability or does this happen very suddenly? Does the system regain its stability at some point in time, and to what developmental incidence can this eventually be related?

In the application of this technique, we have to bear in mind again that we are dealing with a variable that shows a considerable increase, i.e., a growth trend. We do not want the general trend to influence the variability measure. In order to eliminate the influence of the general increase, we have to detrend the data, using a trendline. In order to obtain an optimal fit, we used a flexible regression model. With this model a moving linear regression equation was calculated on a moving window of 19 data points. Thus, slopes and intercepts were estimated

for each (moving) window of 19 data points (the result resembles a loess method smoothing, but the moving regression has the advantage that it can easily be implemented in a spreadsheet program, for instance). We proceeded by calculating the residuals of the original data for this regression model. The critical period was determined as follows. First, we calculated a moving standard deviation (using a moving window of five observation points) on these residuals. We took a timeframe that is relatively stable (in our case the first 21 observations), and calculated the 95% reliability interval. Secondly, we tried to establish at what moment the variability in the system increases. We defined this moment as the moment at which the moving SD exceeds the critical value (which is the upper limit of the reliability interval) for at least six consecutive moving SDs.

We applied this technique to the data of Heleen's spatial prepositions, and plotted both the preposition data and the moving SDs on the residuals of these data in Fig. 6.9. In the case of Heleen, the resulting critical value of the spatial prepositions was 3.61, based on 1.96 times the standard deviation of the first 21 measurement points. As can be seen in Fig. 6.9, this value of 3.16 is exceeded only once at measurement point 29 (September 16) and exceeded again at measurement point 37 (October 29). This value is exceeded for the seventh consecutive time only after measurement point 42 (December 1), which means that point of significant increase in variability is located at this date.

With this method, we do not have the problem of heteroscedasticity that we encountered when we used the SDs as a general index of variability. SDs are much less sensitive to these low values than CVs. We do however have the problem of a higher mean being associated with larger variability. The preposition data show mixed results. First, we see a slow, but some-

**FIGURE 6.9**  Application of the critical moment method to Heleen's preposition data

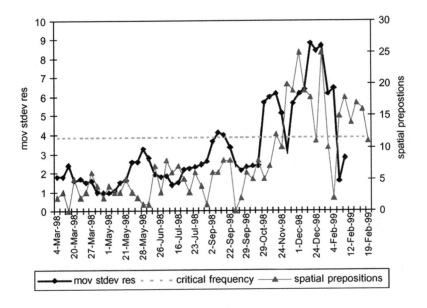

what irregular, increase in the moving CV. We cannot be sure that this is not caused by the increasing mean of the original data. However, we have some indication that the moving SDs decline at the end of the trajectory, while the mean of the original data remains high. Although the decline in our data is not very strong, we suggest that a decline of the moving standard deviation in general can be an important indication of a transition, since such an observation cannot be explained by the external causes such as measurement error. It seems that there has to be some other explanation for this decreasing variability, and this explanation can probably be found in the internal dynamics of the developmental process itself.

### 3.7. The Distribution of Fluctuations

The initial assumptions of the measurement-error-hypothesis suggest another technique to investigate the variability pattern. One of the assumptions is that error, or noise, is supposed to be symmetrically distributed around the central tendency, which represents the best estimation of the true underlying variable. A variability distribution that shows a different pattern does not agree with this assumption. For this reason, the distribution characteristic can give us additional information on the tenability of the error-hypothesis.

When studying the distribution characteristics, there is one property we are especially interested in, namely the skewness. We believe that the skewness can give us information about the degree of consolidation of the acquired developmental variable. When a child begins to discover that he or she can use prepositions to express spatial relations, we expect outliers on the positive side of the distribution. It is highly likely that the child uses this new linguistic category (in this case spatial prepositions) in outbursts, but most of the time this new category is not used and the child simply sticks to his or her usual repertoire (for instance by pointing to a location). This behavior would lead to a positively skewed distribution. In contrast, when the use of spatial prepositions is relatively well-consolidated, we expect the child to use these prepositional utterances most of the time, and only use less sophisticated ways of expressing spatial relations relatively rarely. This well-consolidated state in the acquisition of prepositions would result in a negative skewness.

In dynamic terms, a skewed distribution could possibly be an indication for the existence of bimodality (Alibali & Goldin-Meadow, 1994). Bimodality refers to a situation in which two equilibria exist in a developmental trajectory. In the case of language acquisition, these equilibria represent language rules (or linguistic categories). One equilibrium refers to the old rule and another equilibrium refers to the new rule. Bimodality can be an indication for a developmental transition between the old and the new rule or strategy. A skewed distribution might be indicative of a bimodal equilibrium with considerably different frequencies of occurrence.

What is the distribution of the variability of Heleen's spatial prepositions? In order to eliminate the influence of the general increase, it is important to detrend the data, using a trendline. In order to obtain an optimal fit, we used the flexible regression model we also applied with the critical moment method. We calculated the residuals for this regression line. Consequently, the distribution of these residuals was studied for skewness, using a "moving" skewness factor on a moving window of 13 data points (the choice of the period of the moving window is somewhat arbitrary; we have chosen a period of 13 because that contains enough data to make a reasonable estimation of the skewness possible, without covering too much of our data set and thus concealing changes in the skewness that might occur during the observed trajectory). Note that with this technique we combined the analysis of distribution characteristics with ideas we presented earlier discussing the moving window techniques (e.g., the moving min–max graph). Both the regression equation (slopes and intercepts) and the calculation of the skewness factor are based on so-called moving windows, which move up one position at a time. The result is a flexible symmetry analysis for each part of the developmental trajectory. The values of these moving skewness factors are plotted in a moving skewness graph (see Fig. 6.10).

Evidently, the degree of symmetry is not equal in each part of the developmental trajectory. Instead, an oscillating pattern is observable, with four distinctive parts. The data start out with a near symmetric (only slightly negatively skewed) distribution, which turns into a strong positively skewed distribution from June to September. Then, from September to November, a fairly strong negative skewness is detected, again followed by a part with only moderate positive skewness factor, after November. Note again that error is supposed to be symmetrically distributed around the central tendency, which is supposed to represent the best estimation of the true underlying variable. The oscillating skewness patterns that are found in Heleen's spatial prepositions do not support this symmetry-assumption.

A positive skewness, such as seen in the second part of the moving skewness graph, means that the right tail of the data distribution is longer. There are more outliers on the positive side of the graph. Positive skewness is likely to be associated with a developmental process where the degree of consolidation of a syntactic rule is still low. We expect that later on in the developmental process, this degree of consolidation will increase. This, in turn will lead to a situation in which the new rule will be used most of the time and negative outliers will occur in situations where the old rule is still used. This would lead to a negatively skewed distribution, as is observed in the third part of the moving skewness graph of Heleen's spatial prepositions. We expect that the use of the old rule will finally disappear, which will then lead to a symmetric distribution.

In a standard statistical package, such as SPSS, there is an option to test the normality of a distribution by means of a Kolmogorov–Smirnov test (for studies with n = 50 or more) or a Shapiro-Wilk test (for n = 50 or less). However in studies with a small number of cases per sample, the null-hypothesis of a normal distribution will seldom be rejected. Although it goes well beyond the scope of this article, we would like to point out the possibilities that random sampling techniques have to offer. Bootstrapping techniques can be applied to test the significance of the differences in skewness values of, for instance, the four distinctive periods in Heleen's moving skewness graph. We will elaborate on the possibilities of random sampling techniques further on. Suffice it to say for now that we applied the bootstrap technique to our skewness data and found that the four skewness phases

FIGURE 6.10    Moving skewness graph of Heleen's spatial prepositions

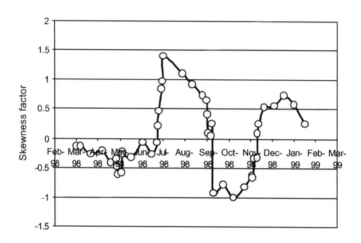

observed in the data correspond with two overlapping skewness distributions with different averages.

### 3.8. Pre-Processing Data for Further Analysis: The Effect of Different Detrending Models

It is important to note that the way the data are detrended in the application of the critical moment method and the moving skewness graph may be essential to the results of this analysis. This may especially be the case if the trendline chosen to detrend the data has a poor fit. For instance, if a simple linear regression is applied to data that show an obviously S-shaped curve, the outcome of the skewness factors can be greatly influenced. We must however, warn against detrending with a too complex model, which eliminates the variability we mean to analyze. The model should only be used to eliminate the effect of trend. As a general rule-of-thumb, we suggest to use the simplest model possible. If the trend looks linear, choose a linear model, if not, choose a simple flexible model, such as our flexible regression model or a loess smoother with a sufficiently long period. The choice of the detrending model is primarily a conceptual matter: one has to decide, on reasonably defendable grounds, what shall be conceived of as the main trend against which the variability will be plotted.

It might however be worthwhile to test the effect of the detrending model on the results. In the case of the critical frequency method for Heleen's prepositions, we applied various detrending models. The results showed that the effect of the model was very small. Although the critical frequency varied somewhat across models, the system lost stability at the same measurement point in all instances. This indicates that the effect found in the analysis is fairly robust. This might however not be the case for other data sets. We also tested the sensitivity of the skewness results by comparing various detrending models. The skewness pattern turns out to be independent on the exact method of detrending, as long as it results in a trend line that follows the general pattern of data sufficiently close. For instance, a qualitatively similar result was obtained when the data were detrended by means of a loess smoother. A completely different way of detrending, differencing, also yielded similar results (differencing means that the residuals are replaced by the difference between a measurement and the preceding measurement, Gottman, 1981).

### 3.9. Random Sampling Methods

Our study of developmental ranges and the variability within those ranges relies, by definition, on extreme values, namely the maxima and minima. If proper care is taken in the language data collection—and imitation games and songs have been removed from the data, for instance—the extremes are as reliable as the more central values. However, in the estimation of a—moving—range, extreme values have a considerably stronger effect on the estimation of the range's boundaries than on the estimation of a central value, such as an average. Take for instance the following imaginary series of observed frequencies: 2, 3, 4, 10, 5, 6, 7. If we calculate the moving maximum for a window of period 4, the maximum is 10 throughout the series of seven measurements. If we compute the moving average with period 4, however, it amounts to 4.7, 5.5, 6.25, 7. This difference should not make us decide to remove the value of 10 from the series as a so-called outlier. An outlier it is, but it has been obtained in a reliable way and thus provides information about the observed child's abilities at that particular moment. In fact, we might have been lucky that we saw the child at a moment where it actually showed a glimpse of a rapidly increasing linguistic capacity. If we had come a day earlier or later, we might have found a frequency of 4 or 5.

### 3.9.1. Bootstrapping as a Technique for Estimating Model Probabilities in Individual Longitudinal Data Sets

Given this possibility, we wish to know to what extent our conclusions, for instance with regard to the average bandwidth of the range, are sensitive to sampling characteristics. In a standard design, we want to know to what extent sampling characteristics prevent us from estimating the correct value of an observed variable for the population from which the sample has been drawn. However, just like in any other comparable case, we have no other information about the "population" of observations than the sample itself. Furthermore, we cannot invoke assumptions about expected distributions, a normal distribution across the population, for instance. First, we usually have no idea of what the distribution of our longitudinally observed data should be. Second, the distribution characteristics (average, standard deviation, skewness, etc.) are not stationary over the observation period, because the variable at issue is rapidly developing. A method that allows us to nevertheless estimate the effect of sampling characteristics on our measurements is the so-called bootstrap method (Chernick, 1999; Efron & Tibshirani, 1993; Good, 1999). The method consists of randomly drawing a large number of subsamples (e.g., 1,000) from our original sample. For each subsample, we compute the test statistic of interest (for instance the average bandwidth of the range of frequencies of spatial prepositions before the "jump"). By comparing the value of the test statistic of the original sample with the distribution of the test statistics from the randomly drawn subsamples, we obtain a fairly good estimation of how subsamples relate to the original sample and thus of how the original sample relates to the population from which it is drawn.

In our design—2-weekly observations interspersed with intensive observation periods—we have a particularly good opportunity for testing the eventual effects of the standard 2-weeks approach on the estimation of the average bandwidth of the observed frequencies of spatial prepositions. For instance, we would like to know to what extent the bandwidth depends on the sampling frequency. Our current data set with its combination of 2-weekly observations and intensive observation periods offers an interesting opportunity to try to answer that question. Our starting assumption is that each of the observations during the intensive periods could have been a potential 2-weekly observation, if all our observations had been scheduled according to the standard 2-weeks interval. We constructed 1,000 randomized observation samples, consisting of all our 2-weekly observations to which we added one observation from each intensive period, randomly drawn from each of those periods. For each randomly drawn sample we computed the average bandwidth of the time period before the jump in the use of spatial prepositions takes place (with observation 38 as the demarcation point) and the average bandwidth of the time after the jump. The band-

**TABLE 6.3   Results of the subsampling procedure**

|  | Average bandwidth | SD | Min | Max | Median |
|---|---|---|---|---|---|
| Subsamples |  |  |  |  |  |
| Substage 1 | 6.69 | 0.62 | 5.48 | 8.69 | 6.62 |
| Substage 2 | 20.05 | 0.5 | 19.67 | 21.17 | 19.89 |
| Data |  |  |  |  |  |
| Substage 1 | 8.03 ($p = 0.015$) |  |  |  |  |
| Substage 2 | 21.17 ($p = 0.115$) |  |  |  |  |

widths are based on windows that cover 58.4 days on average. Table 6.3 summarizes the results of the subsampling procedure.[2]

The table should be read as follows. For the bootstrapped samples, the average bandwidth is 6.69 and 20.05 for the first and second substage, respectively (standard deviations and additional statistics are given in the matrix). The average bandwidth of the original data is 8.03 and 21.17 for the first and second substage, respectively. In our 1,000 bootstrapped samples of the first substage, we found a value equal to or bigger than 8.03 in only 1.5% of the cases. However, the bootstrapped samples of the second substage were equal to or bigger than the empirical bandwidth in 11.5% of the cases. We can conclude, therefore, that the high sampling frequency (as defined by the intensive periods) has led to a significantly bigger bandwidth estimation than the standard sampling frequency of 2 weeks in the case of the first substage, but not in the case of the second substage. It should be noted, however, that also in the case of the second substage, the difference goes in the expected direction (bigger estimated bandwidth if sampling frequencies are higher).

The present subsampling procedure has been carried out for illustrative purposes only and differs from the standard bootstrap technique. A further elaboration of this issue, however, would far extend the scope of the present article.

In summary, bootstrap and resampling methods can be applied to longitudinal data sets of the kind described in the present article to help us understand the effect of sampling characteristics on our estimation of the ranges within which the observed variables vary.

### 3.9.2. Bootstrapping and Generalization of Models over Children

So far, the techniques described applied to individual data trajectories. We have also shown that techniques for visualizing ranges and variability can be as easily applied to cross-sectional data. The problem with intensive individual research is that the number of cases that can be covered in one study is usually quite small (ranging from 1 to a few, e.g., four to five intensively studied children). The question is, how can we generalize our findings to the population (a basic question in social science) given we have only so few cases? Such generalization is possible if every single case is conceived of as a separate study. The generalization problem becomes one of meta-analysis: how can p-values or other test statistics obtained in independent studies, based on their own accidental samples, be combined into an overall p-value or test statistic? In the case of longitudinal studies, the sample is a time series of consecutive measurements of a single child. A simple but effective statistic suitable for meta-analysis is Fisher's combined p-value (Glass, McGaw, & Smith, 1981; Snijders & Bosker, 1999). The technique of p-value combination can be approximated, if it is possible to test individual null-hypotheses by means of bootstrapping (or related permutation techniques). In the preceding paragraph, we have shown that a model of differences in variability over distinct substages can be tested by means of bootstrapping. For each bootstrapped sample of an individual child's data set, we calculate a bootstrap estimation of some statistic of interest (for instance, the aforementioned difference in bandwidths). If we do a bootstrap test for a small number of children, for instance five, we have five series of test statistics based on each child's null-hypothesis. We then randomly draw sets of five test statistics, one from each child, and repeat this a sufficient number of times (e.g., 1,000 times). We can easily compute how many times the average test statistic of the randomly drawn sets of five is equal to or exceeds the average of the five observed test statistics. This number is the combined p-value of our five separate studies, i.e., our five individual children (see for instance Good, 1999).

## 4. SUMMARY AND CONCLUSION

The assumption that (intra-individual) variability in the data is basically an expression of measurement error, is a deeply rooted and often also tacit belief of many developmental psychologists and social science researchers in general. This belief is maintained and even amplified by the use of a standard toolbox of statistical techniques, each of which implicitly supports the error-hypothesis. In addition, developmental theories make little room for variability within individuals as a phenomenon of interest, either as an indicator of development or as cause or condition of change. Against this vicious circle of neglect, we have placed three alternatives. First, we have briefly pointed to an approach to development that conceives of variability as an important phenomenon, namely dynamic systems theory. Second, we have given an overview of studies that have shown that intra-individual variability is an interesting variable in its own right and that it occurs in various forms. Third, and most importantly, we have introduced a number of simple techniques for making variability visible, in order to help researchers explore this interesting source of information.

It is our firm belief that the starting point of developmental studies should be studies of individual trajectories, with as many repeated measurements as possible. Instead of conceptualizing a child's developmental level or developmental state as a hidden true value, concealed by the vagaries of error laden measurement, we invite researchers to look at a child's level as a range, a specific domain of variability, the properties of which change over the course of development. In order to help researchers achieve this goal, we introduced and discussed various techniques.

First, we discussed the most common techniques: visual inspection of raw data (vs. smoothing techniques) and two general variability measures: the standard deviation and the coefficient of variation. We reviewed the complications of these two measures when applying them to developmental (growth) data.

Second, we proposed a range of new techniques that were constructed specifically for the study of patterns of variability. First we presented several methods that show variability in a graph: the moving min–max graph (including the use of altitude or percentile lines), and the progmax–regmin graph. The commonality between these graphs is the representation of the observed score within its score range in a specific time window, for each point in time. These methods are especially useful for obtaining a general impression of the variability pattern (e.g., is it generally increasing or decreasing; are there changes in the bandwidth?) that may be helpful in generating testable hypotheses.

Furthermore, we proposed a technique that is able to detect sudden increases of variability: the critical frequency method. With this technique, we calculated if and when fluctuations become "critically large," and the system loses its stability. We also proposed a technique that is based on a central assumption of measurement-error-hypothesis: namely the symmetric distribution of error. By investigating the moving skewness of the distribution pattern we can test the tenability of this hypothesis in the data. We argued that the direction of the skewness could give information about the degree of consolidation of a new ability (a positively skewed distribution suggests a low degree of consolidation, a negatively skewed distribution a high degree of consolidation). Finally, as traditional statistical techniques offer little in testing variability hypotheses, we suggested the potential benefits of employing random sampling techniques. We have given a example of how sampling techniques can be used to test hypotheses about the pattern of variability.

In line with authors such as Loftus (1996) and Tukey (1977), we believe that psychology in general and developmental psychology in particular will greatly benefit from a more exploratory approach to the data. The approach should be primarily aimed at making the interesting phenomena visible. In developmental psychology, variability is such an interesting phenomenon, although it has long been neglected. If researchers accustom themselves to begin their data analysis by inspecting the patterns of variability within and between individuals, developmental psychology will have a chance to overcome the largely static and in fact non-developmental image that has prevailed in the past decades.

## NOTES

1. A resampling procedure showed that, on average, variability of four infants (followed from age 1;6 to 2;6, among which Heleen [is one]) were larger than that of two adults samples. In all infant cases, samples of six sessions were selected randomly to calculate the CV. For these infants, we only used sessions after the first large increase in preposition use, because of heteroscedasticity (a statistical problem we will discuss later on). While the adults showed CVs of, respectively 0.242 and 0.144, the infants had average CVs of 0.534 (subject Heleen), 0.560 (subject Lisa), 0.459 (subject Jessica) and 0.513 (subject Berend). The resampling procedure based on 2,000 iterations, showed that the probability that these infants acquired the adult CV values of 0.242 and 0.144 and below, were, respectively $<.005$ and $<.005$ (subject Heleen), .068 and .01 (subject Lisa), .04 and .01 (subject Jessica), .01 and $<.005$ (subject Berend). This means that the probability that the adult values come from a distribution similar to that of the infant is in seven out of eight cases below 5% and in 1 case 6.8%. These results indicate that it is highly likely that the adult use of prepositions-in-context shows a lower variability than that of the children.

2. Since the data set contains about twice as much observations as the subsamples, the average bandwidths of the data set were calculated on the basis of windows that were twice as big as those used for the subsamples. Since the average number of days covered by the windows in the subsamples was slightly smaller than that of the data set (with 7%) the average bandwidths of the subsamples were corrected by multiplying the values with 1.07.

## REFERENCES

Alibali, M., & Goldin-Meadow, S. (1994). Gesture–speech mismatch and mechanisms of learning: What the hands reveal about the child's state of mind. *Cognitive Psychology, 25*(4), 468–523.

Arlman-Rupp, A. J. L., Van Niekerk de Haan, D., & Van de Sandt-Koenderman, M. (1976). Brown's early stages: Some evidence from Dutch. *Journal of Child Language, 3*, 267–274.

Bertenthal, B. (1999). Variation and selection in the development of perception and action. In G. Savelsbergh, H. van der Maas, & P. van Geert (Eds.), *Non-linear developmental processes* (Vol. 175, pp. 105–121). Amsterdam, The Netherlands: Royal Netherlands Academy of Arts and Sciences.

Bertenthal, B., & Clifton, R. (1998). Perception and action. In D. Kuhn & R. Siegler (Eds.), *Handbook of child psychology: Cognition perception and language* (Vol. 2, pp. 51–102). New York: Wiley.

Blijd-Hoogewys, E. M. A., Huyghen, A.-M. N., van Geert, P. L. C., Serra, M., Loth, F., & Minderaa, R. B. (2003). *Denken overdacht: De normering van het Theory-of-Mind Takenboek* [Thinking about thoughts: Setting standard norms for the Theory-of-Mind Story Book]. Nederlands Tijdschrift voor de Psychologie *58*(2), 19–33.

Brown, R. (1973). *A first language: The early stages*. London, UK: Allen & Unwin.

Canfield, R. L., Wilken, J., Schmerl, L., & Smith, E. G. (1995). Age-related change and stability of individual differences in infant saccade reaction time. *Infant Behavior and Development, 18*, 351–358.

Chabon, S., Kent-Udolf, L., & Egolf, D. (1982). The temporal reliability of Brown's Mean Length of Utterance (MLU-m) measure with post-stage V children. *Journal of Speech and Hearing Research, 25*, 124–128.

Chernick, M. R. (1999). *Bootstrap methods: A practitioner's guide*. New York: Wiley.

Crockerberg, S. B., & Smith, P. (1982). Antecedents of mother-infant interaction and infant irritability in the first 3 months of life. *Infant Behavior and Development, 5*, 105–119.

Cronbach, L. J. (1960). *The essentials of psychological testing*. New York: Harper & Brothers.

De Weerth, C. (1998). *Emotion-related behaviors in infancy: A longitudinal study of patterns and variability*. Doctoral dissertation, University of Gorningen.

De Weerth, C., van Geert, P., & Hoitink, H. (1999). Intra-individual variability in infant behavior. *Developmental Psychology, 35*(4), 1102–1112.

Dittrichova, J., Paul, K., Tautermannova, M., & Vondracek, J. (1992). Individual variability in infant's early behavior. *Studia Psychologica, 34*, 199–210.

Efron, B., & Tibshirani, R. (1993). *An introduction to the bootstrap*. New York: Chapman and Hall.

Feldman, H. M., Dolaghan, C. A., Campbell, T. F., Kurs-Lasky, M., Janosky, J. E., & Paradise, J. L. (2000). Measurement properties of the MacArthur Communicative Development Inventories at ages 1 and 2 years. *Child Development, 71*, 310–322.

Fenson, L., Bates, E., Dale, P., Goodman, J., Reznick, J. S., & Thal, D. (2000). Measuring variability in early child language: Don't shoot the messenger. *Child Development, 71*(2), 323–328.

Fischer, K. W., Bullock, D., Rotenberg, E. J., & Raya, P. (1993). The dynamics of competence: How context contributes directly to skill. In R. H. Wozniak & K. W. Fisher (Eds.), *Development in context: Acting and thinking in specific environments* (pp. 93–117). Hillsdale, NJ: Erlbaum.

Fischer, K. W., & Granott, N. (1995). Beyond one-dimensional change: Multiple, concurrent, socially distributed processes in learning and development. *Human Development, 38*(6), 302–314.

Frijn, J., & de Haan, G. J. (1994). *Het taallerend kind* (The language-learning child). Dordrecht: ICG Publications.

Gilmore, R. (1981). *Catastrophe theory for scientists and engineers*. New York: Wiley.

Glass, G. V., McGaw, B., & Smith, M. L. (1981). *Meta-analysis in social research*. London: Sage Publications.

Goldin-Meadow, S., Alibali, M. W., & Church, R. B. (1993). Transitions in concept acquisition: Using the hand to read the mind. *Psychological Review, 100*, 279–297.

Good, P. I. (1999). *Resampling methods: A practical guide to data analysis*. Boston: Birkhauser.

Gottman, J. M. (1981). *Time series analysis: A comprehensive introduction for social scientists*. Cambridge, UK: Cambridge University press.

Granott, N. (1993). Patterns of interaction in the co-construction of knowledge: Separate minds, joints efforts and weird creatures. In R. H. Wozniak & K. W. Fisher (Eds.), *Development in context: Acting and thinking in specific environments* (pp. 183–207). Hillsdale, NJ: Erlbaum.

Hadders-Algra, M., Brogren, E., & Forssberg, H. (1996). Ontogeny of postural adjustments during sitting in infancy: Variation, selection and modulation. *Journal of Physiology, 493*(1), 273–288.

Hickey, T. (1991). Mean Length of Utterance and the acquisition of Irish. *Journal of Child Language, 18*, 369–553.

Kelso, J. A. S., Scholz, J. P., & Schöner, G. (1986). Non-equilibrium phase transitions in cooridinated biological motion: Critical fluctuations. *Physics Letters A, 118*(6), 279–284.

Kmenta, J. (1986). Heteroscedasticity. In J. Eatwell, M. Milgate, & P. Newman (Eds.), *Time series and statistics* (pp. 103–104). New York: Norton.

Kuhn, D. (1995). Microgenetic study of change: What has it told us? *Psychological Science, 6*, 133–139.

Lautrey, J. (1993). Structure and variability: A plea for a pluralistic approach to cognitive development. In R. Case & W. Edelstein (Eds.), *The new structuralism in cognitive development: Theory and research on individual pathways* (pp. 101–114). Basel, Switzerland: Karger.

Lautrey, J., Bonthoux, F., & Pacteau, C. (1996). Le traitement holistique peut-il guider le traitement analytique dans la categorisation de visages? [Can holistic processing guide analytic processing for face categorization]. *Annee Psychologique, 96,* 225–254.

Lautrey, J., & Cibois, P. (1994). Application of correspondence analysis to a longitudinal study of cognitive development. In D. Magnusson & L. R. Bergman (Eds.), *Problems and methods in longitudinal research: Stability and change* (pp. 190–211). Cambridge, UK: Cambridge University Press.

Loftus, G. R. (1996). Psychology will be a much better science when we change the way we analyze data. *Current Directions in Psychological Science, 5*(6), 161–171.

Lord F. M., & Novick, R. (1968). *Statistical theories of mental test scores.* Reading, MA: Addison-Wesley.

MacWhinney, B. (1991). *The Childes project: Tools for analyzing talk.* Hillsdale, NJ: Erlbaum.

Minifie, F., Darley, F., & Sherman, D. (1963). Temporal reliability of seven language measures. *Journal of Speech and Hearing Research, 6*(2), 139–148.

Newell, K., & Corcos, D. M. (1993). *Variability and motor control.* Champaign, IL: Human Kinestics.

Nunnally, J. C. (1970). *Introduction to psychological measurement.* New York: McGraw-Hill.

Rittle-Johnson, B., & Siegler, R. S. (1999). Learning to spell: Variability, choice, and change in children's strategy use. *Child Development, 70,* 332–348.

Ruhland, R., & van Geert, P. (1998). Jumping into syntax: Transitions in the development of closed class words. *British Journal of Developmental Psychology, 16,* 65–95.

Siegler, R. S. (1994). Cognitive variability: A key to understanding cognitive development. *Current Directions in Psychological Science, 3,* 1–5.

Siegler, R. S. (1996). *Emerging minds: The process of change in children's thinking.* New York: Oxford University Press.

Siegler, R. S. (1997). Concepts and methods for studying cognitive change. In E. Amsel & K. A. Renninger (Eds.), *Change and development: Issues of theory, method, and application* (pp. 77–97). Hillsdale, NJ: Erlbaum.

Simonoff, J. S. (1996). *Smoothing methods in statistics.* New York: Springer-Verlag.

Snijders, T., & Bosker, R. (1999). *Multilevel analysis: An introduction to basic and advanced multilevel modeling.* London: Sage Publications.

St. James Roberts, I., & Wolke, D. (1984). Comparison of mothers' with trained-observers' reports of neonatal behavioral style. *Infant Behavior and Development, 7,* 299–310.

Thelen, E. (1985). Development origins of motor coordination: Leg movements in human infants. *Developmental Psychobiology, 18,* 1–22.

Thelen, E., & Smith, L. B. (1993). *A dynamic systems approach to the development of cognition and action.* Cambridge, MA: MIT Press.

Thom, R. (1975). *Structural stability and morphogenesis: An outline of a general theory of models.* Reading, MA: Benjamin.

Thordardottir, E., & Weismer, S. E. (1998). Mean Length of Utterance and other language sample measures in early Icelandic. *First Language, 18,* 001–032.

Tukey, J. W. (1977). *Exploratory data analysis.* New York: Addison-Wesley.

van der Maas, H., & Molenaar, P. (1992). Stagewise cognitive development: An application of catastrophe theory. *Psychological Review, 99*(3), 395–417.

Van der Meulen, B. F., & Smrkovsky, M. (1983). BOS 2-30. *Bayley ontwikkelingsschalen, handleiding* [Bayley developmental scales manual]. Lisse, The Netherlands: Swets & Zeitlinger.

van Dijk, M., De Goede, D., Ruhland, R., & van Geert, P. (2000). *Kindertaal met bokkensprongen* [Child language cuts capers]. Nederlands Tijdschrift voor de Psychologie en haar Grensgebieden, 55, 232–245.

van Dijk, M., & van Geert, P. (1999). *Short-term variability in child language.* Unpublished manuscript, The Netherlands: University of Groningen.

van Geert, P. (1994). *Dynamic systems of development: Change between complexity and chaos.* New York: Harvester Wheatsheaf.

van Geert, P. (2000). *Language-analysis Excel add-inn Groningen (LEGro)* [Computer Software]. Groningen, The Netherlands: Author.

van Geert, P., Savelsbergh, G., & van der Maas, H. (1997). Transitions and non-linear dynamics in developmental psychology. In G. Savelsbergh, H. van der Maas, & P. van Geert (Eds.), *Non-linear developmental processes* (Vol. 175, pp. X–XX). Amsterdam, The Netherlands: Royal Netherlands Academy of Arts and Sciences.

Verheul, M., & Geuze, R. (1999). Constraints on the dynamics of bimanual finger tapping. In N. Gantchev & G. N. Gantchev (Eds.), *From basic motor control to function recovery* (pp. 358–362). Sofia, Bulgaria: Academic Publishing House "Prof. M. Drinov."

Wachs, T. D., Morrow, J., & Slabach, E. H. (1990). Intra-individual variability in infant visual recognition memory performance: Temperamental and environmental correlates. *Infant Behavior and Development, 13,* 397–403.

Wimmers, R. H. (1996). *Grasping developmental change: Theory, methodology and data.* Doctoral dissertation, Free University of Amsterdam.

Wimmers, R. H., Savelsbergh, G.-J. P., Beek, P. J., & Hopkins, B. (1998a). Evidence for a phase transition in the early development of prehension. *Developmental Psychobiology, 32,* 235–248.

Wimmers, R., Savelsbergh, G., Beek, P., & Hopkins, B. (1998b). A catastrophic change in the early development of prehension? In G. Savelsbergh, H. van der Maas, & P. van Geert (Eds.), *Non-linear developmental processes* (Vol. 175, pp. 125–136). Amsterdam, The Netherlands: Royal Netherlands Academy of Arts and Sciences.

*Originally published as P. van Geert & M. van Dijk. (2002). Focus on variability: New tools to study intra-individual variability in developmental data.* Infant Behavior and Development, 25, 340–374. *Reprinted with permission of Elsevier Ltd. via Copyright Clearance Center.*

# Afterword

DAVID H. ROSE

After reading this wonderful collection of essays and commentaries, I am reminded of two of my favorite works of art: Julio Cortázar's novel *Hopscotch* and J. S. Bach's *Toccata and Fugue in D Minor*. While in different media, the two works share important thematic and structural similarities with each other and with the essays gathered here.

Cortázar's novel is (or *was*, when it was published in 1963) structurally unique. There are 155 chapters, some of which are as short as a paragraph, some of which are quite long. What is most peculiar about the book, however, is that Cortázar suggests several "options" for how to read the book. One way is to progress through the chapters one at a time as you would in most novels. An alternative is to "hopscotch" through the chapters according to a "table of instructions" given by the author. In this second option, much like a game of hopscotch, some chapters are "landed on" again and again along the journey. The curious result is that the same chapter may have very different meanings on different visits: informed, differentiated, and deepened by new things learned along the way. There is a third option tentatively offered by the author: read the chapters in any order you would like.

Bach's fugue is more linear than Cortázar's book, but there is an underlying structural similarity. In Bach's fugue (as in any fugue) a short theme begins the piece. For the rest of the piece, that same short theme appears again and again—but each time in a different musical context (e.g., heard within different harmonic backgrounds, within a different register, with different antecedent passages, etc.). As a result, the theme is both more familiar and more novel each time it reappears. The magic is in the way that music, which is fundamentally based on repetition, sounds rich and original, all because the surrounding context changes the way the theme sounds and makes its meaning.

Both of these pieces of art reflect—and provide multiple representations of!—some of the most important themes of this book: the centrality of variation and variability, the dynamic interactions that underlie development, the critical role of context, and options in making meaning.[1]

But I wanted to begin with these pieces of art for a different reason: to illustrate my experience of reading this book. Like my experience with Cortázar's and Bach's compositions, reading the classic essays that compose this book seemed both familiar and novel. Revisiting them reminded me of how seminal they were to our thinking and how rich a foundation they prepared for Universal Design for Learning. But revisiting them within their new context—within the added perspective of UDL and the accompanying contemporary commentaries—made them also seem startlingly original, sharpened with new meanings I had missed when I read them before. It is wonderful to have this thoughtful, and thought-provoking, revisiting of the most foundational ideas and research that underlie UDL.

I think, however, that the authors of this collection have set out to do more than revitalize and illuminate some of the foundations of UDL. I think they have set out also to prepare the field—to set the context—for the kind of research that needs to come now. It will be apparent to any reflective reader that this book is merely an opening, a stage setter. What the field of UDL needs now is a robust, varied, active, and interdisciplinary field of research and researchers conducting research that goes far beyond mere foundations and begins to construct a substantial and iterative edifice of evidentiary research on everything from micro-applications and techniques to scalar efficacy and implementation research. That field of research, essential as it is, is barely in its infancy.

What this foundational book makes clear is that the future of UDL will require a probing and iterative research agenda that departs from traditional educational research in several very important ways. The pieces that the authors have chosen, and the commentaries that enlighten them, make it clear that existing research is often too narrow in its questions, too fixed and static in its methods, and too limited in its options for investigation. What is apparent in most of the classic papers, and in each of the commentaries, is that the authors are asking very large, interrelated, and dynamic questions. These questions are difficult to answer within the limited methodologies that still dominate the educational sciences. All of the authors in this book recognize that not to address these questions is to miss the opportunities that educational reform in general—and UDL in particular—will require. They argue that we need to begin to ask more important questions of our educational practices, properly contextualized and properly universalized, and to use methodologies that are robust enough to answer those questions rather than continuing to ask only those questions for which we have simple methods.[2]

I began this afterword with art—Cortázar and Bach. I did that only partly to express (through an alternate representation, a metaphor) the themes of many of these papers and my reaction to them. I also began with art because, as much as anything else, art is a casualty of the limited questions we are asking of our research and the limited goals we are setting for our schools (though, very sadly, not the only casualty).

One of the most pressing (and laudable) goals of present schooling is to narrow the achievement gaps that bedevil our education system and our culture. But the approach too often taken by default—narrowing the curriculum—has potentially disastrous consequences. We don't effectively evaluate those consequences—at least we don't see them with enough urgency—because our research questions (the focus of this book) and our methods (the focus of UDL) are too narrow. To conclude, I want to highlight two kinds of potentially disastrous consequences from that narrowing.

First, consider the possible negative effects *on our students*. In schools across the country, the curriculum has been narrowed for all students in order to devote more time and resources to remediating or accelerating "the basics." For students in the margins—those with disabilities, with economic-related disadvantages, whose first language is not English, etc.—this narrowing is most exaggerated and most pervasive. Those students are more typically pulled out of any art classes that still remain—and also from science, health, music, extracurricular activities —to remediate their decoding skills, written language basics, and so forth. In the short term, this seems inevitable and appropriate. But here's where the larger questions need to be asked: empirically (as opposed to intuitively), what are the consequences of this narrowing?

Most of the essays in this collection either directly or indirectly raise concerns about the effectiveness of narrowing the curriculum, even for those students who are usually targeted for that approach. Instead, the authors like Gardner, Fischer, and Immordino-Yang note the importance, both affectively and cognitively, of providing more options, not fewer, to meet the challenge of effective education for all students. These options, the core of UDL, need careful, extended, and timely research.

Second, consider the effects of narrowing the curriculum *on our culture*. Here the lack of asking larger questions, and the lack of empiricism in answering them, is even more problematic. Elliot Eisner (2011), emeritus professor of art and education at Stanford University, writes more eloquently about this problem than I can in a wonderful essay called "What Does It Mean to Say That a School Is Doing Well?" In that essay he decries the narrowing of the curriculum because it ultimately debases and weakens not only education but our culture itself. Instead, he calls for widening and diversifying the culture of schooling. Considering the goal of equity, for example, he has this to say:

> Can a more informed conception of what constitutes quality in education lead to greater equity for students and ultimately for the culture? Educational equity is much more than just allowing students to cross the threshold of the school. It has to do with what students find after they do so. We ought to be providing environments that enable each youngster in our schools to find a place in the educational sun. But when we narrow the program so that there is only a limited array of areas in which assessment occurs and performance is honored, youngsters whose aptitudes and interests lie elsewhere are going to be marginalized in our schools. The more we diversify those opportunities, the more equity we are going to have because we are going to provide wider opportunities for youngsters to find what it is that they are good at.
>
> And that leads me to the observation that, in our push for attaining standards, we have tended to focus on outcomes that are standard for all youngsters. We want youngsters to arrive at the same place at about the same time. I would argue that really good schools increase variance in student performance. Really good schools increase the variance and raise the mean . . . Merely by conceiving of a system of educational organization that regards productive variance as something to be valued and pursued, we undermine the expectation that everybody should be moving in lockstep through a series of 10-month years in a standardized system and coming out at pretty much the same place by age 18. (p. 370)

The idea that schools need to raise the variance, not just the mean, sure sounds like the question raised by many of the chapters in this book, and the ultimate goal of UDL. That, too, is the kind of question that demands our research energies.

What I like about this book is that ultimately it is not just about the research basis for UDL, or even just about what the research methodology should look like for an adequate evaluation of UDL. It is fundamentally requesting that we expand and deepen the kinds of research questions we need to ask. In the end, and even proximally, larger and better-chosen questions will drive the kinds of research that we will need.[3] This book, and the growing field of UDL, will require research that can ask and answer much larger and more dynamic questions: What should be the goals for an educated and equitable democracy? What are the means for achieving those goals for the largest number of individuals possible? How should we optimize the opportunities as well as the challenges of diversity? How can a school focus effectively on an individual's strengths as well as their weaknesses? What are the effects of raising the variance on raising the mean? How much remediation, how much accommodation, how much adaptation? How much art?

I would like to end with one more reflection on Bach and Cortázar. As you may know, Bach was not a highly regarded composer during his lifetime; he was fairly well known as an organist but not as a composer. Only a century later, when the "measures" of music had expanded and diversified in the romantic period, was his genius discovered. In our era, the opportunities for students to be discovered—a measure of their strengths and their talents, not just their weaknesses—in our schools are far too narrow and outdated. We do harm both to our students and our culture by not setting higher goals and by not providing a much richer and more varied means of achieving them, means that are as varied as our students. And those means must be well validated and researched. In that regard, this book is just a beginning. But already it is Bach's music to my ears and Cortázar's hopscotch for my mind.

## NOTES

1. For a beautiful multiple representation of Bach's piece—visual as well as auditory—that makes it more accessible and meaningful for many, see www.youtube.com/watch?v=ATbMw6X3T40.
2. For a more extended treatment of the importance of asking the right questions, and the dynamic and interdisciplinary methods that they will require, see Rose, Daley, and Rose (2011).
3. For a longer explication of this point, see Rose, Daley, and Rose (2011).

## REFERENCES

Eisner, E. W. (2001, January). What does it mean to say a school is doing well? *Phi Delta Kappan, 82*(5), 367–372.

Rose, L. T., Daley, S. G., & Rose, D. H. (2011). Let the questions be your guide: MBE as interdisciplinary science. *Mind, Brain, and Education, 5*(4), 153–162.

# Acknowledgments

We thank all of the contributors—Kurt Fischer, Howard Gardner, Mary Helen Immordino-Yang, Jeremy Roschelle, Mike Russell, and Paul van Geert—for inspiring us with their own work and ideas and also for taking the time and care to encourage and challenge us. They illuminate these pages with their creativity, experience, and commitment to improving education for all.

Thanks, too, to the publishers and authors who let us republish their work. We are honored to give all of these important articles yet another "life" in this venue.

To Chris Dede, thank you for writing a foreword—and on such short notice! You are an important mentor and colleague of ours.

We wish to thank David Gordon, publishing and communications director at CAST, for encouraging us to do this book and ably guiding us through each step of the process.

Thanks also to Billie Fitzpatrick—writer and editor *extraordinaire* and a wonderful colleague—for helping us prepare for the interviews and for turning sprawling transcripts into clear and useful copy.

Rick Birnbaum gave essential research support, and Brielle Domings worked magic with the graphics. We appreciate their skills and their good humor.

Thanks to Ada Sullivan, president of CAST, for giving us the time and space to do this book amid many other concerns.

Finally, we offer a special note of appreciation and thanks to Anne Meyer and David Rose, cofounders of CAST, for their mentoring and encouragement. They are the pioneers of UDL, and they have charted a path toward more equitable and effective education for all. And in CAST they have built an organization where big thinking and risk taking are prized. This comes through in David's afterword—as it does in our daily work with him and Anne.

# About the Editors

GABRIELLE RAPPOLT-SCHLICHTMANN is director of research at CAST, where she oversees all research activities, supporting her colleagues to work as a team and providing guidance in the areas of research methodology and data analysis. She also coordinates with senior leadership to strategically advance CAST's mission and vision.

Rappolt-Schlichtmann's research is focused on the affective components of UDL. Her area of expertise is in the relationship between emotion and cognition during learning, especially with regard to the impact of children's experiences of stress on emotion and cognitive performance in the context of school. At CAST, she has led multiple research and development projects funded by organizations such as the National Science Foundation, the Institute of Education Sciences, EduCause, and the National Institutes of Health. Her work has been published in many refereed journals, including *Experimental Brain Research, Mind, Brain and Education, Early Childhood Research Quarterly, Development and Psychopathology, Behavioral Neuroscience,* and *Applied Neuropsychology.*

Through her work, Rappolt-Schlichtmann works to make explicit connections between research and practice, developing education technology based in UDL that leverages her research in the areas of developmental neuroscience, emotion, motivation, contextual support, and scaffolding. She is currently serving a three-year term as a member of the National Center for Learning Disabilities Professional Advisory Board and is an adjunct lecturer at the Harvard Graduate School of Education, where she teaches the course Emotion in Development and Learning: Usable Knowledge, Variability and Context.

SAMANTHA G. DALEY is a research scientist at CAST, where she investigates the relationship between emotions and cognitive performance of students, particularly those with learning disabilities. She focuses on the role of emotions in learning activities and how to design instruction to reflect the relationship between emotion and cognition in learning. In addition to this work, she has contributed to projects funded by the U.S. Department of Education's Institute for Educational Sciences and the National Science Foundation to incorporate UDL in middle school and high school science curricula and has led efforts at supporting implementation of the principles of UDL in lesson development and schoolwide change.

Before joining CAST, Daley was a clinical fellow in the Learning Disabilities Program at Children's Hospital, Boston, an instructor in the Language and Literacy Program at the Harvard Graduate School of Education, and a learning disabilities specialist working with high school and college students.

Daley holds a doctorate in human development and psychology from the Harvard Graduate School of Education. She has published her work in *Mind, Brain and Education*, for which she was co-editor of a special section, and the *Journal of Postsecondary Education and Disability*.

L. TODD ROSE brings a background in cognitive neuroscience, dynamic systems, and developmental psychology to his work as a research scientist at CAST. He investigates the ways perception, attention, and working memory interact to shape learning and participates in the development of tools that support the recognition and strategic components of UDL.

Before joining CAST, Rose was a postdoctoral fellow with the Laboratory for Visual Learning (Harvard-Smithsonian Center for Astrophysics), where his work included National Science Foundation–funded research on the link between dyslexia and visual abilities in astrophysics. His previous work includes research on the impact of fixational eye motions on visual learning, the influence of working memory on reading fluency, and the application of dynamic systems concepts to theories of development. He has also served on U.S. and international panels evaluating the promise and future of neuroscience in education.

Rose currently serves on faculty at the Harvard Graduate School of Education, where he teaches a course on educational neuroscience and is co-chair of the summer institute for Mind, Brain, and Education. He lectures nationally and internationally on learning disabilities, the importance of working memory in K–12 classrooms, and the role of neuroscience in education.

# About the Contributors

## PRIMARY CONTRIBUTORS AND AUTHORS

CHRIS DEDE is the Timothy E. Wirth Professor in Learning Technologies at the Harvard Graduate School of Education. Dede has served as a member of the National Academy of Sciences Committee on Foundations of Educational and Psychological Assessment and as a member of the 2010 National Educational Technology Plan Technical Working Group. He is the editor or co-editor of three books, including *Online Professional Development for Teachers: Emerging Models and Methods* (Harvard Education Press, 2006) and *Digital Teaching Platforms* (Teachers College Press, 2012).

JOHN DEWEY (1859–1952) was an American philosopher, educator, and social activist best known as the father of progressive education. After earning a bachelor's degree from the University of Vermont, he worked as a school teacher for two years before taking up graduate studies at Johns Hopkins University, where he earned his PhD. After a decade on the faculty of the University of Michigan, Dewey moved to the fledgling University of Chicago in 1894, where he established the School of Education and published several highly influential works, including "The Curriculum and the Child." In 1904 Dewey moved to Columbia University in New York, where he continued as a prominent public intellectual until his death.

KURT W. FISCHER is the Charles Bigelow Professor of Education and the director of the Mind, Brain, and Education Program at the Harvard Graduate School of Education. Fischer studies cognitive and emotional development and learning from birth through adulthood, combining analysis of the commonalities across people with the diversity of pathways of learning and development. He is the author of a dozen books, as well as more than two hundred scientific articles, and is the editor of the award-winning journal *Mind, Brain and Education*.

HOWARD GARDNER is the John H. and Elisabeth A. Hobbs Professor of Cognition and Education at the Harvard Graduate School of Education. He also holds positions as adjunct professor of psychology at Harvard University and senior director of Harvard Project Zero. The author of twenty-five books translated into twenty-eight languages and several hundred articles, Gardner is best known in educational circles for his theory of multiple intelligences, a critique of the notion that there is a single human intelligence that can be adequately assessed by standard psychometric instruments. Among numerous honors, he has received honorary degrees from twenty-six colleges and universities around the world and a MacArthur Prize Fellowship.

MARY HELEN IMMORDINO-YANG is an affective neuroscientist and human development psychologist who studies the neural, psychophysiological, and psychological bases of social emotion, self-awareness, and culture and their implications for development and schools. She is an assistant professor of education at the Rossier School of Education, an assistant professor of psychology at the Brain and Creativity Institute, and a member of the neuroscience graduate faculty at the University of Southern California. A former junior high school teacher, Immordino-Yang earned her doctorate at the Harvard Graduate School of Education.

ROBERT J. MISLEVY is a Professor Emeritus of Measurement, Statistics, and Evaluation at the University of Maryland. He was previously a Distinguished Research Scientist at ETS and a research associate at National Opinion Research Center. Mislevy's research interests apply developments in statistics, technology, and cognitive research to practical problems in educational assessment. His work has included a National Science Foundation–supported project to develop an assessment design system with a focus on science inquiry. A widely recognized expert in educational assessment, technology, and cognitive science, Mislevy was elected to the National Academy of Education in 2007.

JEREMY ROSCHELLE is director of the Center for Technology in Learning (CTL) at SRI International in Menlo Park, CA. His research examines the design and classroom use of innovations that enhance learning of complex and conceptually difficult ideas in mathematics and science. In addition to directing a staff of more than sixty at CTL, Roschelle founded SRI's Strategic Learning Consulting practice, which translates research knowledge into innovative products.

DAVID H. ROSE is a developmental neuropsychologist and educator whose primary focus is the development of new technologies for learning. In 1984 Rose cofounded CAST, a nonprofit research and development organization whose mission is to improve education for all learners through innovative uses of modern multimedia technology and contemporary research in the cognitive neurosciences. He also teaches at the Harvard Graduate School of Education, where he has been on the faculty for nearly thirty years.

MICHAEL RUSSELL is vice president of Innovation at the Nimble Innovation Laboratory, a division of Measured Progress that specializes in computer-based assessment solutions that are accessible for all students, including those with disabilities and special needs. Prior to joining Measured Progress, Russell was an associate professor at the Lynch School of Education at Boston College, where he directed the Technology and Assessment Study Collaborative. He is the co-author with Peter Airasian of *Classroom Assessment: Concepts and Applications* (McGraw-Hill, 2011).

JUSTIN STORBECK earned his doctorate in social psychology at the University of Virginia and did postdoctoral training in electroencephalography (EEG). His research focuses on the interactions of cognition and emotion—specifically, how affective states regulate cognitive processes such as perception, learning, and memory.

PAUL VAN GEERT is professor of developmental psychology at the University of Groningen, the Netherlands. His research involves longitudinal research into childhood and pays particular attention to cognitive changes, language, and sociocognitive developments. He tries to predict and explain various aspects of development on the basis of chaos theory. Van Geert started his career in his home country of Belgium, where he studied psychology and educational sciences at Ghent University. He earned his PhD in 1975 in developmental psychology, with a thesis on language development, and has worked at the University of Groningen since 1976.

## OTHER AUTHORS

JOHN T. BEHRENS is vice president of the Pearson Center for Digital Transformation.

RANDY E. BENNETT holds the Norman O. Frederiksen Chair in Assessment Innovation at ETS.

DANIEL H. BULLOCK is a professor in the Departments of Cognitive and Neural Systems and Psychology at Boston University.

GERALD L. CLORE is the Commonwealth Professor of Psychology at the University of Virginia.

SARAH F. DEMARK is senior manager of Certifications and Strategic Assessments Systems at Cisco Systems.

DENNIS C. FREZZO manages a games, assessment, and simulations team that creates learning products for Cisco Networking Academy.

ROY LEVY is an assistant professor in the School of Social and Family Dynamics at Arizona State University.

PAMELA RAYA-CARLTON is a research associate at RMC Research Corporation in Portland, OR.

DANIEL H. ROBINSON is a professor in the Department of Educational Psychology at the University of Texas, Austin.

ELAINE J. ROTENBERG is the clinical director of the Alpert Jewish Family and Children's Service in West Palm Beach, FL.

DAISY WISE RUTSTEIN received her doctorate in 2012 in measurement, statistics, and evaluation from the University of Maryland, College Park.

VALERIE J. SHUTE is a professor in educational psychology and learning systems at Florida State University.

KEN STANLEY is a learning and development manager at Cisco Systems.

MARIJN VAN DIJK is on the behavioral and social sciences faculty at the University of Groningen, the Netherlands.

FIELDING I. WINTERS is a postdoctoral researcher and instructor in the Department of Human Development at the University of Maryland, College Park.

# Index